Labour Law in Switzerland

Labour Law in Switzerland

Third Edition

Alexandre Berenstein†
Pascal Mahon
Jean-Philippe Dunand

This book was originally published as a monograph in the International Encyclopaedia of Laws/Labour Law and Industrial Relations.

Founding Editor: Roger Blanpain
General Editor: Frank Hendrickx
Volume Editor: Frank Hendrickx

Stämpfli Publishers

Wolters Kluwer

Published by:
Kluwer Law International B.V.
PO Box 316
2400 AH Alphen aan den Rijn
The Netherlands
E-mail: international-sales@wolterskluwer.com
Website: lrus.wolterskluwer.com

Sold and distributed in North, Central and South America by:
Wolters Kluwer Legal & Regulatory U.S.
7201 McKinney Circle
Frederick, MD 21704
United States of America
Email: customer.service@wolterskluwer.com

Sold and Distributed in Switzerland by:
Stämpfli Publishers Ltd.
Wölflistr. 1, P.O. Box 5662
CH-3001 Berne
Switzerland
E-mail: verlag@staempfli.com
Phone: +41 31 300 66 44
Website: www.staempfliverlag.com

Sold and distributed in all other countries by:
Air Business Subscriptions
Rockwood House
Haywards Heath
West Sussex
RH16 3DH
United Kingdom
Email: international-customerservice@wolterskluwer.com

ISBN 978-90-411-9960-7 (Kluwer)
ISBN 978-3-7272-0746-4 (Stämpfli)

e-Book: ISBN 978-90-411-9961-4
web-PDF: ISBN 978-90-411-9962-1

The Authors

Alexandre Berenstein, 1909–2000, was born in Paris on 19 January. He received the degree of Master of Law from the University of Geneva in 1929, followed by the degrees of *licencié en sociologie* in 1930 and *docteur en droit* in 1936. From 1938 to 1979 he taught labour law, international labour law, social security law and private insurance law in the law faculty of the University of Geneva. Appointed Professor in 1951, he was Dean of the law faculty from 1960 to 1966 and professor emeritus since 1970. He was Vice President and then, from 1970 to 1979, President of the International School for Comparative Labour Law in Trieste. He has lectured in many countries.

Professor Berenstein was a barrister at the Geneva bar from 1939 to 1970. In 1970 he was elected to the Swiss Federal Court and was a judge in this court until 1979. From 1979 to 1987 he was President of the Federal Board of Conciliation for Labour Disputes.

The author of many publications in the field of labour and social law, Professor Berenstein was Secretary General of the International Society for Labour Law and Social Security from 1958 to 1974. In 1974 he was elected Honorary President of this Society. He was President of the International Association for Social Progress and was President of the Swiss Association for Social Politics. A former President of the Workers' University of Geneva he was, from 1983 to 1991, President of the International Peace Research Institute in Geneva (GIPRI) and became the honorary President of this Institute. Professor Berenstein was a consultant expert for the Council of Europe and accomplished various missions for other international organizations, especially for the International Labour Office.

Pascal Mahon was born in Delémont on 4 April 1957. He received the degree of Master of Law from the University of Lausanne in 1980, followed by the degree of *docteur en droit* in 1986. From 1980 to 1984, he was assistant in public law at the University of Lausanne. After a research stay at the University of Bologna (1985–1987), he taught as an associate professor social organization in the political science faculty of the university of Lausanne from 1988 to 1990, and, from 1992 to 1996, labour law and social security law in the law faculty of the University of

Neuchâtel, where he was appointed professor in 1996. Since then, he has taught Swiss constitutional and comparative constitutional law.

Professor Mahon was formerly to be scientific adviser in the Federal Office of Justice, to the Federal Department of Justice and Police from 1988 to 1996. Since 1998, he has been member of the Cantonal Board of Conciliation for Labour Disputes in Neuchâtel.

He was successively Vice-Dean (2003–2004) and Dean (2005–2007) of the law faculty of the University of Neuchâtel and then Vice-President of the same University (2012–2016). He is now also co-director of the Centre of Study on Work Relationships (CERT, www2.unine.ch/cert).

Professor Mahon is author of many publications in the field of constitutional law and of labour and social law.

Jean-Philippe Dunand was born in Geneva on 27 July 1966. He received a master of law from the University of Geneva in 1988. He passed his bar examination in 1991, after a practice at the administrative court of Geneva and in a well-known law firm. He then practised as a lawyer for two years, before becoming assistant in Roman and European civil law at the University of Geneva, from 1994 to 1999. He received his PHD in 1999 and started his teaching career as an assistant professor at the University of Geneva, from 1999 to 2001. He subsequently taught as an associate professor at the University of Neuchâtel (2000–2006), the University of Lausanne (Roman law, 2001–2005) and the University of Geneva (Roman law, 2005), before being appointed professor at the University of Neuchâtel in 2006. Since then he has given labour law lectures to bachelor's and master's students and has organized seminars every year.

He was Vice-Dean (2007–2009) and Dean (2009–2011) of the law faculty of the University of Neuchâtel. He is also co-director of the Center of Study on Work Relationships (CERT, www2.unine.ch/cert).

In 2008, Professor Dunand was certified labour law specialist by the Swiss lawyer association.

Professor Dunand practises other professional activities. He is consultant in a law office in Neuchâtel and is part of the equality federal commission. He also co-edits the website ARV-DTA online and the JAR.

Finally, Professor Dunand has written numerous publications in the domains of labour law, Roman law and history of law.

Foreword to the 2001 Updated Monograph

Professor Berenstein asked me in December 1998 whether I would update with him his earlier version of IEL – *Labour Law and Industrial Relations* – Switzerland.

Unfortunately, just as we finished updating his earlier version of this monograph Professor Berenstein passed away, on 26 June 2000, before he could survey the manuscript.

But this new version is essentially based on his earlier work and has only been updated with the changes which have occurred in Swiss labour law during the last ten years.

With this publication of Professor Berenstein's monograph, I want to pay homage to him: out of respect for his immense and decisive contribution to the development of the science of law, particularly of labour law and, more generally, social law, in Switzerland and in the world.

June 2000
Pascal Mahon[1]

1. I thank my assistants, Mrs Natalie Erard and Mr Bernhard Pulver, for their contribution to updating this monograph.

Foreword to the 2001 Updated Monograph

Foreword to the 2010 Updated Monograph

Unfortunately, Professor Alexandre Berenstein passed away, on 26 June 2000, just as we finished updating the second version of his earlier version of IEL – *Labour Law and Industrial Relations* – Switzerland.

For the third version I asked my colleague, Professor Jean-Philippe Dunand, who is actually teaching labour law at the University of Neuchâtel, whether he would join me to update this monograph. For three years Professor Dunand and I have created at Neuchâtel a new Center of Study on Work Relationships, the Centre d'étude des relations de travail (CERT).

This new monograph of IEL – *Labour Law and Industrial Relations* – Switzerland is essentially based on the earlier work. However it has been updated with the changes which have occurred in Swiss labour law during the last ten years and with important changes which occurred in 2011, with the unification of civil procedure at federal level.

With this third edition of Professor Berenstein's monograph, we want to pay homage to him: out of respect for his immense and decisive contribution to the development of the science of law, particularly of labour law and, more generally, social law, in Switzerland and in the world.

We finally want to thank Mrs Myriam Schaffter Vacheron, who assisted us in the updating of this monograph.

Pascal Mahon
November 2010

Foreword to the 2010 Updated Monograph

Foreword to the 2017 Updated Monograph

This new monograph is essentially based on the first edition of the *IEL – Labour Law and Industrial Relations – Switzerland* of Professor Alexandre Berenstein, as well as on the successive updates of 2001 and 2010.

The present edition has however been completely updated and integrates the numerous changes that the Swiss political system and constitutional law, as well as Swiss labour law, have undergone during the last eight years, in particular with the important changes inferred by the unification of the civil procedure at the federal level since 2011.

We are particularly grateful to Mr Julien Billarant, who assisted us in the preparation of this new edition and undertook a large part of the updating work. We also want to thank Mr Guillaume Jéquier, assistant at the law faculty in the field of civil procedure, for his active collaboration in the establishment of the according chapters.

Pascal Mahon and Jean-Philippe Dunand
September 2017

Table of Contents

Table of Contents

List of Abbreviations

AJP	*Aktuelle juristische Praxis – (Pratique juridique actuelle)*
ARV-DTA	*Arbeitsrecht und Arbeitslosenversicherung – (Droit du travail et Assurance-chômage)* (Labour Law and Unemployment Insurance)
ATF	*Entscheidungen des Schweizerischen Bundesgerichts, Amtliche Sammlung – Arrêts du Tribunal fédéral Suisse, Recueil officiel*
CC	Civil Code of 10 December 1907
CO	Code of Obligations of 30 March 1911
Cst	Federal Constitution of 18 April 1999
EA	Employment Act of 13 March 1964
FF	*Feuille fédérale* (official government publication)
ILO	International Labour Organization
JAR	*Jahrbuch des Schweizerischen Arbeitsrechts*
LTr	*Loi sur le Travail* (Employment Act)
PC	Penal Code of 21 December 1937
RS	*Systematische Sammlung des Bundesrechts Recueil systématique du droit fédéral Raccolta sistematica del diritto federale* (Collection of Federal Law)
SECO	*Staatssekretariat für Wirtschaft – Secrétariat d'Etat à l'économie* (State Secretariat for Economic Affairs)
TF	Federal Court

List of Abbreviations

General Introduction

Chapter 1. The General Background

§1. Geography

1. Switzerland is situated in the centre of Europe, extending from latitude 45° 49' to 47° 48' north and from longitude 5° 57' to 10° 30' east. It is a small continental country, without any direct access to the sea, and falls naturally into five geographic regions: two mountain ranges, the Jura in the north-west (11.9 per cent of the whole territory) and the Alps in the south and in the east (40.7 per cent); between them, on one side the Alpine foreland (16 per cent) and on the other side the middle region (*Mittelland* or plateau – 22.8 per cent); finally the southern side of the Alps (8.6 per cent). The mean altitude is 1,350 m, the highest point (Monte Rosa) being 4,634 m and the lowest Lake Maggiore at 193 m. The total land area is 41,285 km^2. Being in the heart of the Alps, Switzerland gives rise to some of the principal European rivers: the Rhine flows towards the North Sea, the Rhone towards the Mediterranean, the Ticino, a tributary of the Po, towards the Adriatic, and the Inn, a tributary of the Danube, towards the Black Sea. Switzerland is surrounded by five other countries: in the west, France with a border of 572 km; in the south, Italy, with which Switzerland has its longest border – 734 km; in the east, Austria with a border of 165 km, and Liechtenstein which, by virtue of a treaty of 1923, is linked to the Swiss customs system and has a border of 41 km; lastly, in the north, Germany with a border of 346 km.

§2. Political History

2. The mountainous nature of most of the country and the barrier of the Alps have allowed the Swiss, through the centuries, to safeguard their independence. Situated between powerful nations which, in the course of history, have confronted each other many times, Switzerland long sought to obtain recognition of its neutrality. This aim was attained, Swiss neutrality having been recognized as necessary for the balance of Europe by the Congress of Vienna in 1815, and afterwards by the Treaty of Versailles in 1919 and by the League of Nations in 1920.

3. The geographical configuration of Switzerland, and the fact that the country is located at the crossroads of three different linguistic groups – French, German and Italian – help to explain the historical processes which led to the creation of the Swiss nation and its federal structure. An alliance, that had, since the 13th century, united the people of some valleys situated in current central Switzerland, extended progressively to the surrounding regions and to the cities of Bern, Zurich, Lucerne, Fribourg, Solothurn and Basle. The bonds which united these cities or lands in the Holy Roman-Germanic Empire were loosened after the Swabian war by the Treaty of Basle in 1499; and the independence of the Confederates, which had gradually been achieved after many other wars – mainly against the Habsburgs, the Dukes of Milan and the Duke of Burgundy – was definitively recognized after the Thirty Years' War in 1648 at the Peace of Westphalia. Some of the Confederate states were in possession of subject lands, such as the lands of Vaud and Ticino, while on the other hand, bonds of alliance united these states or some of them to other territories, such as the Republics of Geneva, Mulhouse, Grisons and the Valais. In 1798 French troops invaded the country and under French pressure a unitarian state, the 'Helvetic Republic', was created. The allied Republics of Geneva and Mulhouse, and afterwards the Valais, were annexed by France. In 1803, due to the intervention of Napoleon Bonaparte, the Helvetic Republic was replaced by a new Swiss Confederation with 19 cantons (including the old subject territories) as a satellite state of France. After the fall of Napoleon in 1814 Switzerland attained its present boundaries, with the admission of the new cantons of the Valais, Neuchâtel and Geneva. In the same year, a Federal Pact, recreating a very loose confederation of states, was adopted by the Federal Diet.

4. This Confederation lasted until 1848; at that time the Diet, composed of representatives of the cantons, adopted a Federal Constitution which was ratified by a majority of the cantons and came into force on 12 September 1848. Thus was created a modern federal state, the fundamental institutions of which have not been much altered since, except for a continual strengthening of the powers of the central government balanced by an extension of popular rights. With the transformation of the confederation of states into a federal state, the cantons lost their international sovereignty to the newly created state.

5. The Federal Constitution was completely revised in 1874. The Constitution of 1874, having undergone a great number of partial revisions (more than 160 altogether), was also totally revised in 1999. The idea of the 1999 revision was to update (*Nachführung, mise à jour*) the constitutional law in force in 1999: the great number of partial revisions and the unwritten, mostly jurisprudential constitutional contents, had made the text of the 1874 Constitution difficult to understand. Therefore, materially, the new Constitution[2] which came into force on 1 January 2000 only changed a very few aspects of Swiss constitutional law.

---

2. *RS* 101.

§3. Political and Legal System

I. The Confederation

6. The Swiss Confederation (*Schweizerische Eidgenossenschaft, Confédération suisse, Confederazione svizzera*) – this remained the official name of the federal state – is composed of a number of constituent states, the cantons. There are 23 cantons, but three of these are themselves divided into two 'half-cantons' without any organic bond between them, thus making 26 member states. According to the Federal Constitution, the cantons are sovereign in so far as their sovereignty is not limited by the Constitution. This so-called sovereignty is not to be defined in the light of international law, but as a presumption of competence in favour of the cantons: according to Articles 3 and 42 of the Constitution, the Confederation can only legislate in the fields for which Federal Constitution has installed a power for the Confederation. The cantons, which are themselves divided into communes, may organize themselves as they like, provided that they respect a democratic form of government.

II. Popular Rights

7. The federal state is constituted in the form of a democracy – being at the same time a representative democracy and a direct democracy: a representative democracy because it has a Parliament whose members are elected by the people and by the cantons, and a direct democracy because the constituent power lies in the people. A double majority of the voters and of the cantons (this latter majority being expressed by the vote of the citizens of each canton, each half-canton counting for half a voice) is required for any constitutional amendment; 100,000 citizens (out of a total of approximately 4,915,000) may, by means of a popular 'initiative', demand – as may the Federal Assembly – that the draft of a constitutional amendment may be submitted to a popular vote. Furthermore, the people may take part in the exercise of legislative power by using the right of referendum; 50,000 citizens may demand that a bill adopted by the Federal Assembly be submitted to a popular vote (in this latter case only a majority of the voters is required – not a majority of the cantons).

III. The Federal Assembly

8. Otherwise, the legislative powers are entrusted to the Federal Parliament – called the Federal Assembly (*Bundesversammlung, Assemblée fédérale*) – which is composed of two Chambers: the National Council (*Nationalrat, Conseil national*) and the Council of States (*Ständerat, Conseil des Etats*). The National Council has 200 members, elected on the basis of proportional representation within the cantons. Each canton is entitled to a number of members in proportion to its population; the most populous canton, Zurich, is entitled to 34 mandates, while the little cantons of Uri, Obwalden, Nidwalden, Glarus, Appenzell Ausser-Rhoden and

Appenzell Inner-Rhoden each have only one mandate. The Council of States has 46 members, that is two for each canton (the half-cantons being entitled to only one member), who are elected by popular vote. The two Chambers have equal powers. They sit in common for a few matters, such as for the exercise of the power to pardon and for the elections of the Federal Council, the President of the Confederation and the members of the Federal Court.

9. Since the election of October 2015, the National Council has consisted of the following different political groups:

– Swiss People's Party (*Schweizerische Volkspartei, Union démocratique du centre*)	68 seats
– Ticino League (*die Lega dei Ticinesi, la Lega dei Ticinesi*)	2 seats
– Geneva Citizens' Movement (*Genfer Bürgerbewegung, Mouvement citoyen genevois*)	1 seat
– Social Democratic Party of Switzerland (*Sozialdemokratische Partei der Schweiz, Parti socialiste suisse*)	43 seats
– The Liberals (*Freisinnig-Demokratische Partei, Parti libéral-radical*),	33 seats
– Christian Democratic People's Party of Switzerland (*Christlichdemokratische Volkspartei, Parti démocrate-chrétien*)	30 seats
– Evangelical People's Party of Switzerland (*Evangelische Volkspartei der Schweiz, Parti évangélique suisse*)	2 seats
– Christian Social Party (*Mitte Links-CSP*, Centre Gauche PCS)	1 seat
– Green Party of Switzerland (*Die Grünen, Les verts*)	12 seats
– Swiss Party of Labour (*Partei der Arbeit der Schweiz, Parti suisse du travail*)	
– Green Liberal Party of Switzerland (*Grüneliberale Partei, Parti vert'libéral*)	7 seats
– Conservative Democratic Party of Switzerland (*Bürgerlich-Demokratische Partei, Parti bourgeois démocratique*)	7 seats

In the Council of States, the political parties have the following representation: Christian Democratic People's Party of Switzerland: 13; The Liberals: 13; Social Democratic Party of Switzerland: 12; Swiss People's Party/member not belonging to a group: 5/1; Green Party of Switzerland: 1; Conservative Democratic Party of Switzerland: 1.

Women members of Parliament represent 32 per cent of the total membership in the National Council and 15.2 per cent in the Council of States.

IV. The Federal Council

10. Executive power is vested in the Federal Council (*Bundesrat, Conseil fédéral*), composed of seven members elected for four years by the Federal Assembly. This government, the president of which is elected for one year by rotation and who bears the title of President of the Confederation, is a collegiate authority which distributes responsibility for the different administrative departments among its members. It sits, as do the Parliament and the administration, in Bern. The president is the *primus inter pares*; he fulfils the functions of a head of state only for the needs of protocol, the real head of state being the Federal Council as a whole. The Federal Council has often been compared with a governing body; it does not engage its political responsibility before the Parliament. It submits Bills to the latter; if they are rejected by the Parliament or, as the case may be, by the people, it is forced to deliver a new proposition, taking into account the results of the vote. The rejection of a government Bill does not lead to the resignation either of the government or of any of its members.

11. Although the Federal Council is elected by a majority system, a type of proportional representation has in fact existed since 1960. Until 2003, the three political parties which have been the major political forces in the country for decades – the Radical Democratic Party, the Social Democratic Party and the Christian Democratic Party – were each represented by two members, while the People's Party had one member. The elections of 1991, 1995 and 1999 have shown a continual growth of the right-wing People's Party. This tendency continued with the 2003 elections where the People's Party became the most important party of the Parliament. And, for the first time in very many years, the Federal Assembly took the decision not to reelect an outgoing member of the Federal Council of the Christian Democratic Party. Instead, the leader of the People's Party was elected. This non-reelection ended a long Swiss tradition. The success of the People's Party was confirmed after the 2007 federal elections. However, the leader of the People's Party was not reelected in the Federal Council in his turn and was replaced by a member of his own party. It should also be mentioned that, from November 2010 to January 2012, the Federal Council was composed of a majority of women. The parties which compose the Federal Council do not constitute a real coalition; the members of the government are not elected on a common programme and each party retains great freedom of action with regard to the others. Nevertheless, the members of the Federal Council have to observe the principle of collegiality and must respect the decisions taken by the majority of the Council. It is customary for members of the government to be re-elected for as long as they represent themselves – i.e. while their own party represents them. This rule is nevertheless to be nuanced since the 2003 and 2007 tumultuous elections of the Federal Council.

V. The Cantons

12. The cantons are divided into communes, the legal organization of which is determined by the cantonal constitution. All the cantons have a parliament and a government, both elected by the people. In two cantons (Glarus and Appenzell Inner-Rhoden), the members of the executive power are elected publicly by an assembly of the citizens (*Landsgemeinde*), while in the other cantons they, as well as the members of the cantonal parliament, are elected by secret ballot.

13. In the cantons, as in the communes, popular rights are highly developed. The cantonal constitution comes into force when it has been approved by the people, and it has to be revised at least when a majority of citizens asks for it. A new constitution (or an amendment to it) is recognized by the Confederation through a decision of the Federal Assembly ('federal guarantee'). Men and women, at the cantonal as well as at the federal level, enjoy political rights (on the federal level since the popular vote of 7 February 1971, on the cantonal level, the last canton without women's vote had to be forced to introduce women's vote by a sentence of the Federal Court on 27 November 1990).[3] In some cantons, all Acts are voted on or ratified by the people either by secret ballot or, exceptionally, by an assembly of the citizens (*Landsgemeinde* existing still in the cantons of Glarus and Appenzell Inner-Rhoden). In the other cantons, all Acts and some other matters, although they have been voted on by the cantonal parliament, are subject to a referendum if a given number of citizens asks for it. The elections of judges, as well as of certain other officials such as teachers, are often entrusted to the citizens of the canton or of the commune, as the case may be.

VI. The Law

14. Switzerland is a country of written law, with the Federal Constitution as supreme law. It contains in the main, the essential rules on the political organization of the federal state, the competences and duties of the Confederation and a statement of the individual rights guaranteed by the Federal Court. Among the fundamental rules of the Constitution which we ought to mention is Article 8. This article proclaims the equality of all citizens before the law. During the 20th century, the Federal Court has drawn several essential principles from this article, such as the prohibition of arbitrariness, the principle of equality of treatment, the prohibition of excessive formalism, the prohibition of denial of justice, the right to be heard, the right to free legal assistance and the principle of the separation of powers. Most of these principles are now written down in the new Constitution of 1999. Furthermore, the new Constitution contains a complete (but not exhaustive) list of fundamental rights. Many of them have been considered by the Federal Court, because they did not figure in the Constitution of 1874. They include personal freedom, the freedom to hold opinions, freedom of expression, freedom of conscience and belief, freedom of confession, freedom of the press, freedom of association, freedom of assembly, freedom of language, freedom of residence for Swiss citizens, economic freedom, right to property.

---

3. *ATF* 116/1990 Ia 359.

15. Civil law, criminal law, labour law, social security law and procedure in the civil and criminal fields (since 2011) are largely unified; but this is not the case in the fields of education, health, cantonal, communal finances, judicial organization, the police, the law of construction or, last but not least, the political structure and organization of the cantons and communes. In these matters the constitutional and legislative power lie mainly in the cantons. In the fields in which the Confederation has been enabled to legislate (see above, para. 6) federal law, as soon as it has been enacted, it takes precedence over cantonal law.

VII. The Judicial System

16. The judicial system comes mainly within the competence of the cantons but four different courts are in charge of litigations at federal level. The Federal Court is the highest court of Switzerland. The Federal Criminal Court, the Federal Administrative Court and the Federal Patent Court are inferior courts, unless otherwise stated.

17. The Federal Court (*Bundesgericht, Tribunal fédéral*) has been entrusted with ensuring the observance of constitutional rights and supervising the uniform application of federal law (Article 4 of the Federal Act on the Federal Supreme Court).[4] This Court, which sits in Lausanne and Lucerne (for the two social law courts), is composed of 38 judges and 19 substitute judges who are elected for six years by the Federal Assembly and who, in practice, are re-elected until their retirement (Articles 5, para. 1, and 9, para. 1). The Federal Court is the supreme jurisdiction in public (i.e. constitutional and administrative), civil and criminal matters (Article 1, para. 1). It cannot control the constitutionality of federal Acts or of international treaties, but it may declare cantonal acts void. It is divided into several sections, principally the two public law courts, the two civil law courts, the two social law courts and the penal law court. There is no special section for cases involving questions of labour law.

18. The Federal Criminal Court (*Budesstrafgericht, Tribunal pénal fédéral*),[5] situated in Bellinzone, is:

> the ordinary criminal court of the Confederation, adjudicating as the authority preceding the Federal Court, as far as the law does not exclude any recourse to the latter. The Federal Criminal Court has competences in very specific and limited fields, such as, for instance, in cases of specific offences against the Swiss Confederation or members of federal authorities and in the domains of organized and economic crime, if several cantons are concerned or in international matters only.[6]

4. *RS* 173.110.
5. Federal Act on the Organization of the Penal Authorities of the Confederation, *RS* 173.71.
6. See http://www.bstger.ch/.

19. As the Federal Criminal Court, the Federal Administrative Court (*Bundesverwaltungsgericht, Tribunal administratif fédéral*), situated in Sankt-Gallen, represents the federal administrative inferior court before the Federal Court, as long as a recourse is not excluded (Article 1, para. 2, of the Federal Act on the Federal Administrative Court).[7] The Federal Administrative Court is mainly competent for matters relating to the federal administration's rulings in public law.[8]

20. Finally, the Federal Patent Court (*Bundespatentgericht, Tribunal fédéral des brevets*), also situated in Sankt-Gallen, rules before the Federal Court in its field of competence (Article 1 of the Federal Act on the Federal Patent Court).[9]

VIII. International Relations

21. Switzerland joined the United Nations on 10 September 2002 only. It thus became its 190th member state. The accession of Switzerland to the UN was approved by the Swiss Parliament in 1984, but rejected by the people and the cantons in 1986. Several political propositions to reconsider the accession to UN had then been put forward, and a popular initiative on this matter was finally approved by a narrow majority in March 2002. Nevertheless Switzerland has always had regular relations with the UN: indeed, one of the main offices of this organization is located in Geneva.

22. Switzerland is also a party to the statute of the International Court of Justice and has been a member of the International Labour Organization since its creation after the First World War. Other memberships of UN specialized agencies include the World Health Organization (WHO), UNESCO and the FAO. Some of these, including the ILO and the WHO, have their seats in Geneva while the Universal Postal Union (UPU) has its seat in Bern. Switzerland is also part of the OECD and a number of other international organizations. The Bank for International Settlements also sits, for example, in Basel.

23. At a European level, Switzerland is a member of the Council of Europe and of the European Free Trade Association (EFTA),[10] which sits in Geneva. The EFTA has concluded with the European Communities an agreement on the establishment of an European Economic Area, but the ratification of this agreement was rejected by Swiss citizens and cantons on 6 December 1992. In 1992 the Federal Council also submitted the candidature of Switzerland to the European Union, but Switzerland is not yet a member of the European Union: the accession of Switzerland to EU is a matter of a very controversial political debate.

7. *RS* 173.32.
8. See http://www.bundesverwaltungsgericht.ch/fr/index/federal/federal-organisation.htm.
9. *RS* 173.41.
10. Convention establishing EFTA, *RS* 0.632.31.

24. On 21 June 1999, Switzerland concluded seven bilateral agreements with the European Union and its Member States, covering the sectors of agriculture, public procurement markets, research, overland transport, civil aviation and technical barriers to trade and free movement of persons.[11] The latter has an important influence on Swiss social insurance and labour law. Indeed, it is accompanied by different legislative measures (ancillary implementation measures) which aim to avoid social and, particularly, wage dumping (see below, paras. 125–127 and 135).

25. Since a referendum was requested on these bilateral agreements, the Swiss people voted and accepted them on 21 May 2000. Thus, these agreements and the ancillary measures entered into force on 1 June 2002.

26. The European Union and Switzerland then pursued negotiations and concluded a second set of nine bilateral agreements, on 26 October 2004. This second package widens the cooperation to domains other than purely economic, such as security, asylum, environment, culture, statistics and training. These agreements, being independent from one another unlike the bilateral I, entered into force between 2005 and 2008, except for the fight against fraud.

27. Concurrently with the conclusion of the so-called bilateral II, the bilateral agreement on free movement of persons was expanded to eight of the new Member States of the European Union,[12] by means of the signature of a Protocol on 26 October 2004. The other bilateral agreements were indeed automatically extended to the new members. The aforementioned protocol entered into force on 1 April 2006. This extension resulted in a reinforcement of the ancillary implementation measures of the 1 June 2004, which came into effect on 1 April 2006.

28. The same situation occurred once more following the membership of Romania and Bulgaria on 1 January 2007. The EU and Switzerland concluded then a second protocol extending the agreement on free movement of persons to Romania and Bulgaria and coming into force on 1 June 2009. However, the free movement of persons was for them not yet complete and could therefore suffer from restrictions and limitations. Only on 1 June 2016 did Bulgaria and Romania obtain a complete capacity of free movement through the protocol. The same was to be observed for EU-15 + Malta and Cyprus on 1 June 2007, and for EU-8 on 1 May 2011.

29. On 28 November 2008 was voted and accepted the popular initiative for the expulsion of Switzerland of foreign criminals (*initiative sur le renvoi*). On 28 February 2016, Switzerland suffered the refusal of the population concerning the implementing initiative 'For an effective expulsion of foreign criminals' which led to the entry in force of the implementing law on 1 October 2016, modifying the Swiss penal code with articles on the expulsion of foreign criminals. However, pursuant to Article 5 Annexe 1 ALCP, the rights delivered by that Agreement may only be

11. Bilateral Agreement on free movement of persons, *RS* 0.142.112.681.
12. New Member States Cyprus and Malta were indeed already signatories of the Agreement of 21 June 1999.

limited for reasons of public policy, public security or public health. This notion requires the existence of a real menace affecting a fundamental interest of society.

30. In 2013, Croatia entered the European Union. In principle, each accession of a new Member State within the EU provokes the renegotiation of the agreement. Under these conditions, a third protocol started to be negotiated by the Federal Council for the extension of the agreement to Croatia. Unfortunately, in the meantime, on 9 February 2014 the popular initiative 'Against mass immigration' was voted on and accepted. This initiative aims to introduce annual ceilings and quotas as well as the principle of national preference. All residence permits are concerned. The agreement was therefore no longer compatible with the new constitutional provisions governing immigration. The third protocol was signed anyway but has not been ratified by Switzerland; a solution regarding the compatibility of the agreement is yet to be found. In consequences, the situation of Croatian workers was different from that of any other workers bound by the agreement. The accessibility of Croatian citizens to Swiss territory was governed by the Federal Act on Foreign Nationals[13] and not the Agreement on the Free Movement of Persons, and workers suffered from strict quotas and constraints. However, the third protocol came recently into force on 1 January 2017, offering Croatians free movement in Switzerland.

§4. Population

31. In 2014, the total number of inhabitants was estimated to be 8,237,666.[14] Since the beginning of the century, the number of inhabitants has been constantly increasing, as shown by the figures in Table 1.

Table 1. Number of inhabitants (in thousands)

1950	1960	1970	1980	1990	2000	2005	2010	2011	2012	2013
4,717	5,360	6,193	6,335	6,751	7,204	7,459	7,870	7,954	8,039	8,139

Source: Statistical Yearbook of Switzerland 2010; FOS, *STATPOP*, Neuchâtel 2016.

The proportion of women and men was 50.5 per cent and 49.5 per cent respectively in 2014.

32. The cantons with the greatest number of inhabitants are Zurich (1,446,354 inhabitants in 2014), Bern (1,009,418 inhabitants in 2014) and Vaud (761,446 inhabitants in 2014); 84,5 per cent of the inhabitants live in urban and 15.5 per cent in rural areas (in 2014). The largest agglomeration, rounded to the hundred, are

13. *RS* 142.20.
14. Federal Office of Statistics, *Population résidente permanente en Suisse* (*STATPOP*), Neuchâtel 2016.

those of Zurich (1,315,700 inhabitants in 2014), Geneva (570,200 inhabitants), Basle (537,100 inhabitants), Bern (406,900 inhabitants) and Lausanne, in the canton of Vaud (402,900 inhabitants).

33. The Federal Constitution (Articles 4 and 70, para. 1) recognizes four national languages – German, French, Italian and Rhaeto-romanic – but only three of these languages are recognized as fully official languages of the Confederation, i.e. German, French and Italian. These three languages are equal under the law.

34. Each canton has its own official language(s), which is one or more of the national languages. French is spoken in the west, where four cantons (Geneva, Vaud, Neuchâtel and Jura) are French-speaking. Three other cantons (Valais, Fribourg and Bern) are bilingual, being divided into a French-speaking area (the majority language in the Valais and Fribourg) and a German-speaking area (the majority language in Bern). Italian is spoken in the south, in Ticino and in some of the valleys of Grisons, while Rhaeto-romanic is spoken in other parts of Grisons. German (German being the written language), or, more precisely dialects deriving from German, *Schwyzerdütsch*, is spoken in all other cantons (the canton of Grisons has three official languages: German, Italian and Rhaeto-romanic). In 2014, 63.3 per cent of the whole population spoke German or Swiss-German, 22.7 per cent French, 8.1 per cent Italian and only 0.5 per cent Rhaeto-romanic; 20.9 per cent spoke other languages (the total exceeds 100 per cent since people may speak multiple primary languages).

35. The two major religions are Protestantism and Catholicism. In 2014, 31.8 per cent of the Swiss were of the Protestant faith, with Roman Catholics comprising 37.3 per cent. However, the majority of aliens are of the Catholic faith, with the result that, taking the population as a whole, Catholics represent 37.9 per cent and Protestants 25.5 per cent; 23 per cent of the population have no religion.

36. Aliens make up a great proportion of the population of Switzerland. Already at the beginning of the First World War the percentage of aliens was 15 per cent. It now exceeds this proportion. The evolution has been as shown in Table 2.

Table 2. Evolution of the number of aliens

	Number of aliens (in thousands)	Aliens (per 100 inhabitants)
1900	383	12
1910	552	15
1920	404	10
1930	355	9
1941	224	5
1950	285	6
1960	585	11

	Number of aliens (in thousands)	Aliens (per 100 inhabitants)
1970	1,080	17
1980	945	15
1990	1,247	18
2000	1,424	19
2010	1,766	22
2014	1,998	24

Sources: Statistical Yearbook of Switzerland, Die Volkswirtschaft and http://www.bfs.admin.ch/bfs/portal/en/index.html.

37. Among the aliens the most numerous are Italians (306,414 in 2014), Germans (298,027) and Portuguese (262,748). Other countries represented among the alien population are France (116,896), Spain (79,610), Serbia and Montenegro (78,092), Turkey (70,051) and Macedonia (63,516).

38. The distribution of the population by age groups and sexes was in 2014 as shown in Table 3.

Table 3. Distribution of the population by age groups and by sex

Age groups	Absolute numbers (in thousands)			%
	Male	Female	Total	Total
20–39	1,111.6	1,087.4	2,198.9	26.7
40–64	1,464.3	1,445.1	2,909.4	35.3
65–79	495.3	561.6	1,056.9	12.8
80	148.4	260.3	408.7	5.0
Total	4,073.9	4,163.8	8,237.6	100.0

Source: Federal Office of Statistics, STATPOP, Neuchâtel 2016.

§5. The Economy

39. Switzerland is poor in raw materials and its land is partly unproductive: 35.9 per cent of the soil is used as agricultural useful land, forest and woods cover 31.3 per cent, 7.5 per cent represents buildings and infrastructure, and 25.3 per cent is unproductive.

40. Milk, cheese, fruit, grapes, grain and vegetables are the principal products of Swiss agriculture. Two-thirds of the foodstuffs needed to feed the population have to be imported, although Switzerland does have a significant food-producing industry. Other important industries include the machine industry, the watchmaking industry and the chemical industry, all of which export a significant proportion of their production. We ought also to mention in this context the electricity industry, the textile industry and the building industry. Trade, services, banking, insurance and tourism all contribute in large part to the gross national product. Thus, the country is largely open to the exterior. As well as having to import much of the food needed by its people, it also has to import the raw materials – namely the metals – necessary for industrial production; these imports are compensated for by the export of finished products, both food products and industrial products, and by the invisible trade from tourism. Due to the small size of both the country and the population, the internal market is too narrow to permit the machine industry, the watch industry and the chemical industry to dispose of the bulk of their production within the country. Exports are vital for the survival of the Swiss economy.

41. Switzerland operates on the basis of a market economy and a free enterprise system. The constitutional guarantee of economic freedom is considered to be an essential element in economic life. But this freedom is not absolute. It exists, according to Articles 27, 36 and 94 of the Constitution, subject to the limitations provided for by the Constitution and by the Acts which are based on it. The cantons, while they may prescribe rules governing the operation of commerce and industry, cannot derogate from this freedom inasmuch as they are not authorized to do so by the Federal Constitution. So, economic freedom has been restricted by several constitutional articles, including prescriptions on the protection of workmen, of tenants and of the peasantry, as well as on the protection of areas in which the economy is threatened. These measures are intended to remedy the harmful consequences of the cartels and so on.

42. The public and collective sector of the economy is also important. The main public sector areas are the banking sector (with the cantonal banks and the National Bank), communications and transport (railways, buses, trams, post), electricity generating, the supply of gas and water, nuclear energy, building insurance, and, naturally, hospitals, education and social insurance. Nevertheless, the private sector of the economy still predominates, and some public enterprises have recently been transferred to the private sector (especially in the sector of telecommunications).

§6. Employment Statistics

43. Tables 4 to 6 provide some indication of the distribution of employment. Table 4 shows the number of economically active persons of the population. Table 5 distinguishes between Swiss citizens and aliens and shows the importance of aliens as part of the workforce. However, this table does not take into account the foreign workers who work but do not live in Switzerland and who, therefore, are not accounted for in the population statistics. Table 6 shows the distribution of foreign employees working in Switzerland in 2015, according to their status.

Table 4. Total permanent population and active population (2014) (in thousands)

	Men and women	Men	Women
Total population	8,237.6	4,073.9	4,163.8
Persons of working age (15–64 years)	5,547.1	2,800.9	2,746.3
Economically active persons	4,366	2,330	2,036

Source: http://www.bfs.admin.ch/bfs/portal/en/index.html (STATPOP)

Table 5. Distribution of active persons between Swiss and aliens (2014) (in thousands)

Swiss		%
Total Swiss population	6,239.2	(100)
Economically active persons	3,417	(55)
Aliens:		
Total foreign population	1,998.5	(100)
Economically active persons	1,469	(74)

Table 6. Foreign employees (2014)

With settlement authorization	718,000
With residence authorization	386,000
With cross-border authorization	286,000
With short-term authorization	52,000
Other aliens	27,000
Total	1,469,000

Source: OFS, Neuchâtel 2016.

From Table 7 one can see the growing importance of the tertiary sector, which in 1975 surpassed the secondary sector and now represents more than two-thirds of the working population.

Table 7. Distribution of active persons according to economic sectors

	Absolute numbers (in thousands)					
	1970	1975	1980	1985	2009	2014
Sector 1 (agriculture, forestry, fishing)	231	173	189	187	167	173
Sector 2 (industry, crafts, construction)	1,445	1,214	1,204	1,239	1,041	1,057
Sector 3 (services)	1,320	1,324	1,705	2,040	3,314	3,657
Total	2,996	2,711	3,098	3,465	4,522	4,887

Source: Federal Office of Statistics, SPAO, Neuchâtel 2016.

The distribution of active persons according to the size of establishments can be seen in Table 8.

Table 8. Active persons in each sector

	Number of establishments	Active persons
Sector 1	62,486	175,808
Sector 2	77,711	1,061,643
Sector 3	311,454	2,955,194
Total	451,651	4,192,645

Source: Federal Office of Statistics, *Recensement des entreprises 2008*, Neuchâtel, 2009.

Table 9. The distribution of active persons according to the size of establishments

	Size of private enterprises (number of occupied persons)			
	1–9	10–49	50–249	250
Sector 1	93.4	5.9	0.8	-
Sector 2	17	28.7	30.1	24.2
Sector 3	26.5	30.2	25.7	17.6
Total	26.8	28.8	25.8	18.6

Source: Federal Office of Statistics, *Recensement des entreprises 2008*, Neuchâtel, 2009.

44. Unemployment has been virtually unknown for a long time. Although a great number of jobs disappeared after 1974 because of the recession, the departure of a number of foreign workers and the restrictions imposed on the admission of such workers to Switzerland helped to keep the unemployment figures low. There was a new increase from 1981 to 1984, and the number of unemployed has steadily risen since 1990, with a slight drop during the last years, until 2009 when unemployment started to raise significantly. This growth continued until February 2010. There is also an increasing amount of partial unemployment. It should be noted that there has been, in the last few years, a relative increase in the proportion of women among the unemployed.

Table 10. Unemployment rate in December, as defined by ESPA, OFS, Neuchâtel 2016 (in %)

1991	1995	2000	2003	2005	2009	2015
2.2	3.3	2.6	4.4	4.4	5.0	4.5

Source: http://www.bfs.admin.ch/bfs/portal/en/index.html.

In December 2009, the number of the unemployed was as shown in Table 11.

Table 11. Number of unemployed (December 2015), as defined by ESPA, OFS, Neuchâtel 2016 (in thousands)

Men	115
Women	104
Total unemployed	219

Source: http://www.bfs.admin.ch/bfs/portal/en/index.html.

Chapter 2. Definitions and Notions

§1. The Discipline of Labour Law

45. The existence of a legal discipline dedicated to labour law has for a long time not been recognized by all jurists. The idca is nevertheless steadily gaining ground and in the last decades of the 20th century most law faculties have recognized the existence of labour law as a special, autonomous discipline.

46. The main difficulty lies in the fact that the rules of labour law are divided between public law on the one hand and private law on the other. The distinction between these two categories of legal rules is very important. This is particularly so in the field of labour law, since the federal state alone is competent to enact rules of private law; the cantons may enact rules of public law as long as the federal state has not yet enacted laws on the same matter. While the legislative competence of the cantons has been much reduced since the adoption of the Federal Employment Act in 1964 it has not totally disappeared. For a long time, the problem of distributing competence between the Confederation and the cantons in the domain of labour law followed for a large part the line of distinction between public law and private law. The idea of a general codification of labour law has not been accepted, so that provisions on the labour contract are incorporated into the Code of Obligations. This often leads to a failure to recognize the specific character of labour law, while maintaining the labour contract within the framework of the rules of civil law. Another difficulty resulting from the coexistence of rules incorporated in the Code of Obligations, on the one hand, and of rules incorporated in public law Acts on the other hand, arises from the fact that in some matters there is a contradiction between the two different kinds of rules. These contradictions could disappear if the whole of the rules of labour law were incorporated in a single Act, a Labour Code.

47. Nevertheless, despite the division of legislative rules, one may now say that labour law has to be considered as constituting a multiform entity which comprises private law rules, public law rules and collective law rules. It was born from the special situation of working men in the modern world and from the need for protection which derives from it. This situation is characterized, in the framework of contractual relations, by the existence of the labour contract which, although it is one of the contracts regulated by the Code of Obligations, is not a contract like the others. The parties to it are not equal. One of them, the employee, is bound to follow the instructions of the employer while at work; economically, too, he is dependent on the employer, his salary being necessary for the subsistence of himself and his family. In this situation, and bearing in mind the necessity of remedying the lack of balance between the two parties to the contract, the legislator has deemed it necessary to intervene by framing public law provisions which oblige the employer to observe certain rules. Thus some balance is established, the employer for his part being subordinated to the power of the state. The law-maker intervenes in favour of the weaker party to the contract, i.e. the worker.

48. Parallel action has been undertaken by the workers themselves. They have tried, by forming unions both at the industrial level and at the national level, to exert an influence on their conditions of work. In this way they have achieved a strength which can approach that of the employers and even counterbalance it, and has given birth to collective labour law – that is, autonomous law which does not emanate from the state but from groups of individuals. In fact these rules often acquire a value which is as important as that of the law of the state, so that the latter loses its place in the forefront of the development of collective law.

49. While the different constitutive parts of labour law are scattered as regards their legal sources, they are indissolubly bound as regards their effects. They apply to the same human relationships and it is therefore necessary to deal with them in their totality.

50. Labour law applies to dependent labour, that is to labour relations in cases where the person who works – the employee – is subordinated to the authority of the employer. In some cases it also applies to labour relations where the person who is doing the work is in a position nearly equal to that of the employer as regards his economic independence, so-called free workers. It does not apply only to individual relations, but also to relations between a collectivity of workmen on the one hand and an employer or a collectivity of employers on the other. Furthermore, labour law in *lato sensu* also comprises all the protective measures which the authorities may take in favour of workmen because of their special position in society even outside the field of labour relations.

§2. Labour Law and Social Law

51. Labour law may be considered as a part of social law, and social law covers all the rules which are intended to help those individuals whom the legislator deems to be worthy of special protection in the face of the many dangers which may beset them on an economic or social level. The Federal Constitution declares, for example, that the Confederation may, when necessary, in derogation of the principle of the economic freedom, enact provisions with the view of safeguarding the existence of important economic branches or professions; especially with regard to promotion of farms cultivating the land (Article 102, para. 2, Cst). Individuals who are protected by the provisions enacted in pursuance of the constitutional rule, such as those of the Act of 29 April 1998 on agriculture (Farming Act, which replaced the Farming Act of 3 October 1951), are this protected by provisions which fall within the framework of social law.

52. Social law also has as one of its objectives that of ensuring the protection of the essential needs of every human being. One of these needs is the need for housing, which is met by provisions on the protection of tenants (Article 109 Cst), including in particular protection against abusive rents, or as a consumer (Article

97 Cst, dealing with the protection of consumers). On a non-economic level social law deals with the protection of human being in his environment (Article 74 Cst, in line with which the Confederation enacts laws to protect man and his natural sphere against harm or damage). But, naturally, the most important branch of social law – apart from labour law – is that of social security; that is, the system which attempts to ensure, with the provision of benefits in cash or in kind, a minimum degree of security for everybody in the face of the fundamental risks of human life.

§3. Social Security

53. Social security is covered by a number of Acts based on different constitutional provisions; these Acts create an extended system of social insurance. Four of the branches of social security are very closely related to labour law. These branches are accident insurance, unemployment insurance, loss of earnings and maternity insurance, and family benefits.

I. Accident Insurance

54. Accident insurance (today based on Article 117 Cst) was administered until the end of 1983 under the Health and the Federal Act on Accident Insurance of 13 June 1911. This insurance took the place of employers' liability for work accidents, instituted in Switzerland for the first time in the world by the 1877 Federal Act on Work in Factories. By virtue of the Act of 1911, employees in certain groups of enterprises – mainly industrial and transport enterprises – representing two-thirds of all employees were compulsorily insured under a scheme administered by the Swiss Accident Insurance Fund (Suva).

55. From 1 January 1984, accident insurance, according to the Federal Act on Accident Insurance of 20 March 1981[15] and the Ordinance of 20 December 1982,[16] has been compulsory for all employees working in Switzerland, including home workers, unemployed, apprentices, trainees, volunteers and those learning in craft schools or working in protected workshops for the handicapped. The accident insurance – and this is a peculiarity of the Swiss system – covers not only employment injuries – work accidents and occupational diseases – but also other accidents, which are, with some exceptions, covered by the same measure (Article 6 of the Federal Act on Accident Insurance). The financing of non-professional accidents is borne by the insured persons themselves, with the enterprises bearing the costs of employment injuries (Article 91).

56. For the majority of insured persons, i.e. chiefly industrial and transport workers and civil servants of the federal state, insurance is administered by the Swiss Accident Insurance Fund; for other employees, it is administered by public

15. *RS* 832.20.
16. *RS* 832.202.

institutions and health insurance institutions, as well as private insurance companies that, by receiving an approval of the state, are authorized to administrate social security (Article 58). Under the Act of 20 March 1981, the executive organs provided for by the Employment Act as well as the Swiss Accident Insurance Fund administer the prevention of work accidents and occupational diseases. An Ordinance of 19 December 1983 on the Prevention of Accidents and Occupational Diseases[17] lays down the principles which have to be followed by employers and workers with a view to promoting security at work, and the rules for the organization of the said prevention. More than 20 different decrees and ordinances relate to prevention in different special occupations.

57. Furthermore, according to the Federal Act on Navigation under the Swiss Flag of 23 September 1953,[18] shipowners have to insure sailors on sea-going vessels registered in Switzerland against employment injuries (Article 84, para. 2), with a private insurance company.

II. Unemployment Insurance

58. Unemployment insurance, provided for by Article 114 Cst, is now administered under the Federal Act on Compulsory Unemployment Insurance and Benefits on Insolvency of 25 June 1982.[19] The insurance is compulsory for all employees to whom the benefits are to be given in the case of total or partial unemployment. The contribution to the insurance system is paid by the employer, who deducts half of it from the salary of the employee (Articles 3, para. 3 and 5, para. 1). The constitutional provision provides that persons with an independent activity ought to be able to insure themselves on particular terms, but this facility is not available yet.

59. According to the provisions of the Act, unemployment insurance covers four different situations in which benefits are provided. The first one is the 'unemployment benefit', where a worker is totally or partially unemployed (Article 7 para. 2 lit. a and Article 8ss LACI). The second one is the 'benefit in case of reduction of working hours' (Article 7 para. 2 lit. c and Article 31ss LACI). The third one is the 'benefit in case of bad weather' (Article 7 para. 2 lit. d and Article 42ss LACI). The last one is the 'benefit in case of insolvency', where the insolvency of the employer, caused by bankruptcy or seizure, creates a loss in wage for the employee (Article 7 para. 2 lit. e and Article 51ss LACI).

17. *RS* 832.30.
18. *RS* 747.30.
19. *RS* 837.0.

III. Loss of Earnings and Maternity Insurance

60. The scheme of benefits for loss of earnings by members of the army (Article 59 Cst and the Act of 25 September 1952)[20] is modelled, as regards financing, on the system of old-age, survivors' and invalidity insurance. In this system, too, those who are engaged in a self-employed gainful activity are distinguished from those who are engaged in salaried activity.

61. The Constitution has provided since 1945 that the Confederation should create a maternity insurance (Article 116 Cst.). Nevertheless this important provision has failed to be implemented, except for including maternity benefits within the framework of health insurance. An Act introducing an obligatory insurance for the payment of cash benefits in the case of maternity, adopted by Parliament on 20 March 1987, was rejected in a referendum on 6 December of the same year. A new attempt to institute maternity insurance was rejected by the Swiss people in a referendum on 13 June 1999. Switzerland was finally provided with a maternity insurance on 26 September 2004. The new maternity insurance was integrated into the existing Federal Act on the system of compensation for loss of earnings for Persons on Military Service or Civil Protection Duty.

62. The cumulative conditions granting to benefit from maternity allowances are the following (Article 16*b*, para. 1). The assignee must have been insured for nine months before childbirth and working during five months throughout this period of time. In addition, she must, at the time of childbirth, be employed, self-employed or working in her husband's company as a paid employee. The right for allowances finally exists only if the mother gives birth to a viable child or when the pregnancy lasted at least 23 weeks (Article 23 of the Regulation on benefits for loss of earnings).[21] If all conditions are fulfilled, the insurance allocates daily allowances to the amount of 80 per cent of the average salary to a maximal sum of SF 196 per day, for 14 weeks (Articles 16*d*–16*f*). This system is merely a minimum one, free to be improved by cantons in the worker's interests.

IV. Family Benefits

63. Family benefits are partly administered by federal legislation and partly by cantonal legislation. Article 116 Cst provides that the Confederation may enact laws on family benefits; but for a long time, such an Act has been adopted only for the agricultural sector. According to the Federal Act on Family Allowances in Agriculture of 20 June 1952,[22] employees who work for a salary in an agricultural enterprise are entitled to family benefits (household benefits and child benefits) (Article

20. Now the Federal Act on Compensation for Loss of Earnings for Persons on Military Service or Maternity Leave, *RS* 834.1.
21. *RS* 834.11.
22. *RS* 836.1.

1*a*, para. 1). The financing of these benefits is borne by the employers and subsidiarily by the state (Confederation and cantons) (Article 18). Furthermore, self-employed farmers are entitled to family benefits financed by the state (Article 5 *et seq.*). For employees in other branches of the economy, family benefits are provided for by cantonal Acts in all cantons. The latter are 'however' no longer free to fix the benefits since a new federal Act, the Federal Act on Family Allowances of 24 March 2006[23] came into effect on two different dates, that is on 1 March 2007 for a first part and on 1 January 2009 for the major part. This act aims to harmonize the various cantonal systems, but does not modify the dualism existing between family benefits in the agriculture and family benefits in other sectors. Enter the scope of application employees and people without any gainful activity, but the taxable income of which does not exceed a certain amount. However, cantons are free to go beyond federal measures and so to guarantee the granting of family allowances to self-employed workers, for example.[24] The financing of family allowances differs according to the concerned beneficiaries: Article 20, para. 1 provides that family benefits paid to people without any gainful activity are financed by the cantons. Article 16, para. 1 concerning salaried workers provides that the cantons settle the financing and the expenses of administration. Child allowances amount to minimum SF 200 a month and vocational training allowances to minimum SF 250 a month (Article 5, paras. 1 and 2).

64. While accident insurance, unemployment insurance, loss of earnings and maternity insurance, and family benefits are for the main part insurance systems covering employees only and are therefore closely connected with labour law, it is not the case for the other branches of social security[25] which in principle cover the whole population. These other branches are old-age, survivors' and invalidity insurance and health insurance. To these ought to be added benefits for loss of earnings by members of the army and military insurance.

V. Old Age, Survivors' and Invalidity Insurance

65. Old age, survivors' and invalidity insurance (now based on Article 112 Cst), is administered under the Federal Act on the Old Age and Survivors' Insurance of 20 December 1946[26] and the Federal Act on Invalidity Insurance of 19 June 1959[27] with later amendments. All persons residing in Switzerland or engaged therein in gainful activity – and in some cases Swiss citizens residing abroad – are compulsorily insured against these risks (Article 1*a*, para. 1). The pensionable age is currently 65 for men and 64 for women (since 2005) (Article 3, para. 1).

23. *RS* 836.2.
24. See Matthey, F., Mahon, P., 'Les allocations familiales' in SBVR XIV-Meyer, *Soziale Sicherheit*, 3rd edn, Basle, Geneva, Munich, 2016, p. 2023.
25. Except for occupational pensions (see below, para. 57).
26. *RS* 831.10.
27. *RS* 831.20.

66. The fifth revision of the Federal Act on Invalidity Insurance has been in force since 1 January 2008. One of the main purposes of this revision was to improve the invalidity insurance's financial health. The following measures were thus taken: priority is now given to rehabilitation, the granting of new invalid pensions is reduced, complementary pensions were suppressed, child allowances are reduced, etc. However, the sixth revision is already in the pipeline.[28]

67. For the purpose of financing this insurance insured persons engaged in gainful activity are subdivided into those whose activity is 'dependent' and those whose activity is 'independent'. The former have to pay half of the contribution from their salaries (Article 5, para. 1), with the other half being paid by their employers (Article 13). Those considered to be engaged in a dependent activity are not only employees in the civil law sense but other persons too, such as sleeping partners in enterprises, members of the administration of commercial societies, members of public authorities and generally all those whose activity is determined by public law. Thus we have a very broad definition of dependent activity, which not only goes beyond the civil law definition of an employee, but also beyond that of a worker under the public law definition, notably under the Employment Act. With this subdivision, the legislator has found an easier way to organize the financing of the insurance. Persons who are not engaged in gainful activity pay contributions in proportion to the amount of their capital (Article 10, para. 1). The Confederation pays 19.55 per cent of the expenses of the old-age and survivors' insurance (Article 103, para. 1) and finances 37.7 per cent of the expenses of the invalidity insurance (Article 78, para. 1).

68. Under the Federal Act on Benefits supplementary to the Old Age, Survivors and Disability Insurance of 6 October 2006,[29] persons who receive insurance benefits, but whose means do not exceed a prescribed level, may apply for complementary allowances, which are financed by the state (cantons and federal state).

69. According to the Federal Act on Occupational Old Age, Survivors' and Invalidity Pension Provision of 25 June 1982 (Article 2, para. 1),[30] all employees over 17 years old and with a wage over a determined amount (in 2017 SF 21,150 a year) are covered under this scheme. The occupational pension comes as a second insurance cumulated with the old age insurance, in order to guarantee the employee the lifestyle he had under his working years. The employer is obliged to be affiliated to an occupational institution, which has to been chosen in agreement with his employees. He has to pay contributions which are at least equal to the sum of contributions paid by the employees.

---

28. See http://www.bsv.admin.ch/index.html?lang=en.
29. *RS* 831.30.
30. *RS* 831.40.

VI. Health Insurance

70. Health insurance, while administered under the same constitutional provision as accident insurance (Article 117 Cst), is organized quite differently under the Federal Act on Health Insurance of 18 March 1994.[31] Health insurance is composed of two parts: the first part, the insurance for medical and pharmaceutical care, is compulsory for all persons residing in Switzerland (Articles 1*a*, paras. 1 and 3 *et seq.*). Insured persons are affiliated to mutual non-profit institutions (Article 12, para. 1). The benefits are legally determined. The contributions of the insured persons are not calculated in function of the salary: everyone has to pay the same contribution. However, regional differences in the amount of the contributions still exist (Article 61, paras. 1 and 2). The other part of the health insurance is the insurance for loss of earnings (insurance for cash benefits) which is still not compulsory (see below, para. 71) (Articles 67 *et seq.*).

71. By means of collective agreements, insurance for cash benefits (daily benefits) has been made compulsory, at private law level, for a great number of employees.

72. The Federal Act on Navigation under the Swiss Flag requires that sailors are insured against sickness with a private company or a health insurance institution by the shipowners at the expense of the latter (Article 84, para. 2).

VII. Military Insurance

73. Military insurance (the Federal Act on Military Insurance of 19 June 1992)[32] is also generally considered to be a part of social insurance. It provides benefits for members of the army who become ill or have an accident in the course of their military service or due to that service. This system is exclusively financed by the federal state, so that there is no cause to distinguish here between 'independent' and 'dependent' persons.

§4. Labour Law and the Law on Civil Servants

74. The legal provisions regarding the position of civil servants and other federal or cantonal employees and of communal employees may be considered as a part of labour law in the broader sense. The rules governing them are found in the special legislation which relates to their statutory position; namely, as regards the Confederation, in the Federal Act on the Personnel of the Swiss Confederation of 24

31. *RS* 832.10.
32. *RS* 833.1.

March 2000[33] replacing the Act of 1927 and in several Ordinances.[34] For civil servants in the cantons or the communes, it is the cantonal or, as the case may be, the communal public laws that apply.

75. It is generally considered that provisions of this kind are a part of administrative law, and they are studied in this light. But, while it reserves the regulations issued by the Confederation, the cantons and the communes concerning the employment relationship of government employees, the Code of Obligations (Article 342) implicitly considers that such relations are similar to those which are governed by the provisions of the Code on Labour Contracts. In recent years, legislation regarding civil servants has brought these provisions closer to the position of civil law employees, implementing contractual relations between the state and the civil servants and introducing the rules of the Code of Obligations in these provisions.[35] For example, the Act on the Personnel of the Swiss Confederation provides for a contractual relationship between the federal state as employer and its civil servants; thus, this contract presents some analogy with the contract submitted to private labour law, i.e. to the Code of Obligations.

76. On the other hand, the protective public law provisions which apply to employees who are bound by labour contracts also apply in part to public employees. The Federal Act on Work in Public Transport Enterprises of 8 October 1971[36] basically applies to enterprises which belong to the federal state and other public enterprises, although it also applies to private transport enterprises. The Federal Employment Act of 13 March 1964 is in principle applicable to both public and private enterprises, but the federal, cantonal and communal administrations and some other public establishments are excluded from its scope. The ordinance concerning this Act (general ordinance) specifies that the following public enterprises come within the scope of the Act:

(a) those which produce, transform or treat goods or produce, transform or transport energy;
(b) those which transport persons or merchandise (but do not come under the Federal Act on Work in Public Transport Enterprises);
(c) those which deal with waste or with the cleansing and supply of water (Article 4).

77. Nevertheless, for all these enterprises, the regulations enacted by the Confederation, the cantons and the communes or the regulations governing service in public enterprises may derogate Employment Act regulations and take precedence over them (Article 71 EA).

---

33. *RS* 172.220.1.
34. In particular *RS* 172.220.11, 172.220.111.3, 172.220.111.31.
35. See Rosello, H., 'Les influences du droit privé du travail sur le droit de la fonction publique', thesis, Neuchâtel 2016.
36. *RS* 822.21.

78. Civil servants are those who carry out a public function and are appointed by a public authority for a specific period of time. They are bound to the authority by a special relationship, are governed by the regulations enacted by it and are subject to its disciplinary power. But public authorities may engage employees on the basis of a private law contract instead of appointing them to a public law function. In this case the employment relationship is governed by the rules of private law. At federal level, it is expressly provided for by Article 6, paras. 5 and 6, of the Act on the Personnel of the Swiss Confederation.[37] At cantonal level, however, case law and the majority of doctrine consider that private law can only be used in labour relations in exceptional circumstances, unless the law authorizes it expressly. The characteristics of the labour contract itself determine whether it is governed by public or private law; the will of the hiring authority is not sufficient. A court having to decide a case cannot merely rely on the title of the contract in order to determine the applicable law. It has to analyze the details of the labour relation to take its decision.[38] Lastly, it often happens that, even in the case of employees engaged on a public law basis, the applicable provisions refer expressly or implicitly to the rules of private law, which are then applicable in an analogous way.

79. While it can generally be said that the regulation of the conditions of service for civil servants remains outside labour law – coming instead within the sphere of administrative law and so not being eligible for coverage in this monograph – the distinction appears to be somewhat artificial. There is an overlap between the two domains, which means that in practice, they cannot be totally separated from one another.[39]

§5. Characteristics of Labour Law

80. The evolution and present development of labour law in Switzerland cannot be understood without bearing in mind certain existing conditions. One of the essential factors in this evolution is the constitutional organization of the country, dominated as it is by federalism and direct democracy.

81. Switzerland being a federal state, legislative competence is divided between the central state – the Confederation – and the federated states – the cantons. The Confederation may legislate only on those matters which have been attributed to it by the Federal Constitution. The Constitution of 1874 originally gave very limited powers to the Confederation in the field of social law. These powers were progressively extended by constitutional amendments in 1908 and 1947 in the field of labour law and by several other amendments (mainly in 1890, 1925, 1945, 1947,

37. See also Article 2, para. 2(2).
38. See judgments of the Federal Court 2P.181/2002 of 4 February 2003, 2P.63/2003 of 29 July 2003, 2P.136/2005 of 14 December 2005, 4A_219/2012 of 30 July 2012, 4A_238/2015 of 22 September 2015.
39. See Dunand, J.-Ph., Mahon, P. and Perrenoud, S. (eds), 'Le droit de la relation de travail à la croisée des chemins: Convergences et divergences entre le droit privé du travail et le droit de la fonction publique'.

1976) in the field of social security. While its powers had not been extended, the federal authority could not influence the whole of social law, so that federal law coexisted with cantonal law in some matters. On the other hand, federal legislation did not keep pace with the extension of the powers of the federal state and left some matters to the cantons. Numerous uncertainties regarding the distribution of powers between the central and the cantonal authorities resulted from this situation. However, these uncertainties have been proportionately reduced as federal powers and legislation have been extended. Although federal powers in the field of social law are now potentially almost universal, the Confederation has not yet exhausted all the legislative competence it is entitled to under the Constitution. Thus, in certain areas, such as agricultural labour and domestic service, the cantons retain some competence in the field of employee protection.

82. Federalism has naturally had a delaying effect on the development of federal legislation. Switzerland being a small country constituting an economic entity, this diversity of legal provisions has sometimes been inconvenient. Nevertheless, some useful experiments have been possible in the cantons before attempting to incorporate a principle into federal law. This was the case as regards holidays with pay; two cantons, Basle City and Geneva, both predominantly urban cantons, originated the legislation. Their experimentation – as well as that which resulted from collective agreements – served to popularize the institution and finally, in 1964, the principle of holidays with pay became part of the Code of Obligations.

83. The system of direct democracy has been another source of delay in legislation. The people, when called upon to vote expressly or tacitly on Acts adopted by the Federal Parliament or the cantonal parliaments, do not easily accept new institutions. Those citizens and pressure groups who oppose particular reforms will put forward arguments with the intention of frightening public opinion. Their views often meet with a favourable response because of this. The first Factories Act in 1877 was accepted by a small majority of 10,000 people. Some years later, in 1900, the first Sickness and Accident Insurance Act of 1899 was rejected by a majority of more than two-thirds, and it was not until 1911 that a second Act on the same matter was accepted by a majority of 40,000. The evolution of old age and survivors' insurance was identical. The first Act, in 1931, was rejected by a large majority; the second one, in 1946, was adopted in 1947 by a four-fifths majority. Thus, in both cases, a second attempt had to be made in order to obtain the hoped for reform. The first time around the innovation appears frightening; by the second time the people have become accustomed to the idea. In the meantime the experiment has been developed in foreign countries. The somewhat conservative character of the popular vote expresses itself in the opposite sense too: when a reform has been accepted the people do not easily accept a retrogression. Thus, a 48-hour working week having been provided for by the Factories Act of 1919, a new Act passed by the Parliament in 1922 authorizing the government to extend the hours of work was rejected in 1924 by a majority of nearly three-fifths.

84. The institution of the referendum also delays the progress of legislation for another reason: the fact that in most cases, the government does not present a Bill in the field of social law before obtaining, whenever possible, the agreement of the social partners. In the course of framing the law, the government consults with interested economic organizations and constitutes 'expert committees', essentially consisting of members designated by the employers' and workers' organizations, as well as members of other economic groups and of the cantonal governments. This consultation with the cantons, with the political parties and with economic organizations is compulsorily provided for in the Federal Constitution for the framing of legislation in all important fields (Article 147 Cst). It explains that, because of differences between the social partners, the extension of federal law in the field of workers' protection has been obtained by the adoption of the Employment Act in 1964 only, although the adoption of this Act followed a decision taken by the Federal Assembly in 1922!

85. Concerning the factors resulting from the legal system, a historical point has to be added. Due to its statute of neutrality Switzerland was able to stand aside from the two world wars which have stained the 20th century with blood. The great countries neighbouring Switzerland were involved in these two wars, which – during and in their aftermath – provoked a strengthening of national solidarity which led to the adoption of social laws. Switzerland, not being directly affected by the hostilities, remained apart from this movement, and its legislation in the field of labour law did not develop to the same degree as that in neighbouring countries. It therefore remained outside the general evolution in matters such as protection against dismissals, co-determination for employees and union rights within the enterprise.

86. Thus, labour law bears the mark of the predominant 'liberal' character of Swiss legislation. The Constitution effectively protects individual rights; among these rights are included not only 'public liberties' but also economic rights, such as economic freedom and property rights. On the basis of these rights, conservative groups and specifically employers' organizations fight against any intervention made by the state and underline the importance of such rights. On the other hand, progressive groups and the trade unions argue that real freedom can be attained only with the intervention of the state and that the principle of economic freedom is often applied as a brake against the development of labour legislation. For example, in 1954, a Bill proposed by popular initiative in Basle City for the institution in the canton of a minimum wage of SF 2 per hour could not be submitted to the popular vote because the Federal Court considered that this initiative violated the principle of freedom of commerce and industry.[40] More recently, in 2010, the Federal Court delivered a finely shaded judgment in which it held that a popular initiative requesting the registration of the principle of a minimum wage imposed by the state in a cantonal constitution (in that case, Geneva's), was in itself not contrary to federal law and could therefore not be declared invalid (case 1C_357 / 2009 of 8 April 2010). However, another case is currently pending before the Federal Court, in which it will be for the Suprem Court to judge wether the embodiment by the cantonal legislator (i.e. Neuchâtel's) of such a minimum wage guaranted by cantonal

40. *ATF* 80/1954 I 155.

constitution complies or not with federal law and in particular with economic freedom.

87. Cantonal acts instituting holidays with pay were declared to be consistent with this freedom, although only to the extent that they did not exceed what was necessary for safeguarding public health.[41]

88. Meanwhile, the Federal Constitution prescribes that freedom of commerce and industry is limited by the federal constitutional provisions and by the laws which derive from them. Among such restrictive provisions are those which empower the Confederation to legislate on the protection of employees. Furthermore, an important evolution has taken place in the last thirty years of the 20th century, in that the Federal Court has reduced the impact of the economic freedom on measures adopted by the cantons in the field of social law. It has held that what is prohibited by the Constitution are measures of 'economic policy', i.e. measures which aim to hinder free competition or to diminish its effect. Not affected by this provision are 'social' measures or measures of 'social policy', i.e. measures which aim to bring welfare to all citizens or to a great part of them, or to increase this welfare by improving the conditions of life, health or leisure. Nevertheless, these measures still have to be consistent with the constitutional principles which govern all restrictions on individual liberties; that is, lawfulness, public interest, proportionality and equality of treatment. They cannot be deemed to meet the standard of sufficient public interest if they do not satisfy a need that is so commonly recognized that the state has to provide for it.[42]

89. Among the characteristics which have dominated the evolution of labour law in Switzerland, should also be mentioned the importance that the trade unions, as well as the government, confer on collective agreements. Generally, the trade unions seek to regulate industrial relations on the basis of collective agreements and place greater emphasis on their development than on the development of statutory law. Since the conclusion in 1937 of the 'peace conventions' in the machine and metals industry – which in terms of the number of workers involved was the most important in Switzerland for many years – and in the watch-making industry, the trade unions have given preference to collective regulation and some trade union leaders have not been eager to see the development of state law in certain sectors of labour law. For instance, the trade union movement showed a singularly feeble interest in the revision of the Code of Obligations in 1971, even though employees lost ground in some areas of the Code (see below, paras. 152 and 153). However, this situation is changing, and in recent years the trade unions have shown a growing interest in the development of state law.

90. A precarious and atypical employment presents an insecurity, as for the future, the protection of employees, or economic insecurity. Furthermore, employment is precarious and atypical only if the worker concerned has not chosen

41. *Semaine Judiciaire* 1961, p. 33, *ATF* 87/1961 I 186.
42. *ATF* 97/1971 I 499, 116/1990 Ia 414, 130/2004 I 285.

it voluntarily and if its insecurity is not compensated. Examples that illustrate this definition are work on call, pseudo-independence, part-time employment, temporary work, etc.[43] Certain branches of the economy are more concerned than others by the phenomenon of precarious work. That is the case of domestic services, hotel businesses, agriculture and other services.

§6. THE EMPLOYEE, THE EMPLOYER AND THE ENTERPRISE

91. Both public labour law and private labour law have rules regulating labour relations which bind both employers and employees. There is no single definition of an employee under Swiss law; the definition differs according to the category of rules involved. On the public law level the employee is every person in the enterprise with the exception of the employer. On the private law level it is the person who, having agreed to work in the service of another, is bound to him by a labour contract. The employer, in the first case, is the person who employs one or more employees in his enterprise; in the second case he is the person who, being bound to the employee by a labour contract, provides work for him. Later we will see the distinctions which have to be drawn between the different categories of employees in public and in private law.

92. In the field of temporary work, hiring-out agencies hire out employees to other enterprises, without losing their status of employer (Articles 12–23 of the Federal Act on Recruitment and the Hiring of Services of 6 June 1989).[44]

93. Swiss law provides a very broad definition of an enterprise: there is an enterprise, according to the Employment Act, when an employer permanently or temporarily employs one or more workers, even without making use of special installations or premises (Article 1, para. 2 EA). But there is a distinction, according to the Employment Act, between two categories of enterprises: industrial enterprises and non-industrial enterprises.

94. Industrial enterprises are those which use fixed and permanent installations for the production, transformation or processing of goods or for the production, transformation or transmission of power and:

(a) the working method or organization of work is determined by the use of machines or other technical equipment or by the application of mass-production techniques and at least six workers are employed on such activities; or
(b) the working method or organization of work is decisively influenced by the use of automatic processes; or
(c) the workers' life or health are exposed to special dangers (Article 5, para. 2 EA).

43. See Geiser, T., 'Arbeitsrecht Rechtsprechungspanorama' in AJP 2016, p. 1376.
44. *RS* 823.11

95. The distinction between industrial and non-industrial enterprises does not apply to agricultural undertakings as these are excluded from the scope of the Employment Act. The total number of industrial enterprises in 2008 was 73,064. According to the above definition, building and public works enterprises and mines and quarries are not considered as industrial enterprises. The latter are subject to more stringent provisions, especially as regards measures concerning health. Anyone intending to construct or alter an industrial enterprise has to submit his plans for the approval of the cantonal authority. This authority consults the Swiss Accident Insurance Fund (Article 7, para. 1, EA). After obtaining approval the employer may begin construction of the undertaking and installations, but he cannot begin operations until he has obtained a new permit from the authority. The employer also has to have approval of his plans and an operating permit if he wishes to alter internal installations when this means a fundamental change in working methods or when it increases the risks to the life or health of the workers or produces harmful or disagreeable effects for the vicinity. For non-industrial enterprises the authorization procedure is the exclusive responsibility of the cantonal authorities, but the Federal Council may submit certain non-industrial enterprises which present important risks to the same conditions as industrial enterprises (Article 8 EA). Industrial enterprises are supervised by the federal authority.

96. All enterprises have to ask the federal authority to get permission to regularly or periodically work at night or on Sundays and to regularly or periodically continuous work (see below, para. 378).

Chapter 3. The History of Labour Law

§1. Before the Creation of the Federal State

97. Since labour law is so tightly bound up with the social and economic evolution of society, modern labour law was born in the period which followed the industrial revolution at the beginning of the 19th century. This does not, however, mean that before that time labour relations were never regulated by the law. As long ago as the 16th century wage protection measures were being taken in the textile industry in St Gallen; such measures were also taken in the 17th century in Basle and Zurich, along with measures against the truck system. Switzerland was at that time at the forefront of the development of the industry, especially in the form of home work, which has been called the 'scattered factory' system. In 1717 Zurich adopted a Factories Order which applied to all factories and manufacturers and which regulated the rights and duties of workers and employers; but what it was really aimed at was stopping the middle-men (*Trigger*) who were exploiting home workers and at the same time trying to set themselves up as the proprietors of factories. In 1779 a 'mandate' on *Rastgeben* (home work performed by children with a view to making subsistence payments to their parents) in Zurich was the first child protection measure: such work was permitted under supervision only between the age of the first communion and school-leaving age.

98. In the 19th century, with the introduction of mechanization and the creation of factories in the modern sense of the word, the old provisions disappeared. As was the case in other industrial countries at the same time, the exploitation of workers, and especially of children, knew no limits. The duration of work in the factories was 16 hours or more per day and children were employed from the age of 7, both day and night. Some of the confederate states did adopt protective measures: in Zurich, an Ordinance of 7 November 1815 established a minimum age of 12 years for factory work and regulated the duration of work for children. But due to a lack of inspection or any real sanctions these provisions were not observed. In 1837, again in Zurich, an ordinance authorized clergymen and teachers to enter factories with a view to controlling the employment of children. In 1846 an important ordinance was passed in Glarus which regulated not only the minimum age but also the hours of work for all workers (including adult men) in the spinning-mills. Against the opposition of the employers this ordinance was ratified in 1848 by the people in the *Landsgemeinde*.

§2. After the Creation of the Federal State

99. The Federal Constitution of 1848 did not give any competence to the federal authorities in the field of labour law, but it did guarantee freedom of association throughout the whole country and was therefore of great importance for the development of labour law. This freedom made possible the formation and growth of the trade unions, which played an important role in this development. They fought for the establishment and strengthening of protective labour laws and were able to conclude the first wage tariffs or factory rules, i.e. the first collective agreements (for example in Geneva after 1850).

100. The labour movement was influenced by the International Workingmen's Association, founded in London in 1864. Most of the Congresses of the Association took place in Switzerland: the first one in Geneva in 1866, the second in Lausanne in 1867 and the fourth in Basle in 1869. These Congresses stimulated and accelerated the development of the trade unions and the labour movement. On the other hand, the lack of inter-cantonal regulation in the field of workers' protection was lamented by some of the cantons which had already enacted laws and which now feared competition from industrial employers in the cantons with no such laws. The cantons of Glarus, Zurich and Aargau asked for the adoption of inter-cantonal rules, but the conferences called to solve this problem had no practical outcome. Meanwhile, in 1868, the Parliament invited the federal government to proceed with an investigation into child labour. The results of this investigation, published in 1869, revealed some serious abuses.

101. Eventually, in 1874, the revised Constitution gave the federal state the right to enact, up to a certain point, laws in the field of workers' protection; it also made the federal state responsible for contract law. The first federal Act dealing with factory work was adopted by Parliament in 1877 and ratified by the people. This Act was based essentially on the model of the first general Act on labour which had been adopted in Glarus in 1864. It regulated the hours of work in factories (11 hours per day), the minimum working age (14 years), the protection of women and young people and the liability of the employer in the case of work accidents and occupational diseases, all at the federal level. In 1881 the Federal Parliament adopted the Federal Code of Obligations regulating contracts of service.

102. Switzerland was at that time a leader in the field of labour legislation. For the same reasons that the cantons which had adopted protective legislation demanded that the other cantons follow their example, Switzerland was led to demand the adoption of international legislation on work in factories. In 1880 and 1888 the Federal Parliament invited the Federal Council to enter into negotiations with the other major industrial states. The steps taken by Switzerland were at the origin of the Conference of Berlin of 1890, and afterwards the Conferences of Bern in 1905, 1906 and 1913, which marked the beginning of international labour legislation and paved the way for the creation in 1919 of the International Labour Organization.

103. The federal legislation was gradually improved upon and reinforced. The Factories Act was revised in 1914 (the maximum duration of work being reduced to 10 hours per day) and, after the general strike of 1918, in 1919 (introduction of the 48-hour week). The 1881 Code of Obligations was replaced in 1911 by a new one which improved the protection of employees by civil law means. The protection of workers was also reinforced by the adoption of several new Acts: namely the Act of 31 March 1922 on the employment of young persons and women in crafts; the Act of 26 September 1931 on weekly rest; the Act of 24 June 1938 on the minimum age for employment (15 years of age) and the Act of 12 December 1940 on home work. During this period, while employment relations at the civil law level were exclusively regulated by the federal law, there were, besides the federal law which was limited in its scope and on a public protective law level, cantonal Acts. The federal law was mainly concerned with factories, transport enterprises and home work. Other undertakings were, apart from some particular rules about weekly rest and the minimum age, subject to cantonal law – in as much as it existed.

104. But the Employment Act of 13 March 1964, which replaced most of the previous federal Acts at the public protective law level, extended federal regulation to the majority of the branches of the economy – thus sensibly reducing the competence of the cantons (this federal Act was modified by an amending Act of 20 March 1998). As regards civil law, the Code of Obligations, which was first revised in 1956 in respect of collective agreements, was further revised in 1971 when completely new rules governing labour contracts were introduced; other important modifications took place in 1988 (Act on the Termination of the contract of Labour) and 1993 (Act on Collective Dismissals and Transfer of the Employment Relationship). Specific Acts regarding labour law were also recently adopted: 1995 (Federal Act on Gender Equality),[45] 1999 (modification connected with the bilateral agreements with the European Union) and 2005 (Federal Act on Measures to Combat Illegal Employment).[46]

105. It ought to be added that in the field of collective agreements, as in that of protective labour law, Switzerland has historically played a leading role. The Act of 1900 on usage tariffs in Geneva, which gave a special value (force of usage) to collective agreements and instituted compulsory arbitration in collective disputes, was the first law of its kind in Europe. The Federal Code of Obligations of 1911, which gave normative effect to collective agreements, has been an important element in the development of collective labour law; as has been said, the provisions regarding collective agreements were replaced in 1956 by new provisions which took into consideration the evolution of collective relations in the first half of the century. Now, collective agreements play as important a role in the regulation of the conditions of work, as does the state.

45. E *RS* 151.1.
46. *RS* 822.41.

Chapter 4. The Role of Government Institutions in the Administration of Labour Law and Industrial Relations

§1. General Remarks

106. The role of government institutions in the field of labour law and industrial relations is relatively restricted in Switzerland. While this country was one of the first to enact laws for the protection of workers in the classical sense of the term, i.e. for protection as regards the duration of work, industrial safety, the special protection of women and young people and the institution of an inspection service, they did not extend the action of the government authorities much further than this. The fundamental politics relies on the actions of the social partners. In principle, the state does not intervene in the determination of wages in the private sector. It observes the same restraint in the field of industrial relations. The constitutional principle of economic freedom is not just a juridical principle, but pragmatically directs the approach of the public authorities towards labour law and industrial relations.

107. New forms of market control were instituted as a consequence of the adoption of the ancillary implementation measures of the bilateral agreement, particularly to the agreement on free movement of persons. A 'tripartite' commission with specific control competences had to be constituted for every canton and for the Confederation (Article 360*b* CO). In addition, inspectors, whose competences are to control wages according to Article 360*a* CO and to observe the market on behalf of the 'tripartite' commissions, were also introduced (Article 7*a*, para. 1 of the Federal Act on accompanying measures applicable to posted workers and minimum wage control provided by standard employment contracts).[47]

§2. Government Departments and Agencies

108. On the federal level there is no special government department devoted exclusively to the problems of labour. Instead, these problems are dealt with by the Department of Economy, but in fact most government duties are carried out by a subdivision of the Department – the SECO (State Secretariat for Economic Affairs; in German: *Staatssekretariat für Wirtschaft* and in French: *Secrétariat d'Etat à l'économie* combining the former Federal Office for Industry, Crafts and Labour and the Federal Office of Foreign Economy). This office is responsible for the preparation and execution of laws concerning the labour market, manpower, workers' migration, workers' protection and labour law.[48] As there is no incomes policy in Switzerland the competence of the SECO naturally does not extend to the problem

47. *RS* 823.20; Federal Act on Workers posted to Switzerland.
48. Ordinance of 14 June 1999, *RS* 172.216.1. The combining of the two former offices under the new structure SECO was introduced by a revision in 1999. By the term 'labour law' is meant *public* labour law; another department, the Department of Justice and Police, which is generally responsible for civil law, is responsible for the law on labour contracts and collective agreements.

of determining wages. Among the duties which concern the SECO, ought to be mentioned problems regarding the execution of the Employment Act, such as decisions relating to the permits necessary for extending the duration of work or for departing from certain provisions of the Act. The SECO is also responsible for organizing labour inspection and for running the medical labour service. Another subdivision of the Department, Federal Office for vocational training and technology, deals with government duties in the matter of vocational training.

109. The Federal Department of Economy, as such, is itself entrusted with some powers, mainly in the fields of collective disputes and vocational training (see below, para. 749). The Federal Council adopts executive orders for the execution of protective law; it is competent to decree or approve the extension of collective agreements and to adopt standard labour contracts (see below, paras. 696 and 706).

110. Although a matter may lie within the competence of the federal authorities, the responsibility for executing the federal legislation is in large measure conferred on the cantonal authorities. For example, as regards the Employment Act, supervision of its execution is currently entrusted to the cantons, which may in certain cases provide employers with permits for overtime work and so on. While there are federal inspectors, the cantons also have to maintain their own inspection corps. The federal authority nevertheless retains for itself certain competence, especially concerning 'industrial' enterprises. In addition, the general supervision of the execution is the responsibility of the federal authority.

§3. Labour Inspection and Labour Market Control

111. In all countries, labour inspection is one of the most valuable means which can be used for promoting workers' protection. Without an effective service of inspection, the law remains a dead letter. This has been understood for a long time in Switzerland, where the inspection has been introduced since the first Act regarding work in factories, established in 1877. Now, the Employment Act provides that cantons are primarily competent to exert control on the application of their provisions (Article 41 para. 1er LTr).[49] Each canton has to institute an inspection service which must control the observance of the legal provisions and regulations by the undertakings. The federal state exerts supervision over this control. The country is divided into two areas, and in each of them a federal inspectorate of labour has been installed. The federal inspectors, like the cantonal ones, must visit the undertakings with a view to supervising the execution of legal provisions. Moreover, the federal inspectors must deliver advice to the cantons, to employers and to workers; they see whether the application of the Act has been correctly carried out by the cantons. A medical labour service, created by the federal state, also has to visit undertakings and give advice on medical matters in the application of the Act and regulations. The federal inspectors and the medical service may instruct the employer on the measures to be taken.

---

49. *RS* 822.11.

112. The employer is obliged to allow the inspectors to enter the premises of undertakings, of refectories and clubs, to make inquiries therein and remove things and materials to be examined (Article 45, para. 2, EA). Inspectors are empowered to interrogate the employer and, without witnesses, the worker, on any matter concerning the application of the Employment Act or of the regulations or decisions taken in accordance with the Act.

113. If a breach of the legal provisions is established, the employer may be penally responsible for these infractions (Articles 59 *et seq.* EA).

114. Tripartite commissions and inspectors have the right to obtain information and to consult any document necessary for their investigation (Article 360 *b,* para. 5, CO, 7 of the Federal Act on the minimum employment and salary conditions for workers posted to Switzerland and accompanying measures).

§4. Vocational Training

115. According to Article 34*ter* of the former Constitution, adopted in 1947, the Confederation was enabled to legislate on vocational training in industry, crafts, commerce, agriculture and domestic service. It can be deduced from this that the Constitution did not intend to confer upon the federal state universal powers in this respect, vocational training in other areas still lying in the hands of the cantons. A constitutional amendment draft instituting the right to education and giving the Confederation power to legislate on the whole matter of vocational training was rejected in 1975 by a majority of the cantons, even though a majority of citizens had approved it. It would, if it had been adopted, have permitted the federal state to enact laws on vocational training for the professions such as education, nursing and social work. However, the new Constitution, adopted in 1999, contains, in its Article 63 no limitation of the federal power to legislate in the field of vocational training. This is one of the few novelties of the new Constitution (see above, para. 5).

116. Vocational training is administered under the Federal Act on Vocational and Professional Education and Training of 13 December 2002,[50] which succeeded to the Act of 19 April 1978. The scope of application of the new Act is limited to all professional sectors other than those of universities (Article 2, para. 1). From now on, the agriculture domain is also incorporated to the Federal Act on Vocational and Professional Education and Training, while it formerly fell within the scope of the Federal Act on Agriculture of 29 April 1998.[51] This Act is a framework agreement; it demands therefore the adoption of cantonal implementation acts.[52]

---

50. *RS* 412.10. See http://www.bbt.admin.ch/index.html?lang=en.
51. *RS* 910.1.
52. FF 2000, p. 5279.

§5. THE EMPLOYMENT SERVICE

117. The legislation governing employment service is tightly bound up with the measures taken in the fight against unemployment. The Federal Act on Recruitment and the Hiring of Services of 6 October 1989 aims at:

(a) laying down rules governing private employment agencies and the hiring-out of employees;
(b) ensuring a public employment service which contributes to creating or maintaining a balanced labour market;
(c) protecting workers who have recourse to private employment agencies, to public employment services and to agencies which hire out employees (Article 1).

118. Under this Act, whoever intends to act regularly and for a fee as an intermediary between an employer and a worker, with a view to finding employment for the latter, has to apply for a licence with the competent cantonal authority (Article 2, para. 1). For the recruitment of workers for placement abroad as well as for the recruitment of workers from abroad for placement in Switzerland, a supplementary licence has to be applied for with the SECO (Article 2, para. 3).

119. Each canton has to maintain a labour office, whose role is to try and help the workers looking for work. The employer has to give notice of collective redundancies and the closure of enterprises to this office (Article 29). The cantonal labour offices play a great role in the administration of unemployment insurance. Unemployed persons have to register with the cantonal authority, which may, if necessary, decide whether or not they are capable for work and thus eligible for a benefit.

120. In recent years, temporary work has acquired a great importance and the number of hiring-out agencies has increased a great deal. The Act institutes a control over these agencies (Articles 12 *et seq.*). The latter, like employment agencies, have to apply for a licence and to follow a number of rules when going through the hiring procedure (see below, para. 237).

121. The Ordinance on Recruitment[53] distinguishes between:

(a) temporary work; there is temporary work when the aim and the duration of the contract are limited to one single mission in a user undertaking;
(b) labour supply contracts, the aim of the contract concluded between the temporary employment business and the worker being the placing of the worker at the disposal of a user enterprise;
(c) occasional placing of workers at the disposal of a user enterprise, the aim of the labour contract being of putting the worker under the authority of the contracting employer and the hiring-out of the worker being exceptional (Article 27).

53. *RS* 823.111.

122. This last form of hiring-out of workers needs no licence (Article 28 of the Ordinance).

§6. THE ADMISSION OF FOREIGN WORKERS

I. General Remarks

123. The admission of foreign workers to Switzerland is regulated by the Federal Act on Foreign Nationals of 16 December 2005[54] and by several Ordinances[55] as well as by the Agreement on free movement of persons, its additional Protocols and other international agreements. Permits for residence and work are in principle granted by the cantonal authorities. However, some decisions have to be approved by the Federal Office for Migration (FOM) (a subdivision of the Department of Justice and Police). Requests must be submitted to the cantonal labour market authority.

124. Foreign workers do not benefit from the same status and conditions of entry and residency in Switzerland whether they are native from EU/EFTA Member States or nationals of third countries, see below paras. 136 *et seq.*

II. Admission of Nationals of the Member States of the EU and the EFTA

A. The Gradual Opening of the Swiss Labour Market

125. According to bilateral agreements concluded with the European Union and accepted by the Swiss people on 21 May 2000 (see above, para. 24), the Agreement of free movement of persons and its additional protocols are gradually being implemented. Thus, the Swiss system is adapted to the principle of the free movement of persons on the basis of the *acquis communautaire*, in particular by means of gradual opening of the labour market. The agreement covers workers, self-employed persons and persons not gainfully employed who have sufficient financial means. The agreement had an initial duration of seven years. After this initial period, it was prolonged for an indefinite span.

126. As it has been said, the Agreement provides for a gradually opening access to the (Swiss) labour market,[56] over a period of 12 years beginning in 2002 for the 15 older members of the EU, Malta, Cyprus and the Member States of EFTA (EU-17/ EFTA). With the entrance into force of the two additional protocols, two new gradually opening access periods started in 2006 and 2009. The first period concerns eight of the EU new Member States (EU-8) and the second relates to Bulgaria

54. *RS* 142.20.
55. In particular *RS* 142.201.
56. See on this question the Directives of the Federal Office for Migration on the Agreement on free movement of persons of 1 June 2009.

and Romania (EU-2). Recently, Protocol III on the extension of the Agreement to Croatia entered into force on 1 January 2017 (i.e. a new transitional period has started). This protocol was ratified after the adoption by the Parliament of the implementing legislation of Article 121a of the Federal Constitution following the acceptance of the initiative against mass immigration on 9 February 2014. The solution chosen (i.e. the 'reduced national priority') by the Federal chambers enables these new provisions to be applied in respect of the Agreement.

127. Once the agreement takes effect, citizens of the European Union will benefit from equality of treatment and others favourable conditions. During a first period, wage controls, a permit system and quotas ('contingents') are also maintained for the European workers, but with annual preferential quotas for Community citizens within the quota system. These transitional periods lasted until 30 April 2011 for the EU-8 citizens (after two extensions) and until 31 May 2016 for the EU-2 nationals. After the aforesaid periods, the preferential treatment for indigenous workers and all discriminatory practices, in so far as the control of wages and social conditions are concerned, were abolished. After the aforesaid periods, the agreement provides for the abolition of quotas in relation to Community citizens. Quotas are no longer applied to people native of the older members of the EU, Malta and Cyprus and the Member States of the EFTA (EU-17/EFTA) since 1 June 2007. However, in the event of a massive increase (more than 10 per cent in excess of the average for the previous three years) in the numbers arriving from the Community, Switzerland is free to unilaterally reintroduce quotas for the following two years.

B. The Different Types of Authorization[57]

128. If EU/EFTA workers fulfil the conditions regarding the right to residence according to the agreement on free movement of persons, state authorities of the host state are obliged to deliver a residence permit dedicated to this right. Thereby an authorization is required to EU and EFTA workers in order for them to be engaged in a gainful activity in Switzerland. On restricted occasions, the latter can, however, simply announce their arrival. This is the case of ordinary workers native from the EU-17/EFTA, planning to work for a maximum of three months per calendar year. The same is true for self-employed service providers from Member States of the EU-17/EFTA and for offshore workers, staying in Switzerland for a maximum of 90 days. It is nevertheless provided that the authorization and announcement proceedings are governed by the Federal Act on Foreign Nationals (Article 2(4) of Annex I to the Agreement on free movement of persons and Article 9 of the Ordinance on the introduction of the latter Agreement and Article 2, para. 4 of the Appendix to Annex K of the convention establishing the EFTA).[58]

57. See the Directives of the Federal Office for Migration on the Agreement on free movement of persons of 1 June 2009 and the official website of the FOM: http://www.bfm.admin.ch/bfm/en/ home /themen/aufenthalt/eu_efta.html.
58. *RS* 142.203.

129. EU/EFTA workers can obtain two different types of authorization, the granting of which depends, as a rule, on the duration of the labour contract. The first type of authorization is the short-term residence permit (so called L EU/EFTA permit) limited to 364 days. The second type of authorization is the residence permit (B EU/EFTA permit), granted for five years if the employment relationships last more than one year. The duration of both permits can be extended. Their validity covers the whole Swiss territory. However, the Agreement on free movement of persons does not provide any specific provision as to the settlement permit (C EU/EFTA permit), which is ruled by the Federal Act on Foreign Nationals. According to settlement agreements, nationals of EU-15 and EFTA Member States can nevertheless obtain settlement permits, after a regular and uninterrupted stay of five years.

130. EU-25 and EFTA self-employed workers can be granted with an initial residence authorization of five years, provided that they give proof of a gainful employment at the time of the request.

131. A resident permit has to be granted to EU and EFTA workers, assuming required conditions are satisfied. Consequently, if the authority refuses the granting in such cases, the workers can appeal to the Federal Court (Articles 82 and 86, para. 1, of the Federal Act on the Federal Supreme Court).

132. The right of accompaniment is granted to the worker's spouse, their descendants of less than 21 years old or dependants or dependent relatives in the ascending line. The worker must nonetheless have suitable housing as he makes the request and at the time of the arrival of his family.

133. Thanks to the Agreement, EU-17 and EFTA cross-border workers (G EU/EFTA permit) are now free to work in the whole Swiss territory. They, however, have to return to their place of residence abroad at least once a week. The situation of EU-8 and EU-2 cross-border workers is nevertheless different for now, given that they must still stay in the border zones.

134. The Agreement contains specific provisions regarding offshore workers and self-employed service providers.

C. Ancillary Implementation Measures

135. As already said, the Agreement on free movement of persons is accompanied by domestic implementation measures (ancillary implementation measures), which have been adopted simultaneously and reinforced after the adoption of the first Protocol, in order to avoid social and wage dumping. These measures are provided for by the Federal Act on Workers posted to Switzerland of 8 October 1999

(*Loi sur les travailleurs détachés, LDét*).[59] This Act provides in particular for the possibility of fixing minimum wages by means of standard labour contracts (see below, paras. 411, 675, 698, 705 and 710–712). A revision of the ancillary implementation measures entered into force on 1 April 2006. Following improvements were made: in the scope of the Act on Workers posted to Switzerland, the announcement provision was modified (Article 6) and the employment of cantonal inspectors was provided (Article 7*a*, para. 1). Other Acts were also concerned by this revision: Article 330*b* CO (obligation to inform the worker), Article 2, No. 3bis, of the Federal Act on the Declaration of General Application of Collective Employment Agreements,[60] Articles 17, para. 3 and 20 of the Act on Recruitment and the Hiring of Services.[61]

III. Admission for Nationals of Other Countries[62]

136. Unlike EU and EFTA workers (see above, paras. 125 *et seq.*), workers from other countries do not benefit from any facilitated access to the Swiss labour market. Quotas and many restrictive conditions are provided on obtaining working authorizations in Switzerland. The main conditions of admission will be mentioned below.

137. Such workers can enter the Swiss labour market on condition that their admission serves the economic interests of the country (Article 18 of the Federal Act on Foreign Nationals). However, other employees consistently take precedence over workers from other countries (Article 21, para. 1). This is the case for Swiss workers, workers already staying in Switzerland and those coming from the EU or the EFTA. Besides, a worker native of another country cannot be hired at a lower wage than common conditions of the place, the occupation and the branch (Article 22). Personal qualifications also play an important part in the obtaining of a working authorization. Indeed, allowing for exceptions, only executives, specialists or other skilled workers can be admitted to the Swiss labour market (Article 23, para. 1). As well as the aforementioned conditions, the number of various types of authorizations granted every year is limited (Article 20 and Articles 19 and 20 of the Ordinance on Admission, Residence and Employment).[63] An exception to this rule is however provided for short-term residence authorizations of maximum 120 days. Dispensations to the conditions of admission are nevertheless stated (Article 30, para. 1 of the Federal Act on Foreign Nationals).

138. The types of authorization existing for nationals of other countries are similar to those for citizens of the Member States of the EU and the EFTA. A short-term

59. See FF 1999, p. 5440 (5695 *seq.*, 5737 and 5779 *seq.*) for the government's draft and explanation report.
60. *RS* 221.215.311.
61. See FF 2004, p. 6187 for the government's draft and explanation report.
62. See the Directives of the Federal Office for Migration on the aliens' field of 1 July 2010, chapter I.4 and the official website of the FOM: http://www.bfm.admin.ch/bfm/fr/home.html.
63. *RS* 142.201.

residence authorization (Permit L) can thus be granted to workers for a stay of maximum one year. An extension is only possible up to two years. A renewal can be obtained after an interruption of the stay (Article 32). A worker staying for more than a year can receive a residence authorization (Permit B). Its duration of validity of one year can be prolonged, in the absence of motive of revocation (Article 33), such as the dependence on welfare benefits, for example. The settlement authorization (Permit C), as for it, has an indefinite duration. It can be granted only after a stay of at least 10 years, of which the last five years in a continuous way (Article 34). The Swiss law finally provides for exceptional cross-border authorizations (Permit G, Article 35), authorizations for asylum-seekers (Permit N, Article 42 of the Asylum Act), authorizations for people in need for protection (Permit S, Article 74 of the Asylum Act) and authorizations for provisionally admitted foreigners (Permit F, Article 41, para. 2, of the Federal Act on Foreign Nationals). Foreigner holders of Permits L, B, C and G can have gainful employment, whereas holders of Permit S must ask for an authorization. Permits N and S only allow their holders to work in certain circumstances (Articles 43 and 75 of the Asylum Act, 85 of the Federal Act on Foreign Nationals and 52–53 of the Ordinance on Admission, Residence and Employment).[64]

139. The practice of a self-employed activity is, as a rule, only permitted to workers holding a settlement authorization (Article 38, para. 4, of the Federal Act on Foreign Nationals). The restrictive conditions of Article 19 apply indeed to other aliens.

140. Before the approval of the FOM, initial short-term residence or residence authorizations require a preliminary decision of the competent cantonal authority (Articles 83 *et seq.* of the Ordinance on Admission, Residence and Employment).

141. Third-state nationals benefit from a more limited family accompaniment right than workers of the EU and the EFTA. The family accompaniment relating to short-term residence and residence authorization takes into account only the spouse and single children under the age of 18, all forming a common household (Articles 44 and 45 of the Federal Act on Foreign Nationals).

64. *RS* 142.31.

Chapter 5. The Sources of Labour Law

§1. Domestic Law

142. Labour relations are governed primarily – in terms of the hierarchy of sources – by Acts adopted by the legislative power. Apart from the Constitution and, to some extent, from international treaties (see below, para. 1926), statutory law takes precedence over all the other sources of labour law except when the statute itself states otherwise. But legislative provisions may have different aspects and a different scope.

143. The various sources of labour law examined below are classified according to their belonging to private law, public law, mixed law, collective law or other sources.

I. Federal Constitution

144. Article 122 Cst provides that the federal state may legislate on the whole of civil law. Historically, in 1874, the federal state had only a limited power, allowing legislation on some few matters of civil law, especially the law of obligations. The limited provision in the Constitution of 1874 was at the origin of the first federal Code of Obligations in 1881 and of the present Code of 1911 which regulates labour contracts. The adoption of the Code of 1881 had the effect of depriving the cantons of any power to regulate labour contracts, in accordance with the principle of supremacy of federal law (Article 49 Cst which states that federal law takes precedence over contrary cantonal law). Thus the adoption of the Code of Obligations rendered void all legal cantonal provisions concerning labour contracts.

145. The Federal Constitution[65] is indeed the basis for the determination of the distribution of powers between the Confederation on the one hand and the cantons on the other. Some provisions of the Constitution authorize the federal state to enact laws relating to labour. Article 110 Cst empowers the Confederation to enact uniform laws protecting working men. The same article authorizes the Confederation to enact laws governing relations between employers and employees, the general applicability of collective agreements and the employment service. Article 63 empowers the Confederation to legislate in the field of vocational training. All these provisions *permit* the Confederation to enact laws, but as long as it does not do so, the cantons maintain their legislative power. In the field of protective labour law the federal laws, and especially the Employment Act, have extended federal competence to an important degree. The cantons may nevertheless still freely enact laws in areas which have not been affected by federal law.

65. *RS* 101.

146. Other provisions of the Federal Constitution relating to particular matters have also allowed the Confederation to enact rules in the field of labour law. Thus, the Constitution provides that the law on road traffic comes within the powers of the Confederation (since 1921, today's Article 82 Cst), as it does in Article 87 concerning rail traffic, shipping (since 1919) and air transport (since 1921). A 'conjunctural' provision, adopted in 1978, today's Article 100, gives the federal legislator a mandate to take measures to ensure a balance in economic development and, in particular, to prevent and fight against unemployment and inflation.

147. The Constitution does not confine itself to determining the respective competences of the federal and cantonal powers or to giving a definite mandate to the legislator. It may also define the limits within which the legislator can act. Thus, Article 110, giving the federal state the power to declare the extension of the scope of collective labour agreements, also gives the conditions under which this extension may be decided.

148. Naturally, federal Acts – like cantonal Acts – have to be consistent with the Federal Constitution. However, while the Federal Court may declare void a cantonal Act as contrary to the federal (or cantonal) Constitution, or may declare it without effect for the same reason, it cannot control the constitutionality of federal Acts and is bound to apply them (Article 190 Cst). But, if a provision involves different possible interpretations, the Court will apply it in a sense which is consistent with the Constitution.[66]

149. It has already been pointed out that the Federal Constitution (as do the cantonal constitutions) guarantees individual rights (see above, para. 14). Some of these rights are of great importance for labour law. One should mention in this respect Article 26 (right to property), Article 27 (economic freedom), Articles 23 and 28 (freedom of association and freedom to unionize) and the general provision of Article 8 (equality). The third paragraph of this latter provision (adopted in 1981) declares the equality of rights between the sexes, notably in the labour domain, and provides for the right of men and women to receive equal pay for work of equal value; this right can be applied directly by the courts.

II. Private Law

150. Private or civil law Acts regulate relations between individuals themselves – who are theoretically on the same level. As opposed to what will be said about public law, in the field of private law the public authorities do not intervene to ensure the application of the legislation. The individual who maintains that his co-contractor has violated a legal provision has to bring an action before the courts if he wishes to enforce his rights.

66. *ATF* 99/1973 Ia 630, Ib 185, 108/1982 V 235, 119/1993 Ia 241, 131/2005 II 697 and 710.

151. The private law provisions have been wholly codified. Labour contracts are regulated by the Code of Obligations of 30 March 1911.[67] Before 1971, some of the provisions relating to labour contracts were also scattered among other Acts. These provisions have, for the most part, been integrated into the Code by an amending Act of 25 June 1971 which gave a new tenor to Title X of the Code of Obligations concerning labour contracts. The effect of private law provisions can be diverse: they can either have a mandatory effect, or an optional effect.

A. Mandatory Provisions

152. When the legislator has intended to give the law a mandatory effect individuals have to observe it in their conventions. Title X of the Code of Obligations, which deals with labour contracts, contains – more so than do the titles dealing with other kinds of contracts – mandatory provisions. The aim of these provisions is primarily to protect employees from their employers. Although in these cases the legislator did not want to give the legal provisions a coercive – public law – effect, he nevertheless wished to give them a special value, thus depriving agreements which contradict the mandatory provisions of any effect. But the aim of a number of mandatory provisions has at the same time been to ensure the protection of employers – this protection having been one of the objectives of the legal revision of 1971.

153. Indeed, while all the legal revisions of the labour contract had been previously aimed at improving the conditions of employees, with this last revision, the situation of the employee has been worsened in some respects. The federal government, followed by Parliament, held that the worker's state of dependency had disappeared thanks to full employment or over-employment (a situation which was thought to be definitive!), so that not only had the worker to be protected against the employer, but the employer too had to be protected against the worker. Whence the introduction in the Code of provisions from which no departure could be made either to the employee's detriment or to the employer's detriment. Therefore one has to distinguish between two kinds of mandatory provisions: on the one hand there are absolutely mandatory provisions; on the other, relatively mandatory provisions.

154. There are some absolutely mandatory legal provisions, from which no departure can be made, either to the employer's or to the employee's detriment. Article 361 CO enumerates the absolutely mandatory rules regulating labour contracts and states that agreements and clauses of collective agreements and standard labour contracts which depart from them are void. Many of these provisions mark a setback, giving employers protection they apparently do not need. But the protection thus given to the employers has been somewhat attenuated by the legal revision of 1988. However, the nature of a provision can change in course of time (see below, para. 364).

67. *RS* 220.

155. Article 362 CO enumerates relatively mandatory legal provisions, i.e. provisions from which the contracting parties may not depart to the employee's detriment, although departures to the employer's detriment can be made. In these cases if the provisions of the contract are more favourable for the employee they are perfectly valid. For instance, provisions regarding the payment of remuneration when the employee is unable to work may be more favourable to the employee under his individual contract than according to the Code (Article 324*a* CO). It is admitted that the lists of Articles 361 and 362 CO are, however, not exhaustive. Indeed, as an example and according to case law, Article 321 *c,* para. 3, CO relating to overtime pay is partly mandatory, even if not included in the lists of Articles 361 and 362 CO.[68]

156. The relatively mandatory provisions are typical in labour law and especially in the contract of labour. As has been said (see above, para. 47), one of the main characteristics of the labour law provisions is that they are deemed to ensure the protection of the workers. The relatively mandatory provisions of the Code are one of the means the legislator can use to that effect. These provisions have been conceived with the view to protecting the weaker party to the contract, i.e. the worker.

157. But the following question arises: what is the meaning of the 'invalidity' of contractual clauses which are contrary to the mandatory provisions of the law? Does it only mean that one cannot validly renounce in advance the ability to avail oneself of the rights vested in the contract, or is the waiver also void when it has been expressed at the time the right falls due, or even afterwards? This question has been expressly solved by the law. Article 341, para. 1, CO states that the employee may not waive any claims arising from the mandatory provisions of the law while under contract or during the month which follows its termination. Thus, this provision protects only the employee and not the employer.[69] The Federal Court ruled that it excludes any waiver; not only an express, but also a tacit waiver,[70] and that the simple passage of time until he uses his right to claim does not mean that he renounces to the right.[71]

B. Optional Provisions

158. Optional provisions apply only when there are no contrary contractual clauses. They are deemed to express the will of the parties which has not otherwise been expressed. As regards provisions of the Code of Obligations dealing with the labour contract, provisions which are not mentioned as being mandatory (especially by Articles 361 and 362) are in principle considered as being optional. The parties

68. *ATF* 124/1998 III 469, see also *ATF* 132/2006 III 32.
69. Examples: *ATF* 124/1998 II 436 (453) and III 469 (where the Federal Court ruled that the worker cannot validly waive the supplement wage for the supplementary hours he has already worked).
70. *ATF* 105/1979 II 39.
71. *ATF* 110/1984 II 273, 116/1990 II 428, 126/2000 III 337.

may depart from the optional provisions to both the employer's and the employee's detriment.

C. *Impact of Public Law Provisions on Private Law*

159. In the field of labour law, the public law provisions have a direct impact on private law. Indeed, the person who is bound by a labour contract and in favour of whom an obligation has been imposed by public law on a third person may institute civil proceedings to bring about the discharge of that obligation (Article 342, para. 2, CO). Since civil law is the exclusive domain of the federal authorities, the cantons may not enact laws in this field except when federal law specifically authorizes them to do so.

D. *The Individual Labour Contract*

160. Although the individual contract is not considered formally as a source of labour law, its place in the hierarchy of sources has to be examined. From what has already been said, it may be concluded that the individual contract takes precedence only over those statutory provisions which have an optional effect or, as the case may be, over relatively mandatory statutory provisions. It takes precedence over the provisions of a collective agreement only when it is more favourable for the employee. This does not mean that the clauses of the individual labour contract have little practical importance. Indeed, many of the conditions of work are still determined by the individual contract. In most cases wages are fixed by it. Wages are not determined by statutory law or by collective agreements, which may fix only the minimum or average wages; effective wages have, therefore, to be fixed by the individual labour contract.

161. In some cases the law distinguishes between an ordinary contract (which may be oral or even tacit) and a written contract, conferring a greater value on the latter. The legal provisions may have a mandatory character in the face of an unwritten contract but only an optional character in the face of an arrangement in writing (as well as in the face of a collective agreement or of a standard labour contract). This is, for instance, the case with respect to the wage supplement for overtime (Article 321*c* CO). The same may occur in this connection between standard labour contracts or usage on the one hand and arrangements made in writing on the other.

III. Public Law

A. *Legislation*

162. Public law Acts involve orders given by the state to individuals. This type of legislation (protective legislation) has a coercive action. Its provisions are compulsory for the employer as well as the employee. Derogation may be consented to only within the limits set by the Act. Its application is under the control of the state and any breaches are subject to penal sanctions. Now, in the field of labour law, most of the public law Acts are federal Acts. As we have already said (see above, para. 146), the cantons may legislate mainly in domains where there is no federal Act (protection of agricultural workers, domestic servants and apprentices in those professions which do not come within the scope of federal public law) and some have done so.

163. The federal public law Acts regulating the conditions of work are as follows:

- No. 1. The Federal Act on Employment in Business, Trade and Industry (Employment Act) of 13 March 1964.[72] This Act applies to all enterprises and employees, with some exceptions, more particularly the following:
  - (a) agricultural enterprises and related services, horticultural enterprises and fishing;
  - (b) private households;
  - (c) public administrations;
  - (d) churches and monasteries;
  - (e) enterprises covered by another federal public law Act (public transport, maritime shipping, home workers);
  - (f) aircrews in international air transport undertakings;
  - (g) persons in senior management positions, employees engaged in independent artistic or in scientific work, commercial travellers, teaching staff in private schools and teaching, welfare, educational or supervisory staff employed in institutions;
  - (h) family enterprises.
- No. 2. The Federal Act on Work in Public Transport Enterprises (Act on Hours of Work) of 8 October 1971. This applies to employees in postal services, federal and private concession railways, motor transport concessions, shipping and telepheric enterprises.
- No. 3. The Federal Act on Home Work of 20 March 1981,[73] which applies to home workers in industry and crafts.
- No. 4. The Road Traffic Act of 19 December 1958,[74] Article 56 of which mandates the Federal Council to regulate the hours of work of professional drivers.[75]
- No. 5. The Federal Act on Information and Consultation of Workers in the Enterprise (Act on Participation) of 17 December 1993.[76]
- No. 6. The Federal Act on Measures to Combat Illegal Employment of 17 June 2005.

---

72. *RS* 822.11.
73. *RS* 822.31.
74. *RS* 741.01.
75. On basis of this provision the Federal Council has adopted the *Drivers' Ordinance* of 19 June 1995 (*RS* 822.221, see below, para. 138).
76. *RS* 822.14.

164. Regulations or orders of the executive power have to be based on a provision in an Act which empowers the executive authority to issue provisions for the execution of that Act. Such regulations are issued mainly in the field of public law. They have the same executory force as acts of the legislative power. Naturally they have to be consistent with the Act concerned and cannot depart from it, except when the Act itself empowers the executive authority to do so. Among the numerous ordinances issued by the Federal Council and affecting the protection of employees ought to be mentioned:

(1) the ordinances for the execution of the Employment Act, namely:
   (a) Ordinance I, or General Ordinance, of 10 May 2000;[77]
   (b) Ordinance II, or Ordinance on Special Provisions for Certain Categories of Enterprises or Employees, of 10 May 2000;[78] this ordinance contains rules which may depart, for such enterprises or employees, from the provisions of the Act on hours of work;
   (c) Ordinance III, or Ordinance on Industrial Hygiene in Industrial Enterprises, of 18 August 1993;[79]
   (d) Ordinance IV, or Ordinance on Construction and Set up of Enterprises (planning approval procedure), of 18 August 1993;[80]
   (e) Ordinance V, or Ordinance on Protection of Young Workers, of 28 September 2007;[81]
(2) the Ordinance to the Act on Work in Public Transport Enterprises of 26 January 1972;[82]
(3) the Ordinance to the Act on Home Work of 20 December 1982;[83]
(4) the Drivers' Ordinance of 19 June 1995 which applies to all professional car drivers, whether employed or self-employed;
(5) numerous ordinances on the prevention of accidents and occupational diseases; namely the Ordinance on Prevention of Accidents and Occupational Diseases of 19 December 1983.

B. *Standard Labour Contracts*

165. In some professions where collective agreements are not usual, the federal or cantonal authorities will establish standard labour contracts (Articles 359 to 360f CO), i.e. rules which apply to relations between employer and employee when a matter has not been regulated by an individual labour contract. These rules have the same binding force as the clauses of a contract. Under the same circumstances as for collective agreements, however (see below, para. 202), the standard labour

77. *RS* 822.111.
78. *RS* 822.112.
79. *RS* 822.113.
80. *RS* 822.114.
81. *RS* 822.115.
82. *RS* 822.211.
83. *RS* 822.311.

contract may take precedence over legal provisions which are described as being absolutely or relatively mandatory. The standard contract may provide that some of its provisions apply to individual relations even when a matter has been regulated by the individual contract, as long as that contract is not a written one. In these cases the standard labour contract takes precedence over the individual contract.

166. The ancillary implementation measures to the bilateral agreements with the European Union (see above, para. 24) provide for mandatory provisions in standard labour contracts, in particular provisions regarding minimum wages. Then, such provisions outweigh those of the individual contract (see below, paras. 411 and 704–721).

C. *Work Rules*

167. Work rules have to be established by the employer in 'industrial enterprises' according to the Employment Act (Articles 37 to 39 LTr); they may also be established in other enterprises. They cannot contain anything contrary to a mandatory provision of the law or to any collective agreement binding the employer. They bind both employers and employees and, therefore, having a mandatory effect, take precedence over individual contracts. However, they have a limited scope, containing only provisions on the protection of health and accident prevention, as well as provisions on internal order and the behaviour of employees in the undertaking. When the work rules have been agreed upon by the employer with a freely elected delegation of employees, they may also contain provisions about the relations between the employer and the employees, provided that these matters are not usually settled in the branch by collective agreement.

IV. Mixed Law

168. The following federal Acts contain both public law and private law provisions:

- No. 1: Federal Act on Gender Equality of 24 March 1995;
- No. 2: Federal Act on Recruitment and the Hiring of Services of 6 October 1989;
- No. 3: Federal Act on Data Protection of 19 June 1992;[84]
- No. 4: Federal Act on Vocational and Professional Education and Training of 13 December 2002;
- No. 5: Federal Act on Navigation under the Swiss Flag of 23 September 1953, which applies to the crews of ships registered in Switzerland;
- No. 6: Federal Act on the minimum employment and salary conditions for workers posted to Switzerland and accompanying measures;
- No. 7: Federal Act on Itinerant Trade of 23 March 2001;[85]

84. *RS* 235.1.
85. *RS* 943.1.

– No. 8: Federal Act on the Declaration of General Application of Collective Employment Agreements of 28 September 1956.

169. Some of the Acts mentioned above are completed by corresponding Ordinances:

(1) the Ordinance on Recruitment of 16 January 1991;
(2) the Ordinance to the Federal Act on Data Protection of 14 June 1993;[86]
(3) the Ordinance on Vocational and Professional Education and Training of 19 November 2003;[87]
(4) the Ordinance on Navigation of 20 November 1956;[88]
(5) the Ordinance on Workers posted to Switzerland of 21 May 2003;[89]
(6) the Ordinance on Itinerant Trade of 4 September 2002.[90]

170. In particular, the federal legislator has adopted, on 24 March 1995, a Federal Act on Gender Equality. Its aim is to bring about equality in the occupational field. To that end, it contains a prohibition of every kind of discrimination based on the sex of the worker, especially in the fields of hiring, remuneration and sexual harassment. It also contains provisions on procedure, which were partly transferred to the Code of Civil Procedure (see below paras. 565 *et seq.*), and federal encouragement measures. It applies both to civil labour contracts and to federal, cantonal and communal civil servants. Thus, this act has a double nature, covering both the fields of public and of civil law. Several rules of this Act could also have been introduced into the Code of Obligations.

V. Collective Law

171. Collective agreements constitute a very important source of labour law (Article 356 to 358 CO) Conditions of work are to a great extent regulated by such agreements, which may also regulate relations between employers' and workers' organizations.

172. A collective agreement has, in principle, a binding effect on individual labour relations: it takes precedence over individual contracts concluded between the employers and employees who are bound by it. The provisions of an individual contract or arrangements which conflict with a collective agreement are void, except when they are more favourable for the employee. In this case, and inasmuch as they are more favourable, the clauses of the individual contract take precedence over the collective agreement. The employer may, for instance, validly undertake to pay a higher wage than that provided for by the collective agreement, or to give longer

86. *RS* 235.11.
87. *RS* 412.101.
88. *RS* 747.301.
89. *RS* 823.201.
90. *RS* 943.11.

holidays, and so on. As is the case for the mandatory provisions of the legislation, the worker cannot, while under contract and in the month following, waive any claims arising from the mandatory provisions of the collective agreement. Nevertheless, the collective agreement may itself provide that it will have no mandatory effect.

173. Public law and private law with mandatory effect take precedence over the provisions of a collective agreement, but departures made in favour of the employee are still valid except when the legislation expressly opposes it (Article 358 CO). The collective agreement, on the other hand, takes precedence over the provisions of optional legislation. However, in some cases the collective agreement will take precedence over legal provisions described as being mandatory. This is true, for instance, as regards the reduction of leave in the case of sickness (Article 329*b* CO), where the collective agreement may offer a solution which differs from that of the Code, when it brings at least equivalent advantages for the employee. However, in these cases it is the consequence of a special provision of the Code, and that really means that the said provisions are only partly mandatory.

174. If required by all contracting parties, competent authority can, by a specific decision, extend the scope of a collective agreement to employers and workers belonging to the aimed economic branch or profession and who are not bound by this convention (Article 1, para. 1). Such opportunity is provided for by the Federal Act of 28 September 1956 on the Declaration of General Application of Collective Employment Agreements. Extension can only be pronounced if numerous conditions are fulfilled (Article 2).

VI. Others

A. Usage

175. Usage is also a source of law. The Code of Obligations expressly refers to it in some specific cases when no statutory or contractual provision applies to the matter; for instance, as regards the determination of wages (Article 322, para. 1 CO). Usage may also take precedence over a disposing or relatively mandatory legal provision: for instance, remuneration must be paid at the end of each month unless usage or the contract provides for shorter intervals or other dates (Article 323, para. 1 CO). In one case usage even takes precedence over the contract if the contract is not a written one. This is so for commercial travellers whose main working conditions are determined, when there is no written contract, by the usual conditions (Article 347*a*, para. 2 CO). Usual salaries in a branch or profession also represent the measure of an important decrease of salaries requiring a state intervention (Article 360*a*, para. 1, CO, see below, para. 710).[91]

91. See Aubert, G., 'L'usage en droit du travail' in: *Droit du travail*, 2001, no 3, pp. 95–102.

B. Custom

176. Custom, that is, long practice which is generally recognized as the expression of law, is a subsidiary source of law, as opposed to mere usage, which has to be considered only when expressly referred to by statutory law, custom – when it exists – has to be applied by the judge in a general way with a view to filling gaps in the law (Article 1 of the Civil Code).[92] But customary law is very rare and does not play any practical role in labour law.

C. Doctrine and Judicial Precedents

177. Doctrine and judicial precedents can also be considered as auxiliary sources of law. The judge has, according to Article 1 CC, to take this into account in framing his decisions. Doctrine plays an important role in the decisions of the Federal Court. Jurisprudence has a great impact not only on judicial decisions, but also on the legislator. The law on collective agreements, as adopted in 1956, is to a large extent the result of past decisions of the Federal Court.

§2. International Law

178. Besides domestic law, international private law and international public law also have to be considered as sources of labour law.

I. International Private Law

A. Conflicts of Law

179. The conflict of law is dealt with by the Federal Act on International Private Law, of 18 December 1987.[93] Article 121 of this Act deals especially with the contract of labour. The law which has to be applied is the law of the state in which the work is usually performed. If the work is performed in several states, the applicable law is that of the seat of the undertaking or, in default, of the domicile or of the usual residence of the employer. The parties may choose another law, but it has to be either that of the state in which the employee has his usual residence or that of the state where the employer has the seat of his undertaking, his domicile or his usual residence.

180. By virtue of the principle of territoriality, public law is applied to workers who are employed in Switzerland even when private relations between employer and employees are governed by another law. The scope of application regarding location of the Employment Act is not clear. The provisions apply to workers

92. *RS* 210.
93. *RS* 291.

employed in Switzerland by an undertaking having its head office abroad in so far as circumstances permit (Article 1, para. 3), i.e. as far as the legal provisions may be effectively applied to such an undertaking. However, the law is, for instance, silent concerning the hiring of foreign workers by Swiss firms.[94] The provisions of the Act on Home Work apply to those employers who have their domicile abroad, but who employ home workers in Switzerland (Article 1, para. 3). Those of the Drivers' Ordinance apply to all those driving a vehicle registered in Switzerland, even when they are driving abroad, unless international agreements to which Switzerland is a party, provide for more severe rules; some of the provisions apply also to those driving a vehicle registered in an other country (Article 3). According to the Federal Act on Navigation under the Swiss Flag, the provisions of Swiss labour law, and especially those contained in this Act, have to be applied in principle to all sailors who are serving aboard Swiss boats, whatever their nationality (Articles 63 and 68).

181. The Federal Act on Workers posted to Switzerland is also to be mentioned. It governs minimum work and wage conditions applying to workers detached during a limited period of time in Switzerland by an employer having his seat or domicile abroad (Article 1, para. 1). Two different kinds of detachment are admitted by the law: detachments in order to work on behalf and under the direction of the employer (1), or in a subsidiary company or a firm belonging to the group (2) (Article 1, para. 1). According to Article 121, para. 1, of the Federal Act on International Private Law, these forms of labour relationships are still governed by the law of their state of origin. The Act on Workers posted to Switzerland must however assure the stability of Swiss salaries. The latter imposes consequently minimum work and salary conditions provided for by Federal Acts and Ordinances, extended collective agreements and standard labour contracts according to Article 360*a* CO in certain domains (Article 2, para. 1). The aforementioned minimum conditions are mandatory provisions of the Swiss legislation applying whatever applicable state law is designated by the Federal Act on International Private Law (Article 18).[95]

182. Some of the mandatory provisions of civil law which are designed to protect the weaker party to the contract – i.e. the employee – such as the provisions regarding the protection of the employee's person or individuality, may be considered as being of public order and have to be applied even if the relations between the parties are governed by foreign law. The Federal Act on International Private Law expressly reserves the mandatory provisions of the Swiss law which, due to their particular aim, have to be applied whatever the national law indicated by the Act is (Article 18 LDIP).[96]

---

94. See Geiser, T., Von Kaenel, A., and Wyler, R. (eds.), p. 33.
95. See Portmann, W., 'Die flankierenden Massnahmen I und II zum Abkommen über die Freizügigkeit', in: *Bilaterale Verträge I & II Schweiz – EU*, Zurich, 2007, pp. 367–368.
96. See judgments of the Federal Court 4A_106/2009 of 1 October 2009, 4A_339/2009 of 17 November 2009.

B. Competent Judge

183. In litigation arising from labour contracts, where the work is not or not totally performed in Switzerland or where the employer or the employee have their domicile abroad, the competent judge is either that of the defendant's domicile or that of the place where the worker usually performs his work. Furthermore, the worker may also bring his action before a judge of his domicile or usual residence in Switzerland (Article 115 of the Federal Act on International Private Law). That meant that the Swiss judge was not competent when the worker, sent abroad by an employer, performed temporary work in the country. However, the ancillary implementation measures of the bilateral agreement on free movement of persons with the European Union (see above, paras. 24, 125–127 and 135) provided for a modification of Article 115 of the Federal Act on International Private Law: according to the new disposition, the Swiss judge is also competent for certain claims when the worker, sent abroad by an employer, performs temporary work in Switzerland.

184. The parties may, nevertheless, agree to choose another judge. However, their choice may be considered null and void if it abusively aims to deprive a party of the protection which Swiss law would have provided for him (Article 5 of the Federal Act on International Private Law).

185. Where there is no other competent judge in Switzerland and litigation in another state is not possible or when it is unreasonable to require that litigation should be brought before a judge abroad, the authorities of a place with which the case has a sufficient relation are competent (Article 3 of the Federal Act on International Private Law). Competence may also be given to a Swiss court in the case of litigation against a defendant living abroad if a sequestration of the defendant's property has been ordered in Switzerland at the plaintiff's request (Article 4 of the Act).

186. If one of the parties has his domicile in another state bound by the revised Convention of Lugano of 30 October 2007 – which has been ratified with some reservations by Switzerland – the provisions provided for by this convention apply in principle instead of those of the Swiss law and therefore instead of the Federal Act on International Private Law.

187. The state immunity is limited. Thus, the foreign state's immunity from jurisdiction does not apply if this one acts *jure gestionis* and not *jure imperii*. In the field of labour law, case law admits that the state has an important interest not to see litigations opposing itself to members of its embassies exercising superior functions before foreign courts. The situation is however different when subordinate employees are concerned, such as chauffeur, gate-keeper, gardener, cook, translator, office worker and house cleaner. The latter indeed do not appear as tools of national power. In these circumstances, according to case law, courts of the place of jurisdiction are competent in most cases.[97]

II. International Public Law

188. Switzerland is bound, in the field of labour law, by a number of multilateral international conventions and by some bilateral treaties. It may be recalled that the first international labour treaties were adopted in Bern in 1906 on the initiative of Switzerland. These were the convention on the prohibition of night work for women in industrial employment and the convention prohibiting the use of white phosphorous in the manufacture of matches.

189. Now Switzerland is bound by about 50 conventions (including those which relate to social security) of the International Labour Organization. Among them are the following important conventions on human and social rights: No. 87 on the Freedom of Association and Protection of the Right to Organize; No. 154 on Collective Bargaining; No. 11 concerning the Right of Association in Agriculture; Nos. 29 and 105 on Forced Labour; No. 111 concerning Discrimination in Employment and Profession and No. 100 on Equal Remuneration. Switzerland has also ratified Convention No. 81 on Labour Inspection, as well as various conventions on conditions of work and on the protection of women and young persons. These conventions include No. 14 on Weekly Rest in Industry; No. 138 on Minimum Age; No. 6 concerning Night Work by Young Persons. Switzerland had ratified convention No. 89 on Night Work by Women, but, like other countries, renounced it in 1992. Recently, Switzerland has ratified Convention No. 183 on maternity protection, Convention No. 189 concerning the domestic workers and the Convention on maritime labour.

190. Switzerland signed the European Social Charter of the Council of Europe, but has not ratified it yet; indeed, in 1987, ratification was rejected by the Federal Assembly. Proposals have been made in the Federal Assembly in order to submit it once more to the latter.[98] However, at present, the Social Charter is at a standstill. The National Council indeed did not grant a new extension of time to its social security and public health commission to produce its report and propositions. On 17 December 2004, the last parliamentary initiative was therefore classified.[99] However, in the beginning of 2010, the Federal Council was put in charge to report on the compatibility of the Revised European Social Charter with the Swiss legal order. It must also examine the opportunity to sign and to ratify it shortly. Switzerland ratified the European Convention on the Protection of Human Rights and Fundamental Freedoms[100] in 1974 and, in 1992, the two general Human Rights Covenants of the

97. *ATF* 134/2008 III 570 (572–573), Federal Court 7 July 2015, decision 4A_618/2014.
98. See FF 1996 II, p. 717, for the relation and proposal of a Parliament's commission, and FF 1996 IV, p. 1273, for the government's advice on the question.
99. BO 2004 N. 2169.
100. *RS* 0.101.

United Nations – the International Covenant on Economic, Social and Cultural Rights and the International Covenant on Civil and Political Rights.[101] Switzerland has also ratified during the last five years the UN Covenant on the Rights of the Children[102] and on the Elimination of all kinds of Discrimination against Women.[103]

191. As mentioned above, Switzerland has also concluded bilateral agreements with the European Union. One of these provides for the free movement of persons and undoubtedly has had a great influence on Swiss labour law (see above, paras. 24 and 125–127, 135, below, paras. 411, 675, 698, 705 and 710–712). Yet, European law in general also influences the Swiss legislator. Numerous European directives have indeed directly inspired Swiss laws and the Code of Obligations' provisions in the field of labour law. This is for example the case of the provisions about work relation transfer in case of enterprise transfer (Article 333 CO),[104] provisions about mass dismissal (Articles 335*d* to 335*g* CO)[105] and the Federal Act on Gender Equality.[106] So, Swiss courts can, in these particular domains, take inspiration from the concerned European directives and from the Court of Justice of the European Communities' jurisprudence.[107]

192. International treaties approved by the Federal Assembly are considered a part of Swiss law. When containing legal rules that can be directly applied (i.e. rules that are self-executing), both the authorities and the citizens are bound to it.[108] A treaty is not self-executing if it merely contains a programmatic statement or guidelines applying to the domestic legislator and no precise rules that can be applied directly by the courts.[109] Thus, conventions such as those concerning the right of association are self-executing and do not need to be transformed into domestic law; on the other hand conventions concerning hours of work need such a transformation by the adoption of domestic legislation. The former can be invoked before the courts; the latter cannot.

193. In 2003, the Swiss Federation of Trade Unions (USS) registered a complaint to the ILO against Switzerland for violation of trade union freedom (violation

101. *RS* 0.103.1 and 0.103.2.
102. *RS* 0.107. The Covenant has been in force since 1997 for Switzerland.
103. *RS* 0.108. This Covenant has also been in force since 1997 for Switzerland.
104. See Directive 77/187/EEC of 14 February 1977.
105. See Directive 75/129/EEC of 15 February 1975.
106. See Directives 75/117/EEC of 10 February 1975, 76/207/EEC of 9 February 1976, 97/80/EC of 15 December 1997.
107. See, for instance, *ATF* 132/2006 III 32, 132/2006 III 406.
108. See, for instance, *ATF* 119/1993 V 174, 124/1998 III 90, 126/2000 I 240, 133/2007 I 286.
109. See, for instance, *ATF* 100/1974 Ib 226, 118/1992 Ia 112 (117), 120/1994 Ia 1 (10, regarding Article 13 of the UN Covenant No. 1 (right to education)), 121/1995 V 229 (232, regarding Articles 3 and 9 of the same Covenant (equality between women and men and social security)) and 121/1995 V 246 (248, regarding Article 2, paras. 2, and 9, of the same Covenant (discrimination based on nationality in the social security system)). *See* also *ATF* 125/1999 III 277 (about self executing character of Article 8 of the UN Covenant No. 1, which provides for the right to strike: the Federal Court let the question open).

of Article 1 of Convention No. 98). In the recommendation of 15 November 2006 (report No. 343, case No. 2265),[110] the Committee demanded that Switzerland, among other, things to take measures to assure a protection of trade union representatives against wrongful dismissal which is identical to that granted by the Federal Act on Gender Equality, and which guarantees reinstatement of concerned workers. The Federal Department of Economy took note of this recommendation which was subject of an examination and discussions especially with social partners. The file was then communicated to the Federal Council in order to obtain its opinion. In its previous standpoints, the Federal Council however considered that the litigious Convention did not contain directly applying rules in the Swiss legislation.[111]

194. In 2008, the Federal Council estimated in a report that the existing protection was sufficient.[112] After the responses of the social partners, the Committee made some observations and asked the Government to start the discussions again and to keep it informed regarding the evolution of jurisprudence.[113] The Government agreed to continue discussions and invited the social partners to improve protection against wrongful dismissal through collective labour agreements.

195. In October 2010, the Federal Council put in consultation a pre-project regarding the review of wrongfull dismissal in the code of obligations. Unfortunatly, although the pre-project tried to reinforce the protection in case of such dismissal, it did not, contrary to ILO recommendations, provide any reinstatement or nullity.

196. In September 2012, the Swiss Federation of Trade Unions (USS) asked the ILO to reexamine the case, as their 2006 recommendation had not been respected. Finally, in November 2012, the Federal Council decided to suspend any legislative work concerning the protection of trade union dismissals in order to ask for complete and deep study regarding the matter.

197. Another case was brought beyond the ILO in April 2013 by the Swiss Federation of Trade Unions (USS) against Switzerland for a violation of the conventions Nos. 87 and 98. The complaint concerns the insufficient protection for workers in case of dismissal delivered for the use of the right of strike. This complaint is a consequence of the '*Providence* case'. This case saw 22 strikers dismissed from the Providence hospital of Neuchâtel following the taking over of the establishment by private hospitals. Despite some observations delivered on 26 March 2014, the

110. Vol. LXXXIX, 2006, Series B, No. 3.
111. See Dunand, J.-P., *Entre flexibilisation et protection: le droit du travail en évolution (2005-2006)*, La pratique de l'avocat, Bern, 2007, pp. 342–343.
112. See http://www.news.admin.ch/NSBSubscriber/message/attachments/13164.pdf.
113. See http://webfusion.ilo.org/public/db/standards/normes/appl/appl-displaycomment.cfm?hdroff=1&ctry=0590&year=2008&type=O&conv=C098&lang=EN.

Federal Council refused to rule on the case, penal and civil proceedings still waiting for a decision. However, aware of the fact that such situations should be considered as preoccupying, the Federal Council entrusted some administration services competent in the matter to deliver a deep and meticulous study on every points raised by the complaint.

Part I. The Individual Employment Relationship

Chapter 1. Definitions and Concepts

§1. The Individual Labour Contract

198. The term 'contract of labour' means the instrument with which contractual relations are engaged and at the same time the bond of a permanent character which unites the contracting parties. Under the latter meaning, the contract includes not only what has been agreed on at the time of the engagement, but also the conditions fixing the contents of the contractual relationship. These conditions arise from the initial instrument; they also arise from both the rules of public and private law which have an effect on the contents of the contract and from those rules which in the course of the labour relationship have attached themselves, expressly or impliedly, to this relationship. Thus, it is considered that certain employment conditions prevailing in an enterprise at the moment of the engagement and being applied to all employees, can be deemed as conditions which are agreed to tacitly and which become part of the contract. The same may be said about employment conditions which, under analogous circumstances, have been introduced in the enterprise after the engagement. From the fact that, in a given enterprise, a special bonus has been paid regularly and without reservation to the employees at the end of every year, for at least three years in a row, case-law and doctrine have deduced that this bonus has become a contractual element, entering impliedly into the employment conditions and constituting a part of the wage. Moreover, even with the existence of a reservation, the employer may be forced to deliver a special bonus to his employee if this former appears to be a mere formality. This could be the case, for exemple, when the employer keeps offering a bonus to his employee throughout the years, even when his financial means are at his worst.[114]

199. On the other hand, individual labour relations are not limited to the scope of the individual contract as regulated by the Code of Obligations. Indeed, public law creates a broader framework in which certain individual labour relations which do not come within the scope of those being regulated as such by civil law are also regulated.

---

114. Federal Court 25 October 2004, decision 4C.244/200; Federal Court 22 August 2012, decision 4A_172/2012.

200. The individual labour contract is essentially regulated by the Code of Obligations. Part X of this Code, dedicated to labour contracts, provides a definition of the contract and indicates its effects. According to this definition, the individual labour contract is the contract by which the worker undertakes to perform work in the employer's service for a specified or unspecified period and by which the employer undertakes to pay a wage (Article 319 al. 1er CO). This definition clearly shows the element of subordination which derives from the establishment of the contract: the worker is in the employer's service and he undertakes to personally perform the work for him, i.e. he puts his own force of labour at the disposal of the employer who, according to the instructions he gives, may dispose of it to the extent provided for by the contract and by the law. Unlike the other contracts regulated by the Code of Obligations, the labour contract always implies a personal undertaking on the part of the worker, who must be a natural person. In other contracts regarding the performance of work, those who undertake to perform the work can be legal entities. The period of time during which the worker performs his duties is at the disposal of the employer; this idea being rendered by the term 'for a specified or unspecified period'. As the Federal Court has said, the Swiss concept of the labour contract implies subordinated labour.[115] As for the employer, his main undertaking, deriving from the legal definition, is to pay a wage fixed either on a time basis or on the basis of the work performed.

201. Public protective labour law is based on the same criterion of subordinated labour, but does not require, for the application of its provisions, that a contract in the private law sense be established. The existence of a labour relationship is sufficient; in other words, a person working in an enterprise or in a household in the employer's service is acceptable. Thus, even labour relationships where the employer did not undertake to pay a wage and is not bound to pay such a wage are still covered by public labour law.

202. According to the Employment Act and Ordinance I, a worker is considered, in the sense of the act, as any person employed in an enterprise subject to this act, permanently or temporarily, during the whole or part of the labour schedule (Article 1, para. 1, Ordinance I); while an enterprise, as we have already said, is deemed to exist if an employer employs one or more workers permanently or temporarily, even without using specific installations or premises (Article 1, para. 2, EA). *Stagiaires*, volunteers and other persons who work in an undertaking mainly for training purposes or to prepare themselves for the choice of a profession are also workers in the sense of the Act (Article 1, para. 2, Ordinance I). Even those who work in an undertaking belonging to a member of their family (husband, same-sex partner, parents) are deemed to be workers in the same sense although they may, according to civil law, be bound not by a contract of labour but rather by family ties. In fact, family members are, by virtue of a special provision of the Act, excluded from the application of most of its provisions, but some of them (the children) are not excluded from all these provisions (Article 4 EA) (see below, para. 517).

115. *ATF* 95/1969 I 21; Federal Court 3 September 2015, decision 4C_200/2015, 4.2.1.

§2. THE DIFFERENT CATEGORIES OF EMPLOYEE

I. Blue-collar and White-collar Workers

203. Until its revision in 1971, part X of the Code of Obligations distinguished between three main categories of employees: blue-collar workers, white-collar workers and domestic servants. The legal provisions for these different categories of workers differed only on some points, such as the intervals for the payment of wages, the trial period and the period of notice. These differences have, as a rule, been suppressed by the amending Act of 1971 and the above categories have been melded into one: that of the *Arbeitnehmer* in German, the *travailleurs* in French and the *lavoratori* in Italian.

Meanwhile, even though the distinction between blue- and white-collar employees has disappeared from the Code of Obligations, it still partly subsists in the Employment Act. In two particular areas, the hours of work and overtime payment, blue-collar and white-collar employees are subject to different regulations. Office workers, technical staff and other salaried employees are classified as constituting a special category – that of white-collar workers – and included in this same category are some sales staff, but only those in large retail undertakings; i.e. those undertakings which employ more than 50 employees in retail sales in the same building or in nearby buildings (Articles 9 and 13 EA, Article 2 Ordinance I). From this formulation, it appears that the distinction between white-collar workers and other workers is not an easy one to make. There is indeed no precise definition of a white-collar worker (*Angestellte, employé, impiegato*). For the purpose of applying the former version of the Code of Obligations it was generally considered that white-collar workers were those who were neither blue-collar (i.e. who performed manual work) nor domestic servants (performing household work). It was a very heterogeneous category, including all those workers who exercised intellectual or commercial functions or who did office work. While it is quite easy to understand what is meant by the term 'office workers', it is not so easy to draw a line between technical staff and blue-collar workers. Questions have often arisen about foremen. According, for instance, to their technical training, they may or may not be included among the 'other salaried employees'. Whatever the case may be for foremen, one thing is certain: members of the sales staff in the retail trade are not, according to the Employment Act, generally to be considered as 'other salaried employees'. Rather, only those who are employed in *large* retail shops are to be put in this category.

II. Professional Persons, Managerial and Supervisory Staff

204. In its 1911 version, the Code of Obligations expressly stated that its provisions respecting the contract of labour also applied to professional persons when the contract by which they were bound had the characteristics of a labour contract. This provision has been suppressed by the amendment Act of 1971 which contains no provision at all about these persons. The government, influenced by the German doctrine, wrote in its explanatory report to Parliament that work performed on an 'independent basis', such as that of a physician or a barrister working as an employee, had to be excluded from the scope of the labour contract and considered instead as entering into another type of contract, such as the mandate or that of an independent contractor. But, before Parliament, the government finally abandoned this distinction, which had no basis in the terms of the Act.[116] Therefore, it has to be admitted that professional persons working in the service of an employer are bound by an individual labour contract. Members of the managerial and supervisory staff of an enterprise are also bound by a labour contract in the sense of the code. But some of them are not protected by federal public law; senior managerial staff and those who carry out an independent artistic or a scientific activity are, due to a special provision of the Employment Act, excluded from its scope (Article 3 EA).

205. According to continuous case law, workers benefit from the application of protection rules of labour law, whatever their position is.[117] There are however two exceptions: some rules are interpreted differently towards executives (duty of loyalty, supplementary hours) and, as said above, some of them are not protected by rules of public law.

III. Commercial Travellers

206. The Code of Obligations contains special provisions for those commercial travellers whose principal and permanent activity consists in negotiating or concluding business of any kind outside the employer's business premises on behalf of the owner of a commercial or industrial undertaking (Articles 347–350*a* CO). Other travellers – such as those who are not principally employed as travellers or who work for the employer only occasionally or temporarily, or those who merely present lines of samples – are not affected by these provisions, except perhaps sometimes by analogy. The reasons for the special treatment given to commercial travellers are evident. They do not work under the direct control of the employer, their work being done outside the premises. The question of their remuneration and of the payment of their travelling expenses has to be regulated by special provisions: their remuneration necessarily differs from that paid to workers who work within the precincts of the enterprise and who are subject to the permanent control of the employer. Travelling expenses are often significant and must be met by the employer. The powers of the traveller to negotiate and to conclude deals have to be specified (Article 347*a*, para. 1, CO). Commercial travellers, being outside the scope of application of the Employment Act (Article 3 EA), are not protected by federal public law.

207. Commercial travellers are very similar to commercial agents who, like themselves, can negotiate or conclude business. But the latter work independently and their working time does not come, even indirectly, under the control of their principal. The position of agents is like that of commercial travellers in that they

116. *See* on this question Berenstein, A., *Etudes de droit social*, Geneva, 1979, p. 152.
117. ATF 141 III 23; Federal Court 19 February 2013, decision 4A_611/2012.

are bound permanently and are frequently economically dependent on their principal. As far as social security is concerned, most commercial agents are considered to be performing a dependent activity since they do not bear the risk of enterprise.[118]

208. Thus the agency contract, regulated by Articles 418*a* to 418*v* CO, is on the borderline of labour law. The legal provisions concerning commercial agents include some of a social character, derived from those concerning other workers. This is the case for those agents who, by virtue of the contract, are prohibited from simultaneously representing another principal. If they are prevented from working through illness or another similar event, their right to remuneration is protected along the same lines as that of other workers (Article 418*m* CO).

209. The Federal Act on Itinerant Trade of 23 March 2001 provides for special provisions relating people who exercise itinerant trade on the Swiss territory, such as stallholders, pedlars and circus owners. The latter workers must generally be in possession of an authorization given by the competent cantonal authority (Article 2). A regime of exception is established for the participation in markets and fairs (Article 3).

IV. Home Workers

210. Home workers are those who work for an employer and for a salary, but operate from their homes or in another place of their own choosing, either alone or with the help of members of their family. 'With the help' means that the home worker is not bound to these members of his family by a contract of labour. The home worker is not subject to the control of the employer as would have been the case had he worked on the premises of the enterprise. He normally organizes his own work and is not bound to observe a fixed schedule.

211. These characteristics of home work explain the difficulties which have been encountered in distinguishing between the home worker and the self-employed craftsman. The latter may indeed undertake to perform work like the home worker, but he is not 'in the service' of the employer; he does not promise his work, only the results of it – i.e. the completed work. It has been proposed to accept the existence of a labour contract when there is a permanent bond between the employer and the home worker, and when the worker does not possess important materials and tools and so could not be considered as an independent contractor. In such cases the home worker is in fact, although not always juridically, economically dependent on the employer.

212. These doubts have been removed by legislation. Home workers are now protected by two Acts: a public law Act – the Federal Act on Home Work – and a

118. See, for instance, the sentence of the Federal Insurance Court of 14 September 1971 (*ATF* 97/1971 V 134); *ATF* 129 III 668 c. 3.2; Federal Court 29 April 2015, decision 4A_86/2015, 4.1.

civil law – the Code of Obligations. Neither Act depends, for the purpose of defining home workers, on the legal definition of the labour contract. The home worker is thus protected without reference to the extent to which he fulfils the conditions of the general definition of the labour contract.

213. The special protection given by the law to home workers derives, in Switzerland as in other countries, from the fact that they are often exploited: not being concentrated in factories but scattered, they do not organize themselves in unions; furthermore most of them are women for whom the remuneration for home work is often considered a means of making up their income.

214. The Federal Act on Home Work applies only to those workers who carry out, in their homes or in another place of their own choosing, industrial or artisanal work, either alone or together with family members. The provisions of this Act cover the communication of the conditions of employment, wages, the reimbursement of costs, tools and materials, instructions, minimum age, protection against overexertion, protection of life and health, and dangerous work.

215. The Code of Obligations considers the home work contract as a special type of labour contract (Articles 351–354). Contrary to the public law, the private law provisions relating to home workers apply to any kind of home work and not only to industrial or artisanal work; for instance, translations done at home and employees in the commercial field doing telework may be covered by the provisions of the code if the worker is economically dependent on the principal.

216. Regarding the employees doing telework (online home work, i.e. work in other fields than industrial or artisanal work, for instance office or telecommunications work), recently, on 16 November 2016, the Federal Council delivered a report, in response to Meier-Schatz postulate no. 12.3166, providing answers on the legal consequences of telework. The report states that the ordinary rules of labour contract apply and that those should prove sufficient in order to regulate telework even if some shortcoming clearly exist, but not without the possibility to address them throughout the tools that are the collective agreements. The Federal Council also develops the assets of this particular way of working, such as the motivation presented by the employee pursuant to the regulation of his own working time or the advantage regarding the policy on transport and environment. Concerning the flaws, the Federal Council merely states that the social, spatial and temporal boundaries between professional and private life might crumble and that measures should be taken in order to prevent such problems.

V. Seamen

217. Switzerland has no seaboard but nevertheless possesses a merchant fleet which is registered in Basle (Article 2, para. 2, of the Federal Act on Navigation under the Swiss Flag), the only Swiss port which is connected to the sea – in this case by way of the Rhine. Swiss shipping is regulated by the Federal Act on Navigation under the Swiss Flag.

218. The position of the crew is, of course, very different from that of ordinary workers; seamen work under special conditions and are subject to special discipline. The said Act, like thc Ordinance on Navigation, includes both public and private law provisions, although the public law provisions are particularly important. The ships are subject to special control by the public authorities. Thus, the Federal Office for Maritime Shipping may order, in the interests of the country, the immediate dismissal of a member of the crew (Article 60, para. 3, of the Act).

219. The members of the crew are the captain and the seamen (Article 60, para. 1). The captain and the officers have to be holders of a special certificate of vocational education (Articles 60, paras. 2 and 62). All crew members have to undergo a periodical medical test and be holders of a certificate of fitness (Articles 17–18 of the Ordinance). The captain, while subject to the provisions of the Act relating to the crew, also represents, at the same time, both the ship-owner – being, in this respect, the superior of the other members of the crew – and the public authority (Articles 54–55). He exerts disciplinary power (Article 54), which even permits him to place members of the crew under arrest in the case of disciplinary transgressions (Articles 156, para. 2 and 157, para. 1).

VI. Family Members

220. Ascertaining the legal position of persons who work in an enterprise and who are bound to the owner by family ties is often difficult. This question arises in the following terms: when are these persons to be considered as employees, i.e. bound by a contract of labour, and when is their cooperation to be considered as falling under the legal provisions respecting family obligations?

221. The problem arises mostly in the case of a spouse, a same-sex partner or a cohabitant who works in his consort's enterprise. The spouses, the same-sex partners or the cohabitants may expressly conclude a contract of labour between themselves, binding them in this case by such a contract. A contract may also be concluded impliedly, when the spouse, the same-sex partner or the cohabitant works in the enterprise like an employee and receives a wage. The same questions arise should a child work in the enterprise of his parents.

222. Before the revision in 1984 of the provisions of the Civil Code concerning marriage, the fact that a woman worked for her husband's enterprise gave rise to different interpretations. After having decided that, in such a case, the wife is presumed to have acted within her marital obligations, the Federal Court, in the last development of its practice, said that the existence of a contract of labour had to be admitted when the activity of the wife exceeded what was required from her by virtue of her marital obligations.

223. Now, and since 1988 (date of the coming into force of the revision of 1984), the situation is quite different. According to Article 163 of the Civil Code, the spouses agree between themselves how they will contribute to the maintenance of the family, either by contributions in cash, or by work at home, or in taking care of the children, or by the help given to the other partner in the exercise of his profession or in his enterprise. The spouse who helps the other in his profession or enterprise (or who works at home or is taking care of the children) is entitled to receive regularly from him a reasonable amount (Article 164). When a spouse has given his collaboration to the profession or enterprise in a manner which exceeds notably what he had to give, he is entitled to a reasonable remuneration, unless his contribution has been given on the basis of a contract of labour or of another contract (Article 165).

224. In this situation, either it is admitted, in a particular case, that the spouse, in giving his help in the enterprise, has accomplished his contribution to the maintenance of the family, and he is then entitled to receive a reasonable amount (as it is also the case when he brings his help to the maintenance of the family by his work at home). Or if his help notably exceeds that which is required from him, and he is entitled to receive reasonable remuneration, unless he is bound by a contract of labour (and receives a wage) or by another contract (for example, partnership agreement). It ought then to be considered that in such a case, the existence of a contract of labour will be admitted only if such a contract has been formally concluded.

225. It is, however, still controversial to know whether Article 320, para. 2, CO can also apply when the spouse works in the other's enterprise. The latter provision provides indeed that a labour contract is considered to be concluded when the employer accepts for a given time period the execution of a work, which, according to circumstances, must only be performed for a salary. The Federal Court has not come to a decision on the subsidiarity of Article 320, para. 2, CO towards Article 165 of the Civil Code yet. Some observations have nevertheless been made by analysis of jurisprudence. Thus, the spouses can exclude the application of Article 165 of the Civil Code by means of an agreement. Furthermore, Article 165 of the Civil Code does not apply when the spouse is not the only person interested in the other spouse's work. An indication in favour of the existence of a labour contract is finally the payment of social insurance contributions by the spouse who employs the other.[119] The doctrine, for its part, remains rather divided on the relationship between Articles 320, para. 2 and 165, of the Civil Code.[120]

226. In spite of the absence of a similar provision to Article 165 of the Civil Code in the Federal Act on the Registered Partnership between Persons of the Same Sex (SSPA),[121] the jurisprudence concerning the first paragraph of the

119. See Wyler, R. and Heinzer, B., p. 40 *seq.*
120. See on this question Staehelin, A., N. 23 ad Article 320 CO.
121. *RS* 211.231.

aforementioned article can also apply to a same-sex partner helping the other in her/his enterprise.[122]

227. In the case of a woman who has worked for the enterprise of a man with whom she has lived in a free union, the practice of the Federal Court has undergone many changes: after having decided that the work of such a woman had to be remunerated, it said that the services she rendered were not necessarily given in expectation of a wage, and that there was no reason to give the mistress a better treatment than that received by a spouse. Lastly, it has ruled that relations between those living together may be founded, according to the circumstances, on the provisions of the Code relating to partnership (*société simple, einfache Gesellschaft*), or, as the case may be, a labour contract according to Article 320, para. 2, CO.[123] Such a conclusion depends on the circumstances of each case. Critera speaking either in favour of the existence of a tacit labour contract or in favour of a partnership are the subordination relationship, the shared interest in pursuit of an enterprise, a reason other than the cohabitation for helping the partner, payment expectancy and the existence of a 'marital equity' in case of the partnership liquidation.[124]

228. Finally, according to Article 4 EA, the Employment Act does not apply to undertakings in which the chief's spouse, the same-sex partner, his ascendants and descendants and their spouses or same-sex partners, as well as the children of the chief's spouse or same-sex partner are the only one to work. When other persons than those mentioned above work in the enterprise, the Employment Act only applies to them.

VII. Persons in Training

229. The contract of apprenticeship, which used to be considered as a contract *sui generis* while being very close to the contract of labour, has – since the revision of 1971 – been classified as a 'special type of individual labour contract' (Articles 344–346*a* CO). It is, nevertheless, obvious that the definition of a contract of labour does not apply to a contract of apprenticeship. While in the contract of labour the primary purpose of the worker is to receive a wage, in the contract of apprenticeship his purpose is to acquire a vocational training with a view to being able to carry on a given occupation: the employer undertakes to train the person in training in accordance with the skills of the trade, while the person in training undertakes to work in the employer's service in order to acquire such training (Article 344 CO).[125] There is, of course, an obligation on the part of the person in training to work in the service of the employer as in a contract of labour, but the essential aim

122. See FF 2003, pp. 1215–1216.
123. *ATF* 108/1982 II 208, 109/1983 II 230, and in a sentence of 23 August 1999 (*FamPra* 2000, p. 151).
124. See Wyler, R. and Heinzer, B., pp. 43–44.
125. See Aubert, D., in Dunand and Mahon, p. 917 *seq.*

of this obligation is different from that which is pursued in the labour contract. Nevertheless, the bond of subordination in the contract of apprenticeship is similar to that which results from the contract of labour. The person in training enters the enterprise and has to obey the employer's orders. Being in most cases a minor, he needs, like other employees and undoubtedly even more so than them, particular protection from the law.

230. The contract of apprenticeship, as regulated by the Code of Obligations, applies to all those who come within the above mentioned legal definition. However, the position of most persons in training is also regulated by the Federal Act on Vocational and Professional Education and Training, the provisions of which, being partly of a public law character, take precedence over those of the Code. The contract of apprenticeship, concluded by means of an official form, has to be approved by the cantonal authority (Article 14, para. 3).

VIII. Volunteers and *Stagiaires*

231. Volunteers are persons who work in an enterprise under the control and instructions of an employer without being entitled to a wage and, thus, without being bound by a contract of labour. *Stagiaires* are those persons who work in the enterprise with a view to familiarizing themselves with the methods of production, sale, etc., but who are not bound by a contract of apprenticeship. It is unclear whether this type of person is bound by a labour contract. Doctrine suggests that if the *stagiaire* undertakes a *stage* that provides interests exclusively in his favour and not in the employer's one, the latter has no obligation to pay the former. Therefore, since labour contract is an onerous contract, this type of stage cannot be qualified as a labour contract. However, if the employer has a personal interest in hiring a *stagiaire*, this same *stagiaire* should be entitled to request a salary to his employer (Article 320 para. 2 CO).[126] This last and specific hypotheses should prevent cases of hidden labour contracts where an employee is employed as a *stagiaire,* but with the same work rate and assignments of a normal worker and usually for a long period of time, in order for the employer not to have a salary to deliver.

§3. Different Categories of Labour Contract

I. Contracts for a Definite or Indefinite Period

A. Contracts for a Definite Period

232. A contract of labour is deemed to be a contract for a definite period either if the contracting parties have specified at the establishment of the contract the duration for which it has been concluded or if this duration is a consequence of the stated purpose of the work contracted for. However, in this last case, the duration of the

126. See Brunner *et al.*, p. 42.

contract is deemed to be a definite one only if both parties are aware of this duration and the worker knows exactly by which date he has to seek a new engagement. The duration may depend on a future event if it is objectively foreseeable and does not depend on the will of one of the parties.[127] The contract for a definite period terminates automatically at the end of the specified duration or when the purpose is accomplished (Article 334, para. 1, CO).

233. If, however, at the end of the period the contract is tacitly continued in the sense that the worker, with the express or implied agreement of the employer, is continuing his work, then the contract is deemed to be converted in a contract for an indefinite period (Article 334, para. 2, CO). Nevertheless, the parties may agree that the continued contract be a new contract for a definite period. But such an agreement may be deemed to be void in case of intended fraud, for example if its purpose is to prevent the originating of claims which are based on a minimal duration of labour relations.

234. A contract in which it is stipulated that it may be terminated upon notice, for instance for the end of one month, but, if not terminated beforehand, will terminate at the end of a specified period, is a maximum duration contract; at the beginning, it is a contract for an indefinite period; at the end, if not terminated before, it is a contract for a definite period and has the effects of such a contract.

B. *Contracts for an Indefinite Period*

235. Most contracts of labour are stipulated for an indefinite period. The duration of these contracts has not been provided for at the moment of their establishment. In such cases, the contract terminates after notice has been given by either of the parties (Article 335 CO).

236. In contracts for an indefinite period, the first month is deemed to be a preliminary *trial period*. This period may be suppressed or extended by a written contract, a collective agreement or a standard labour contract. Nevertheless, it cannot be extended beyond the total duration of three months. If, during this period, the worker has been prevented from doing his work because of illness, accident or accomplishment of a legal obligation he did not ask to assume, the trial period is extended for the time of the impediment. In the course of the trial period, the contract may be terminated by the parties at a very short notice (Article 335*b* CO). The fact that the trial period is still in operation involves other consequences; namely, during this period there is no protection against a termination of the contract at an improper time.

127. See Carron, in Dunand and Mahon, p. 556 *seq.*

II. Labour Subcontracting

237. As has been said, temporary work and other hiring-out agencies are subject to the provisions of the Federal Act on Recruitment and the Hiring of Services of 6 October 1989. According to this Act, there is a hiring-out agency when the worker is bound by a contract of labour with the primary employer, who has towards him the main obligation of an employer – namely, the payment of wages. But there are also, between the secondary employer and the worker, contractual or quasi-contractual relations, which allow the secondary employer to avail himself of certain obligations on the part of the worker arising out of the contract of labour, and vice versa – namely, on the part of the worker, the care to be exercised, and on the part of the employer the obligation to protect the worker against the hazards of work. According to Article 10 of the Ordinance on the Prevention of Accidents and Occupational Diseases, the employer has, concerning safety at work, the same obligations with regard to hired-in workers as he has with regard to his own workers.

238. Temporary workers are, by the nature of their engagement, deprived of a part of the protection which is given by the law to ordinary workers (period of notice, situation as regards unemployment insurance).

239. In June 2008, swissstaffing and the trade union Unia finally concluded a collective agreement on temporary work. This result was the conclusion of almost a year of difficult negotiations. The collective agreement reinforces protection for all temporary workers, as all domains fall within its scope of application. Thus, according to the new collective agreement, all workers benefit from a minimal salary, provided for by an existing collective agreement or by the collective agreement on temporary work itself. The collective agreement also standardizes other subjects, such as contributions for vocational training and the right to sickness benefits.

240. In November 2008, the social partners made a request to extend the scope of application of the collective agreements on temporary work. Following 265 oppositions, the process stopped.[128] However, it was finally extended on 1January 2012 by the Federal Council and lastly modified on 1 May 2016 to stay in force until 31 December 2018.

III. Group or Teamwork

241. In a relatively old and isolated court ruling, the Federal Court recognized the existence of teamwork. The employer may, instead of contracting with a single worker, contract with a group or team of workers. This is, for instance, often the case with an orchestra which can be engaged by the owner of a café or restaurant.

128. Common press release of swissstaffing and Unia: http://www.swissstaffing.ch/UserData/Publikation_fr_00113_00.pdf, Interpellation of Carobbio Guscetti, M. of 10 December 2009.

The situation may present itself in different forms. When the café owner contracts only with the conductor or teamleader, and the latter, himself, engages the other members of the orchestra, then the conductor may be according to the terms of the contract either an independent contractor, or an employee, bound by a contract of labour; when he engages the other members of the group without giving their identity to the owner and in his own name, then a so-called 'cascade contract' is created; the members of the group are auxiliaries of the conductor, bound with him by a contract of labour. He can also conclude the contract with the owner in the name of the other members of the team as their representative, and the contract is in such a case concluded with the team as an entity (partnership) or, as the case may be, personally with each member of the team.[129] However, some part of the doctrine appeared reluctant toward this position, considering that the employer was transferring his responsibility to someone that was not in a position to assume them. The 'cascade contract' should therefore be allowed merely in a restrictive manner.[130]

§4. The Establishment and Form of the Contract

I. The Individual Contract of Labour in General

A. *The Normal Establishment of the Contract*

242. The establishment of an individual contract of labour does not require any special form (Article 320, para. 1, CO): the contract can be established in writing, verbally or even impliedly.

243. However, for labour contracts concluded for an indefinite period or for more than one month, the new Article 330*b* CO binds the employer to inform his employee in writing about the following points: the parties' name, the date of the beginning of the work relationship, the worker's function, the salary and possible wage supplements and the weekly duration of work. This information must be given at the most one month after the beginning of the work relationship. In case of violation of Article 330*b* CO, the law provides no sanctions, leaving the one possibility for the employee to invoke Article 97 CO and its action for damages.[131]

244. According to Article 320, para. 1, CO, the writing form can also be provided by special provisions. As examples, one can mention Articles 344 *a*, para. 1 (contract of apprenticeship), 347 *a,* para. 1, CO (hiring contract of commercial travellers), 8, para. 1, 19 para. 1, of the Act on Recruitment and the Hiring of Services and 69, para. 2, of the Federal Act on Navigation under the Swiss Flag.

---

129. *ATF* 112/1986 II 41.
130. Dunand, J.-Ph., in Dunand and Mahon, p. 49.
131. See Aubert, D., in *ibid.*, pp. 463–464.

B. The Acceptance of Work

245. According to the general rules of the Code of Obligations, a contract is deemed to be concluded as soon as the parties have manifested their mutual assent with regard to all essential points (Articles 1 and 2 CO). But, as regards the contract of labour, a departure has been made from this principle: this contract is deemed to have been established when the employer has accepted the performance of work in his service for a given time under circumstances in which it cannot be presumed that such work would be performed without remuneration (Article 320, para. 2, CO). This legal provision has been inserted in the Code with a view to protecting the worker who, with the agreement of the employer, has furnished work even though the employer has not demonstrated his will either to conclude a contract or to pay a wage. If, in such a case, the general rules of the law of obligations were applied, the contract would not exist, since the undertaking to pay a wage is an essential point of a contract of labour. But the fact that, in this case, a labour relationship exists, has led the legislator to consider it necessary to admit the existence of a contract of labour and so entitle the worker to claim his wage. If the wage cannot be fixed according to a collective agreement or a standard labour contract it will be fixed by the usual norms (Article 322 para. 1er CO).

246. Thus, the fact that the employer has, in the circumstances indicated above, accepted the work, constitutes the irrefutable presumption of the establishment of a contract, thus giving rise to an obligation on his part to remunerate the worker for the work performed. It is not the private intention of the parties, but the external circumstances which are decisive. It does not matter if, thinking perhaps that he would be remunerated afterwards in some other manner, the worker has temporarily renounced his wages for the work done.[132] Thus, a worker on picket service, by so-called 'work on call' (*service de piquet, travail sur appel; Pickettdienst, Arbeit auf Abruf*) outside the enterprise has to be remunerated by the employer.[133]

C. The Void Contract – the de facto *Contractual Relationship*

247. Where a worker has, in good faith, performed work in the employer's service under a contract of labour which has subsequently proved to be invalid, both parties are bound to fulfil the obligations arising from the employment relationship as if the contract had been valid (Article 320, para. 3, CO). Therefore, despite the invalidity of the contract, the worker may claim remuneration for his work, considering that a *de facto* contractual relationship has been created. But, as has been said, he may do so only if he was 'in good faith'. However, according to the recent jurisprudence, the interpretation to give to the scope of good faith relating to Article 320, para. 3, CO is broad. A worker is in bad faith only when it can be proved that he

132. *ATF* 95/1969 II 126.
133. See the sentence of the Federal Court of 6 May 1998, *ATF* 124/1998 III 249.

knew of the invalidity of his labour contract and of the consequences of such a defect.[134]

248. This provision is indeed open to criticism, for, if it had to be interpreted literally, it would mean that the employer who has used the services of a worker under the legal minimum age while the young worker, his parent or guardian was conversant with the prohibition of work, would be unduly favoured; he would not be bound to pay him a wage, but only, as the case may be, compensation for unjust enrichment or unlawful action. However, in a sentence of 21 June 1988, the Federal Court avoided this consequence of this provision. It had to deal with a case where a foreign worker had been engaged without having obtained the official permit to work in Switzerland and who wanted to receive payment of his wage. Could it be said that the contract was void, and the wage was not due? In such a case, the Court ruled, the invalidity of the contract would give an undue advantage to the employer and would not be appropriate in view of the purpose of the legal prohibition on engaging an alien who does not have the permit to work. It would, moreover, be contrary to the principle of the protection of the weaker party in a contract of labour. Such a sanction has to be reserved when it is required by an overwhelming public interest, for instance for the purpose of social protection.[135] In this way, the inequality of the legal provision has been corrected by judicial practice.

249. It has to be added that, in the case of the discovery of the invalidity of the contract, each of the parties may terminate it immediately.

D. The Content of the Contract

250. While no special form is required for the establishment of the contract, some of the provisions are valid only if they have been made in writing. This is the case for the undertaking of non-competition agreed to by the worker (see below, para. 545). In other cases, contractual provisions which depart from legal provisions are valid only if they have been made in writing (see above, para. 161).

II. Hiring-out Contracts

251. The employer who hires out the services of a worker to another employer and leaves to the latter the main power of direction over the worker is considered as the hirer-out. The contract of labour concluded between the hirer-out and the worker must contain written stipulations on the essential points, i.e. (Article 19, para. 2, of the Act on Recruitment and the Hiring of Services):

(a) the kind of labour;
(b) the place of work and the beginning of work;

134. *ATF* 132/2006 III 242.
135. *ATF* 114/1988 II 279.

(c) the duration of the contract or the period of notice;
(d) the hours of work;
(e) the wages, the fringe benefits and the deductions for social insurance contributions;
(f) allowances for supplementary work and in case of illness, maternity, accident, military service, vacations;
(g) the time of payment.

252. In cases of urgency, it is not necessary to make the contract in writing before the beginning of the work, but then the contract has to be made in writing as soon as possible, unless the duration of the work does not exceed six hours (Article 48 of the Ordinance). In the absence of a written contract, the relations between the hirer-out and the worker are governed by the usual conditions in the place and in the profession, or by the legal provisions, unless more favourable conditions for the worker had been agreed upon (Article 19, para. 3).

253. Any stipulations which require from the worker the payment of emoluments or other previous financial benefits, or which aim to prevent the transfer of the worker to the hiring-in enterprise after the termination of the contract are null and void (Article 19, para. 5).

254. The agency also has to conclude a written contract with the hiring-in employer; if the worker has worked for less than three months for the agency and was engaged by the hiring-in employer less than three months after the expiration of the engagement with the hiring-out undertaking, this contract may provide for the payment of an indemnity to the agency, this indemnity not exceeding the fee for three months (Article 22).

255. The contracts with the worker and with the hiring-in employer are void if the hiring-out enterprise has no licence (Article 22, para. 5).

III. Contracts for Commercial Travellers and Home Workers

256. In the case of a commercial traveller's contract, the main provisions are valid only if they have been made in writing (Article 347*a* CO); in the absence of a written contract, these matters are governed by the statutory provisions and by the customary conditions of employment.

257. For home workers, if the amount of wages and the allowance for materials and accessories supplied to the worker are not indicated in writing, then the customary conditions of employment apply (Article 351*a*, para. 2, CO).

IV. Contracts of Apprenticeship

258. In contrast to the individual contract of labour, the contract of apprenticeship is valid only if made in writing (Article 344*a*, para. 1, CO). When the contract is subject to the Federal Act on Vocational and Professional Education and Training (as most contracts of apprenticeship are) it has, moreover, to be approved by the competent authority (Article 14, para. 3, of the Federal Act on Vocational Training) and be written on an official form (Article 8, para. 6, of the Ordinance on Vocational and Professional Education and Training).

259. The written contract has to regulate the following points: the nature and duration of the vocational training, the wage, the trial period, the hours of work and the vacations (Article 344*a*, para. 2, CO). Any stipulations which aim to deprive the apprentice of his liberty to decide on his activity after the end of the apprenticeship are null and void (Article 344*a*, para. 4, CO).

260. The consequences of the absence of a written contract are not always very clear. It is necessary in such a case to distinguish between two types of circumstances. If the relationship between the parties is a real apprenticeship relationship then the legal provisions concerning the contract of apprenticeship have to be observed; the conditions of the relationship between the parties being determined by the customary conditions. Recently the Federal Court applied Article 320, para. 3, CO in this domain and inferred the learning person's wage from common practice.[136] If, on the other hand, it cannot be said that there is an apprenticeship relationship between the parties – for example, if the employer does not possess the necessary qualifications and is, therefore, not authorized to train persons learning – then the alleged contract of apprenticeship is converted into a contract of labour in accordance with Article 320, para. 2, CO.[137] According to Article 14, para. 6, of the Federal Act on Vocational and Professional Education and Training, the provisions of the aforesaid law are applicable to apprenticeship even though the parties leave out to conclude a contract, do not propound the contract to the approval of the cantonal authority or propound it late.

V. Contracts for Seamen

261. The establishment of a contract for seamen, according to the provisions of the Federal Act on Navigation under the Swiss Flag, requires the observation of a very particular form. The enrolment has to be made before a Swiss consul: the captain and the seaman set their hand on a list of the crew, which is then countersigned by the consul (Articles 64–65 of the Act). The contract has to be made in writing and must include all the necessary provisions, such as those about the nature of the service, a mention of the ship or ships on which the seaman is to be engaged and,

136. *ATF* 132/2006 III 753.
137. See Aubert, D., in Dunand and Mahon, p. 917 *seq.*

if possible, the journey, the wage and so on. It must also reproduce the statutory provisions regarding hours of work, holidays and insurance (Articles 69–70). Captains or shipowners who do not respect these provisions are liable to a fine (Article 150).

§5. Restrictions on the Right of Contracting

262. The right to conclude a contract of labour is naturally restricted by the civil law provisions about contractual capacity. It may also be somewhat restricted by special provisions regarding the statute of aliens and public law protective provisions.

I. Civil Capacity

263. In order to conclude a contract of labour the parties must have the capacity to effect a legal transaction. A contract of labour can be concluded with every major person – i.e. one who is 18 years old – who has not been declared incapable and who is not devoid of discretion. A contract of labour can also be concluded with a person who is a minor or who has been declared incapable, but with the assistance, or at least with the express or implied consent, of their parent or guardian (Article 19 CC).

II. The Statute of Aliens

264. As mentioned above, EU-17 and EFTA workers now benefit from a total freedom of movement in Switzerland, on the basis of the Agreement on free movement of persons (see above, paras. 126, 127). Thus, only the latter and alien holders of a settlement permit are empowered to conclude a labour contract without any restriction, on the Swiss territory. Other foreigners may take employment only with the consent of the competent authority. An employer may not engage an alien who is not native from EU-17/EFTA Member States or not holder of settlement permit or whose engagement has not been authorized by the competent authority. However, a contract concluded with a worker who does not have a permit to work is not void (see above, para. 248).

III. The Public Law Protective Provisions

A. Minimum Age

265. A contract of labour may be concluded only with a worker who is above the minimum age provided for by public law (see below, paras. 520 and 521).

B. Protection of Young People and Women

266. The Employment Act (Articles 29 to 32) and its Ordinance V contain specific provisions relating to the protection of young people. This regulation is different from the ordinary one in terms of working and resting time and for certain types of occupation. Several dangerous jobs are indeed prohibited to young workers. So are for example activities when they are exposed to high or low temperatures, dangerous substances or significant noise.[138] Others protective provisions were enacted for women in relation with pregnancy, maternity and breastfeeding (Articles 35 to 35*b* EA and Articles 60 to 66, of the Ordinance I).

C. Prohibition of Certain Jobs on Health Grounds

267. The Swiss Accident Insurance Fund may forbid workers to be employed in certain enterprises if they have, after a medical test, been declared unfit for such work. In such cases it is prohibited for enterprises to employ them (see below, para. 339).

D. Special Provisions Regarding Vocational Training

268. With regard to vocational training, special provisions have been enacted with a view to ensuring that the trainer has the requisite occupational skill, proficiency and personal qualities; moreover, he must have attended a training course (Article 44 of the Ordinance on Vocational and Professional Education and Training). The cantons are responsible for the surveillance of the initial vocational training (Article 4). The Ordinance allows the cantonal authority not to deliver an authorization to train or to withdraw it if the training is insufficient, if the trainers do not meet the legal requirements anymore or if they infringe their obligations (Article 11).

---

138. See the Ordinance of the Federal Department of Economy on Dangerous Work for Young People (*RS* 822.115.2).

Chapter 2. General Rights and Duties of the Parties

269. The establishment of a contract of labour gives rise to a series of mutual obligations and rights for both parties. The essential obligations are for the employee to furnish work and for the employer to pay a wage; but these obligations – essential for the establishment of the contract – which square with corresponding rights, are accompanied by other obligations, which, while they may theoretically be deemed to be secondary, are sometimes very important.

270. We will see, hereafter, those obligations, which are of a general kind, principally those which are related to the obligation of the employee to work and others which are derived from them.

§1. Duties of The Employee

I. The Obligation to Carry out the Work

A. Personal Performance of Work

271. The employee has, as a rule, the duty to perform personally the work, which he has undertaken to execute; he may not, therefore, be replaced by another worker. But this rule is liable to exceptions: especially for accessory work, it could, according to the circumstances, be contrary to the duty of the worker not to be assisted or replaced by a third person. Indeed, the Code states that the right for the worker to be helped or replaced by a third person may result either from an agreement or from the circumstances (Article 321 CO).[139] It is, for instance, customary for a house porter to sometimes be replaced by his fellow workers or even by other persons. For home work, it is expressly provided that the worker may be helped by members of his family (Article 351 CO).

B. The Work to be Performed

272. The work that the employee has to perform is the work which has been assigned to him, expressly or impliedly, by the contract of labour. But it is generally not possible to describe in the contract, in every detail, the activity which is required from the employee. In this connection, the worker has to follow the instructions which may be given to him by the employer (below, paras. 278–281).

273. A change in the work which has been assigned to the worker may be ordered in certain circumstances. One of such particular situations that should be mentioned is the change in the place of work. Theoretically, when written in a contact, the place of work shall not be modified unilaterally by the employer. However,

139. See Dunand, J.-Ph., in Dunand and Mahon, p. 46 *seq.*

an employee should not be aloud to refuse a mutation if temporary and if necessary to the employers' legitimate interests. In any case, a modification of the employer's workplace should be demanded in accordance to the rules of good faith. In particular, the employer must take into account the family obligations of the employee concerned, as well as the travel time and additional costs incurred by the change. According to the Federal Court, a modification of the workplace, which requires a change of canton and a displacement of more than 50 km, usually results in a transfer of domicile in Switzerland. This is therefore a significant change in the agreed position, which requires the worker's agreement.[140]

274. The lack of profitability of a branch constitutes an economic risk that must be borne by the employer and consequently does not authorize the modification of the place of work.

275. In general, the more precise the contractual specifications are, the more difficult it will be for the employer to change the employee's tasks, even temporarily. If new tasks presented to the employee appear too distant from the ones provided by the contractual specifications, these should be considered as a new offer from the employer to modify the contract, therefore waiting for an acceptance of the employee in order to become valid.

276. Furthermore, the extent to which the worker has to comply with such demands also depends on his position in the enterprise and on the kind of work he does.

277. Apart for the temporary mutation, the above-mentioned rules are liable to an exception in the case of commercial travellers. The employer of such travellers may himself modify the contractual provisions relating to the area or group of customers assigned to the traveller when there is a valid reason to do so. However, the commercial traveller may, in such a case, claim compensation and revoke the contract for an important reason (Article 349, para. 2, CO). But in fact, the contract may exclude such a right for the employer.

C. Observance of Directives and Instructions; Disciplinary Sanctions

1. Directives and Instructions

278. One of the effects of the element of subordination which characterizes the contract of labour is to oblige the employee to follow the orders which are given to him by the employer for the execution of the work. The fact that, in this type of contract, the working time is at the disposal of the employer means that the employer may decide, in the course of the execution of the work, its organization and the manner in which it is to be executed.

---

140. Federal Court 2 July 2002, decision 4C.115/2002, c. 2.3.

279. The employer may establish general directives on how the work is to be performed and on the conduct of workers in the enterprise or household; he may also give them specific instructions (Article 321*d*, para. 1, CO).

280. The general directives which may be given by the employer have to be distinguished from the work rules which have to be established in industrial enterprises (and may be established in other enterprises) and which make provision for health and accident prevention and, when necessary, bear on the internal order and the behaviour of the workers in the enterprise (Article 38 EA). The work rules adopted by the employer after consultation with the workers are binding on both the employer and the workers (see above, para. 167), while the general directives are established by the employer alone within the limits of the contract. These directives may be established within the framework provided by the work rules. They may apply to all the workers in the enterprise or to some categories of them. They may bear on the execution of work, the control of work, order in the enterprise and so on. The *specific instructions* state how the work is to be performed in a particular case and how the worker is to behave under particular circumstances.

281. Workers who live in their employer's household are, moreover, submitted to the *rules of the house*, which are established by the head of the family and which regulate the behaviour of persons living in the common household (Articles 331–332 CC).

282. Meanwhile, the right of the employer to give directions and the duty of the worker to respect the orders he has been given are not unlimited. The right of the employer to give instructions about the behaviour of his employees is, as a rule, limited to what is done during work or inside the enterprise. While the employer may control and supervise the manner in which his orders are obeyed, he may do so only to an extent consistent with due respect for the person and individuality of the worker (Article 328, para. 1, CO).

283. For his part, the worker is bound to follow the orders of the employer only within the limits of what can be asked from him in good faith (Article 321*d*, para. 2, CO). The orders have to be related to the employment relationship and must be consistent with the conditions of the contract. They may not have an unlawful or immoral content; in particular, they may not be contrary to the health and safety regulations. The employer may not demand an activity which is not within the scope and capacity of the worker as it appears from the contract.

2. Disciplinary Sanctions

284. The Federal Act of 1914 on work in factories laid down that the employer could fine a worker who had breached the regulations on work and security in the factory. The same provision regulated the applicable procedure very strictly and provided that the fines had to be used in favour of the workers, especially for relief funds. This right of the employer to personally establish sanctions on the basis of his disciplinary powers has rightly been criticized, and there was no provision to this effect in the original version of the Employment Act of 1964. But the 1971 Act amending the Code of Obligations reintroduced into the Employment Act (Article 38) the right of the employer to apply *disciplinary sanctions* to workers as long as such sanctions are provided for by the work rules 'in a proper manner'. It is, indeed, surprising that Parliament thus reinstated the obsolete system of self-justice. It ought to be added that the restrictions which had been provided for by the old provisions have not been taken up again, but it is considered that they are implied in the words 'in a proper manner'.[141]

285. Disciplinary sanctions based on provisions in the labour contract or in enterprise regulations are also possible (Article 321*d* CO gives the employer right to give general directives and specific instructions to the worker, see above, para. 280). As the employer may establish work rules on the internal order and the behaviour of the workers in the enterprise, these rules may include disciplinary sanctions. But, as the Federal Court decided, these disciplinary sanctions have to be considered as conventional penalties for the case of violation of the contract (Article 160 CO) and as such, they have to respect the principle of proportionality and have to be determined precisely by their nature and by their amount in the labour contract or in the company regulations. In a private law relationship, like the labour contract, there is no place for freely and unilaterally fixed penalties as fines or other disciplinary sanctions.[142]

D. *The Duty of Care and the Liability of the Employee*

1. Duty of Care

286. The worker has to carry out the work which he has undertaken to perform with due care. He has to operate the employer's machinery, working tools, computer equipment, technical equipment and plant, as well as vehicles, in a proper manner and handle them with care; he also has to handle with care any materials supplied to him for the performance of his work (Article 321*a*, para. 2, CO).[143]

2. The Employee's Liability

287. The violation of the obligation of due care may give rise to liability on the part of the worker for the damage done to the employer. According to the Code, the worker is responsible for any damage which he has done wilfully or through negligence (Article 321*e* CO). His fault is presumed, according to Article 97 CO. He is deemed to have acted negligently when he has not exercised the required care. The extent of the care so required is determined by the particular contract, taking into

141. *ARV* 1971, p. 75 and 79.
142. *ATF* 119/1993 II 164.
143. See Dunand, J.-Ph., in Dunand and Mahon, p. 52 *seq.*

account certain objective factors on the one hand and certain subjective factors on the other.

288. The first of the *objective* factors to be taken into account is the occupational risk: responsibility in the performance of work may be diminished or even suppressed according to the importance of the risk. Another objective factor, which may produce the opposite effect, is that of the level of education or technical proficiency required for the work: the employee's responsibility is aggravated if he undertakes to do a job without having the necessary knowledge for this purpose.

289. The *subjective* element relates to the person of the worker. The employer cannot reproach the employee for damage done when, while being aware of it, he has hired an employee who does not have the aptitudes and personal qualities necessary for the given work, or when he did not care whether the employee had or did not have the said aptitudes and qualities.

290. In the event of conflict, the judge has to take into account all the above elements with a view to deciding whether the worker is responsible and, if he is, to what extent. The fact that damage has been caused is not, in itself, enough to entitle the employer to receive damages. Although the worker may be deemed to have been negligent and to be responsible, he will seldom – except naturally in the case of wilful damage – be condemned to compensate for the whole of the damage. In these cases, the courts will very often apply the general principle according to which the judge may reasonably reduce the amount of compensation when payment of the total amount would cause undue hardship to the worker (Article 44 CO).[144]

291. A special responsibility is laid upon the home worker due to the particular nature of his work: if, through his fault, there are forthcomings in the finished work he has to remedy such forthcomings at his own expense as far as possible (Article 352, para. 2 CO). If this is not possible, then the general rules on employee's responsibility apply. If, through his own fault, the home worker spoils any materials or tools put at his disposal, he may be bound to pay damages to the employer, but his liability in such a case is limited to the cost of replacement (Article 352*a*, para. 3 CO).

II. The Duty of Loyalty

292. Besides his duty to perform the work, the worker is bound to observe a duty of loyalty towards the employer, i.e. he is bound to faithfully protect the employer's legitimate interests (Article 321*a* CO). This duty arises from the personal nature of the contract of labour. According to this contract, the worker is obliged, in the course of his work, and – within given limits – also outside his work, to endeavour to promote the said legitimate interests and to avoid taking any action which would

144. See, for instance, *ATF* 80/1954 II 247.

be detrimental to the employer.[145] This general duty of loyalty is more particularly expressed in special duties which are specified in the Code: the prohibition of competition and the prohibition against divulging secrets.

A. *Prohibition of Competition*

293. The establishment of a contract of labour normally gives rise to a duty on the part of the employee not to compete with his employer – a duty which ought not to be confused with the covenant of non-competition which may take effect after the termination of the contract (see below, para. 544). In the course of the execution of the contract, the employee is not authorized to do remunerated work for another party, to the extent that he would thereby be compromising his obligation to be loyal to his employer – notably by competing against him (Article 321*a*, para. 3, CO).

294. This provision is, in the first place, directed against so-called 'black work' – especially work done after normal working hours for a competing enterprise. But, of course, this does not mean that *any* work performed for a third person or enterprise is forbidden. For instance, the employee may be employed in two different enterprises for half a day – or for some days in the week – in each one. In such a case the employment conditions generally show the presence of an express or implied agreement which allows the employee to work for part of the day – or, as the case may be, part of the week – in each enterprise. The Code of Obligations itself alludes to the case of the employee who performs piece-work or task-work for more than one employer (Article 326, para. 1, CO), and to that of the commercial traveller who works for two or more employers at the same time (Article 349*d*, para. 1, CO). Although there is no express or implied agreement, work for a third party is forbidden only to the extent that in performing it, the employee really compromises his duty of loyalty; and this is not necessarily the case, especially when he does not work for a competing enterprise.

295. It has been said that the exercise of a competing activity is not the only case where the prohibition against working for a third party is transgressed. Indeed, the exercise of such an activity is only mentioned in the Code as an example. Another example – a very theoretical one – is the case where the worker, without competing with his employer, performs another job which reduces his capacity to work. But it is dubious that in doing such work he transgresses his duty of loyalty. If this were the case, one could also consider involvement in exhausting sporting activity as constituting such a violation. The question which arises in this case appears to be one which does not affect the duty of loyalty, but may perhaps affect the duty of care.

296. The prohibition against working for a third person constitutes the basis of a special provision respecting holidays with pay (Article 329*d*, para. 3, CO; see below, para. 394).

---

145. On this duty of loyalty in general, see *ATF* 124/1998 III 25.

297. The prohibition against competing with the employer finds particular expression in the legal provisions respecting the contracts of commercial travellers. Commercial travellers may not negotiate or conclude business on their own account or for a third party without their employer's written permission (Article 348, para. 1, CO).

B. Prohibition against Divulging Secrets

298. The duty not to divulge secrets is another consequence of the duty of loyalty. The worker is obliged not to make use of or to divulge confidential matters such as manufacturing or business secrets which come to his knowledge in the employer's service (Article 321*a*, para. 4, CO). The duty to keep secrets is not, however, limited to manufacturing or business secrets; it extends to other confidential matters which ought to be kept secret.

299. This duty is not extinguished at the end of the contract. The worker is bound to keep secrecy after the termination of the contract in so far as is necessary to safeguard the employer's legitimate interests. At this time, the worker is no longer bound to keep all confidential matters secret, but only those which would be particularly prejudicial to the employer if disclosed. The worker may, with a view to improving his economic position, make use of the aptitudes and proficiency he has acquired in the enterprise, but he may not 'abuse his right'.[146] The legal position here is very unclear: this provision can conflict with the rules respecting the covenant of non-competition, which strictly limits the right of the employer to oppose the exercise of a competitive activity by his former employee (see below, para. 544). As a rule, the duty which thus binds the employee disappears in the course of time, but the period after which it disappears varies according to the circumstances of the case.

300. The worker who has disclosed a manufacturing or business secret may be liable to criminal punishment: the Penal Code punishes those who have disclosed such secrets even though they were bound to keep them under a legal or contractual obligation (Article 162 PC).

III. The Obligation to Render Account and to Restitute

301. The worker is bound to render account to the employer for anything he has received from third parties on the employer's behalf in the course of his work and to remit to the employer anything he has received or produced in the course of his work (Article 321*b* CO).

302. Nevertheless, the employee to whom the employer owes money may, according to the general rules of law, set off his debt against the wages due to him

---

146. See the explanatory report of the Federal Council, FF 1967 II, p. 310.

(Article 120 CO). The commercial traveller may, as a guarantee for claims arising from the contract, retain personal property and securities as well as moneys paid to him by customers by virtue of his authority to collect outstanding amounts; this right does not apply to transport tickets, price lists, lists of customers and other documents (Article 349*e* CO).

§2. Duties of the Employer

I. The Obligation to Provide the Employee with Work

A. In General

303. The employer is, as a rule, not obliged to provide the employee with work. The employee is primarily interested in receiving the remuneration due to him according to the contract. The employer has to pay the agreed wage whether he has provided the work or not. When the work cannot be done through the fault of the employer, or when the employer fails to accept performance of the work for other reasons, he continues to be liable for payment of the remuneration without any obligation on the worker to do the work at a later date (Article 324, para. 1, CO). This is, for example, the case when the employer tells the employee he has no work for him or when he prevents the employee from having access to the premises of the enterprise. The provision in Article 324 CO is related to that in the general part of the Code concerning the default of the obligee: according to Article 91 CO the obligee is in default if he refuses – without justification – to accept performance duly tendered, or if he refuses to do any preliminary acts which he is obliged to perform and without which the obligator is unable to perform. Article 324 CO is, thus, a special case of application of Article 91.

304. For the application of Article 324 CO, the most important question is to know in which cases it can be deemed that the employer has 'justification' for not providing the employee with work. Does, for instance, an economic crisis or the impossibility of the employer providing the employee with work because of a lack of materials or a loss of electricity etc., constitute such a justification? The subjective impossibility of the employer providing work does not constitute a justification in this sense. The employer gets the profits of the enterprise and must bear the risks also.[147] The situation is, indeed, no different from that of the obligator who is in default on payment of a debt because, whatever the cause may be, he does not have the necessary money at his disposal; the absence of fault does not prevent him from bearing the financial consequences of this situation.

305. The position of the employer in the face of an objective impossibility due to *force majeure* is controversial. Some authors and certain judicial decisions admit that such an objective impossibility can be invoked by an employer; for instance, when it arises from a general disaster – such as a natural catastrophe – which strikes

147. *ATF* 125/1999 III 65.

everyone. However, this opinion is not generally followed, the employer having to bear the risk of the enterprise.[148] But, for some authors, in exceptional cases, where the existence of the enterprise is at stake, the employer may revoke the contract without prior notice (Article 337 CO). In this case, the employee may ask for damages according to Article 337*b*, para. 2, CO. The difference between the two situations is quite thin.

306. In view of the above stated principles, the interruption of work due to the weather (for example, because of the cold) should not, in itself, justify a refusal to provide work; it is the same in the case of reduction of work due to an economic crisis.[149]

307. It is stated in the Code of Obligations (Article 362), that the provision of Article 324 CO, according to which an employer who does not accept the work has, nevertheless, to pay the wage has a mandatory character. In its explanatory report, the federal government stated that this provision did not prevent the parties from concluding an agreement, according to which the work is interrupted or the working hours are reduced without payment of a wage for the days or hours during which the work has not been performed; the mandatory character would only appear in those cases where the employer decides 'unilaterally' on the interruption of work.[150] But, if one had to apply the provision establishing the mandatory character of the consequences of the obligation of the employer in relation to the provision in Article 341 CO which renders void the renouncement by the worker of the benefit of his rights arising from a mandatory provision of the law, this would mean the invalidity of every decision by an employer to reduce working time without compensation whether this decision had or had not been accepted by the employee. Nevertheless, it has generally been admitted that, in practice, when the worker has accepted a reduction in working hours – and consequently partial unemployment – with a view to avoiding dismissal, there is, in this case, no renunciation by the worker of his rights but rather an agreement binding him. Thus, the provision in Article 362 CO remains here a dead letter.

308. Besides, the legislation on unemployment insurance provides for the payment of benefits in the case of partial unemployment due to a temporary reduction of working time because of economic factors, and of benefits in case of bad weather (Federal Act on Compulsory Unemployment Insurance and Benefits on Insolvency, title 3, chapters 3 and 4).[151]

---

148. *ATF* 124/1998 III 346 admits that, in a general manner, the employer has to bear the risk of the enterprise.
149. *ATF* 57/1931 I 371, 124/1998 III 346.
150. FF 1967 II, p. 338.
151. See the sentence of the former Federal Insurance Court, of 24 July 1979, *ATF* 105/1979 V 234. The Court has ruled that the worker is deemed to renounce the full salary in accepting the reduction of working time if objectively necessary, but that he has no valid reason to renounce if the contract has been repudiated by the employer; in the latter case, being entitled to the full salary, he is not entitled to receive unemployment benefits during the period during which the working time has been reduced.

309. It is often admitted that, when the employer does not provide the employee with work, the latter has to summon the employer to give him work. If the employee does not, he should be deemed to waive his rights. Indeed, there is no such general obligation, and its existence depends on the circumstances; for example, if the employer has unmistakably expressed his will not to provide the employee with work, the summons is superfluous.

310. The employer who does not provide the employee with work and has to pay him remuneration, may deduct from the wage any amounts which the latter has not disbursed as a result of being prevented from doing his work, or which he has earned by doing other work, or the amount of any earnings he deliberately forgoes (Article 324, para. 2, CO) (*see* also *below*, para. 443).

B. The Right to be Occupied

311. The principle according to which the employer who continues to pay the wage is not bound to provide work, does not apply in occupations where the employee has an interest, not only in receiving the wage, but also in performing the work effectively. This is the case for artists, who have an interest in appearing before the public, as well as sportsmen, and for journalists, who have an interest in seeing their articles published and for producers, etc. All these people need to be able to work effectively with a view to enhancing their fame and reputation; to provide them with work is an obligation of the employer. The payment of the agreed remuneration is not sufficient to compensate them for the damage they suffer because of a lack of work. They are, therefore, entitled to damages, which are due to be paid to them by the employer if he is not able to prove the absence of fault (Article 97 CO).[152]

C. The Case of Workers Employed to do Piece-work or Task-work

312. The obligation of the employer assumes another shape when, under contract, the employee has to perform only piece-work or task-work. In this case, the work itself constitutes the basis of the wage computation. Therefore, the employer has to supply a sufficient amount of work in order for the worker to be normally remunerated (Article 326, para. 1, CO). But he may prevent the consequences of his failure to accept work if assigning to the employee, instead of the piece or task-work, work at a time rate. He may proceed in such a manner if, through no fault of his own, he is unable to supply the amount of piece-work or task-work provided for in the contract or if operational conditions temporarily require the performance of work at time rates (Article 326, para. 2, CO). If neither of these conditions is realized, or if for some other reason the employer does not supply the employee with

152. See Dunand, J.-Ph., in Dunand and Mahon, p. 268 *seq.*

work at time rates, he then has to suffer the consequences of his failure to provide work (Article 326, para. 4, CO).

313. Nevertheless, except in the case of an express or tacit undertaking, the employer is not bound to supply an employee who also works for another employer with a sufficient amount of work (Article 326, para. 1, CO); in this case, the consequences of the employer's default do not occur.

314. As regards home workers, when the employer has failed to provide the home worker with work, he is obliged to pay remuneration to the worker only when he supplies the latter with work on a continuous basis (Article 353*b* CO).

D. The Case of so-called 'Workers on Call'

315. During the last years a new quite widespread form of labour relationship has appeared, so-called 'work on call' (*Arbeit auf Abruf, travail sur appel*). The worker does not have a fixed and guaranteed minimal work schedule, but remains at the disposal of the employer, on 'picket service' (*Pickettdienst, service de piquet*), and the latter calls him when he has some work to provide him with. While this form of relationship is controversial, the Federal Court, in a sentence of 6 May 1998, admitted that it is not contrary to the law (Code of Obligations), but that the employer has to pay the employee for the time he remains at the disposal of the employer outside the enterprise.[153]

316. In another sentence, of 14December 1998, the Federal Court ruled that 'work on call' has to respect the mandatory dispositions of the Code of Obligations. Thus, the possibility of the employer deciding 'unilaterally' on substantial reduction of the quantity of furnished work is contrary to Article 335*c* CO, because it does not respect the protection conferred by the terms of notice provided for by this disposition. Accordingly, the worker must be remunerated until the end of the term of notice.[154]

317. Recently, the Federal Court made a distinction between two different types of work on call: the properly named work on call and improperly named work on call (*travail sur appel proprement et improprement dit*).[155] The main difference between those two works on call is the possibility the employee has, in an improperly named work on call, to refuse the mission his employer is offering him. However, improperly named work on call should still be distinguished from occasional work as it still presents an open-ended relationship when the latter is a fixed-term relationship. In order to qualify the contract as one or the other, clues showing the continuity of the relationship such as its length in time or the rate of its missions should be used.

153. *ATF* 124/1998 III 249.
154. *ATF* 125/1999 III 65.
155. Federal Court 21 May 2015, decision 8C_318/2014.

II. The Protection of the Person and the Duty to Grant Suitable Treatment to the Employee

318. The employer has to respect the person and the individuality of the employee in the employment relationship; he is bound to pay due regard to the employee's health and the observance of morals (Article 328, para. 1, CO). Naturally he also has to observe the general provision on respect for the personality provided for by Article 28 CC. When the employer is a legal entity, the reprehensible acts of its governing body must be imputed to it (Article 55, para. 2, of the Civil Code). Besides, the employer answers for his subalterns' actions (Articles 55 and 101 CO), i.e. for all his employees, whatever the hierarchy level.

319. The protection of the personality of the employee has acquired a greater importance in the last years. Article 328 CO is indeed widely applied by courts. The employer has to organize work in a rational and harmonious way to avoid conflicts in the company. Numerous decisions deal with mobbing, defined as 'a chain of hostile comments and/or acts, frequently repeated during a rather long period, by which one or several persons try to isolate, marginalize, or even exclude a person on his workplace'.[156] Case-law also deduced from Article 328 CO a right for the employee not to be discriminated towards his colleagues.[157]

320. The most important collective agreements include provisions which guarantee the protection of a worker's privacy. The Federal Act of 19 June 1992 on Data Protection has introduced in the Code of Obligations an Article 328*b*, according to which the employer can process data concerning the employee only to the extent that these data relate to the aptitude of the employee to fulfil his or her job or are necessary to the performance of the contract of labour. Furthermore, the employee, according to the said Act, can ask the employer if data concerning him have been processed; the employer must communicate to him all the data concerning him which are contained in the data files as well as the purpose of the processing and the identity of the users of the data (Article 8); the employer cannot, without justifiable reasons, communicate to third parties sensitive information (e.g. personal data on religious, philosophical, political or union opinions or activities, health, intimate matters or race, criminal prosecutions) or personality profiles (Article 12, para. 2). The employer who evades the obligation to give access to a data file, notably because the file has been kept secret, is subject to punishment (Article 34, para. 1). Means of control of workers such as surveillance, global positioning system, video and Internet must be used only with prudence. Employees are to be informed about control measures.

321. The personality of the person learning is especially protected, inasmuch that any agreements which infringe upon the free choice of the apprentice concerning his professional activity after the end of the apprenticeship are null and void (Article 344*a*, para. 6, CO).

156. Federal Court 9 July 2007, decision 4A_128/2007.
157. Federal Court 6 July 2007, decision 4A_63/2007.

322. The Federal Act on Gender Equality, adopted in 1995 (see above, paras. 168 and 170), guarantees equality between women and men in the occupational field and contains provisions against sexual harassment. This Act also modified Article 328 CO obliging the employer to ensure that workers will not be the object of sexual harassment.

323. The question whether the employer has to observe, in a general manner, between his employees the principle of equality of treatment (in other fields than the question of sex) is disputed. Under the conception sustained in the Swiss legal system, the right to equality of treatment is a fundamental right that can only be raised against the state. Contractual freedom should therefore prevail and as a consequence no general right to equality of treatment should emerge from it. However, in cases of situations treated collectively by the employer, such as social plans, collective dismissals or health protection, the Federal Court may grant a right to equality of treatment.[158] We thus agree with the approach taken by the Federal Court that Article 328 CO prohibits the employer from discriminating a worker when such an attitude reveals an undervaluation of the employee' personality being injurious to the employee. Such an underestimation will only be recognized if the employee is placed in a clearly less advantageous position than a large number of other employees, but not when the employer favors only some of his employees. Thus, the employer is free to determine or agree, depending on the circumstances, criteria for the inclusion or exclusion of certain categories of workers in collective treatment, provided that these criteria are recognizable, that they are not arbitrary and do not violate respect for personality and are not unlawful.

324. When the employee lives in the household of his employer, the employer has particular duties towards him. He is responsible for the preservation and security of property belonging to members of his household (Article 332 CC). He has to provide the employee with sufficient food and suitable accommodation. In the case of sickness or accident, as well as during pregnancy and confinement, he has to provide nursing and medical care for the same period as that for which he is bound to pay the wage (see below, paras. 452 and 453). He has, moreover, to provide such care not only after the first three months as for the payment of wages, but from the beginning of the contract (Article 328*a* CO).

III. The Duty to Provide Tools and Materials

325. It is the duty of the employer to provide the worker, in the absence of an agreement or usage to the contrary, with the working tools and materials he needs to perform his work (Article 327, para. 1, CO).

326. When the worker himself, with the employer's consent, supplies the materials and accessories necessary for the performance of his work, he is entitled to fair compensation unless a different arrangement has been agreed on or is customary

158. See *ATF* 129/2003 III 276; Dunand, J.-Ph., in Dunand and Mahon, p. 290.

(Article 327, para. 2, CO). This situation, called BYOD (bring your own device), typically presents an information system of a given company on the one hand, linked to personal devices of the employee such as a smartphone or computer on the other hand.[159]

327. In the case of home work, the employer has to indicate to the home worker, before issuing the work, the materials and accessories which have to be supplied by that worker and to record in writing the allowance payable for the said materials and accessories. If this allowance is not indicated in writing, the customary conditions apply (Article 351*a* CO).

IV. Guarantee for the Surety

328. The employer, in certain cases, may ask the employee for the deposit of a surety as a pledge for the discharge of his contractual obligations. Such a manner of proceeding usually occurs with regard to employees such as cashiers, commercial travellers who are entrusted with a costly collection, stock-keepers, etc. In such cases the employer may not himself retain the sum deposited but must keep it separate from his own assets and provide a guarantee for its safekeeping. Normally, the surety will be deposited with a bank which then gives the guarantee to the employee (Article 330 CO).

329. This provision falls within the scope of civil law. Meanwhile, in the canton of Geneva, it has been strengthened by a public law provision: the sum has to be deposited with a bank, unless it exceeds SF 10,000, and the non-observance of this rule is subject to punishment.[160]

V. The Certificate

330. The employee is entitled to obtain from his employer a certificate which will be useful or even essential to him when it comes to finding a new job. This certificate may be requested at any time, i.e. during the course of employment as well as at the end of the employment relationship or even afterwards. In this certificate the employer has to attest to the nature and duration of the employment relationship and to furnish data on the quality of the employee's work and his conduct (Article 330*a*, para. 1, CO).

331. The employee may, on the other hand, require that the certificate bears only the nature and duration of the employment relationship, without any appreciation of the quality of his work or conduct (Article 330*a*, para. 2, CO).

---

159. Fanti, S., in 'Internet au travail', p. 166.
160. Cantonal Act of 22 March 1930.

332. In the case of a contract of apprenticeship, it is only at the end of the contract that the trainer is bound to deliver a certificate. Furthermore, this certificate only has to indicate the occupation that the person has learned and the duration of the apprenticeship. At the request of the person learning, his parents or guardian, the certificate also has to include indications of the learner's aptitude, work and conduct (Article 346*a* CO).

333. Similar provisions apply to the seamen (Article 80 of the Federal Act on Navigation under the Swiss Flag).

334. If his claim for the delivery of a certificate has not been satisfied, the employee may bring an action before the court. He may also bring an action against the employer if he claims that the certificate he has received is untrue or contains assessments which are not objectively founded.

335. The employee's repudiation of the delivery of a certificate is not valid (Article 362 CO).

VI. Protection of Health and Prevention of Accidents: the Responsibility of the Employer

A. Health and Security

336. The duties of the employer regarding health and safety are among the most important of his obligations which derive from the contract of labour or, more generally, from the labour relationship. These duties are prescribed by public law as well as by civil law. In both cases, the relevant Acts are expressed in nearly the same terms.

337. According to the Employment Act, it is the duty of the employer, in the undertakings which are subjected to the provisions of the Act, to make all the arrangements which have been shown by experience to be necessary, that the present state of technology permits and that are suited to the operating conditions of the enterprise, with the object of protecting his workers' health. The employer has to arrange his installations and adapt the organization of work so as to protect his workers as far as possible from the dangers threatening their health and from undue fatigue (Article 6, paras. 1 and 2, EA). These provisions apply by analogy to public transport enterprises (Article 24, para. 1 Ordinance of 26 January 1972). Similar provisions are provided for in the Federal Act on Accident Insurance, which applies in principle to all the branches of economy, for the prevention of work accidents and occupational diseases (Article 82). For maritime shipping, its Ordinance (Article 12) states that the complement of the crew has to be sufficient to ensure the security of the ship.

338. The public law provisions also include detailed rules prescribing the concrete measures which have to be taken by the employer. Thus, the construction and transformation of industrial enterprises are submitted to the control of the public authorities in the labour sector – independently of the control of the authorities in the building sector (Article 7 EA). Ordinance III for the execution of the Employment Act of 18 August 1993 deals with health protection. The Ordinance of 19 December 1983 on the prevention of accidents and occupational diseases contains detailed provisions governing security at work. Besides, the Federal Council has enacted a series of ordinances with a view to preventing labour accidents in different groups of enterprises.

339. According to Article 84 of the Federal Act on Accident Insurance and to the provisions of the Ordinance on the prevention of accidents and occupational diseases, the executive organs of the accident insurance may submit workers in certain categories of enterprises or activities to a medical examination and, according to the result of the examination, the Swiss Accident Insurance Fund may, when necessary, declare them temporarily or permanently unfit for work in the relevant activity; the affected worker may, under certain conditions, receive a benefit to compensate for the change of occupation. Such measures are mainly applied in jobs which carry a risk of silicosis.

340. These public law measures bind workers as well as employers. For their part, the administrative authorities (cantonal authorities, federal labour inspectorate) may bring a contravention of an Act or a decision to the offender's notice and instruct him to comply with the provision or decision concerned. If the offender does not act then, the cantonal authority may take the appropriate decision under threat of a penalty. If this decision is not acted upon it may then take the necessary measures to enforce the law. When there is a serious danger to lives or health it may prohibit the use of certain premises or installations or even close the enterprise for a specified period (Article 52 EA) or until the danger is averted (Article 86 of the Federal Act on Accident Insurance).

341. Specific jobs which are deemed to be dangerous may not be given as home work (Article 9 of the Act on Home Work, Article 9 of the Ordinance on Home Work).

342. The prevention measures are reinforced by the financial system of the accident insurance. Enterprises are classified, in each group of activities, according to the risk of accidents and the preventive measures they have taken; thus, the contributions which have to be paid by employers are fixed in such a manner that the employer, in whose enterprise there have been many accidents, has to pay a higher contribution, which in turn induces him to take preventive measures.

343. The Federal Act on Accident Insurance deals with the co-operation of the medical services of enterprises, with the prevention of work accidents and occupational diseases. The Ordinance of the 19th of December 1983 on the Prevention of Accidents and Occupational Diseases has contained, since its modification of 1993, a legal provision obliging enterprises to engage doctors or labour security specialists if the waste of the enterprise or the specific risks of the activity of the enterprise requires it (Article 11*a*). The Ordinance contains also detailed provisions about the tasks and rights of labour security specialists in the enterprise. The inspection of health conditions falls mainly to the medical labour service of the SECO and the medical service of the National Institute for Accident Insurance. The participation of workers in security committees has been recognized in the collective agreement for the chemical industry and in some enterprises in the machine industry. An Ordinance of 25 November 1996[161] deals with the qualification of labour security specialists. It prescribes minimum requirements for their vocational training.

344. In civil law terms the statutory provisions are, in principle, almost identical to those of public law. Article 328, para. 2, CO corresponds to Article 6 EA and to Article 82 of the Federal Act on Accident Insurance inasmuch as they deal with the obligation of the employer to take preventive measures. It specifies that the necessary arrangements are required from the employer only to the extent that may reasonably be expected of him, considering the nature of the employment relationship and of the work performed.

345. With a view to meeting this obligation, the employer has to inform the worker of any unusual risks which the latter does not know of, and of the measures to be taken to avoid them; he has to ensure the scrupulous application of these measures. The safety obligation which lies on the employer includes the prevention of any accident which is not due to unforeseeable behaviour of the worker, implying a serious fault of the latter.[162] Moreover, the employer may be forced to take heavier measures in some specific cases. Regarding this matter, the Federal Court ruled that the duty of protection emanating from an employer regarding an employee allergic to the smoke of cigarettes was to go beyond what is ordinarily required to protect employees against detrimental effects of passive smoking pursuant to Article 19 OLT 3.[163]

346. Article 328 CO is a civil law provision and as such is not penally sanctioned, but sanctions are provided for by the Employment Act and the Federal Act on Accident Insurance. When the health or life of the worker has been impaired by corporal injury through negligence (Article 125 PC) or manslaughter (Article 117 PC), this is taken into account in the application of the Penal Code, or, as the case may be, in the frame of special provisions, such as that which punishes the suppression or lack of installation of protective devices (Article 230 PC).

B. The Employer's Liability

347. In 2003, the entrance into force of the Federal Act on General Aspects of Social Security Law[164] and the corresponding repeal of Article 44 of the Federal Act

161. *RS* 822.116.
162. *ATF* 112/1986 II 138.
163. *ATF* 132/2006 III 257.
164. *RS* 830.1.

on Accident Insurance had an impact on the system of the employer's liability. The privilege of appeal took indeed the place of the responsibility privilege (Article 75).

348. At the time, the responsibility privilege used to release the author of a damage from his liability towards the victim as well as towards the surrogate insurance.

349. Nowadays, and since 2003, Article 75, para. 2, of the Act on the General Part of Social Insurances, newly conferring a privilege of appeal for occupational accidents on the insured person's employer, his employees and the employer's family members, cancels the insurance's appeal against all the latter but not the victim's appeal, the wrongdoer having to answer of his damage regarding her.[165] However, this privilege ceases in case of deliberate damage or of grave negligence, except if the person has an obligatory liability insurance.

350. Regarding occupational pension funds, the exact same limitation of appeal is provided at Article 27c OPP 2.

VII. Staff Welfare

351. As has been said (see above, para. 69), all employees whose wages exceed the amount of SF 21,150 a year, are covered by the Occupational Pensions scheme. Many employers are, furthermore, affiliated to voluntary provident funds. The obligations of these funds are fixed in the Code of Obligations (Articles 331–331*f*).

352. If the employer makes payments for the purpose of staff welfare, or if the workers pay contributions to that effect, the employer has to transfer such payments or contributions to a foundation, a cooperative or a public body. This is not the case when the payments are made to an insurance company or to a recognized sick fund with a view to insuring the worker against sickness, accident or disability or for taking out a life or endowment insurance policy in his favour, provided that the worker has a direct claim against the insurance carrier or the fund as soon as the contingency arises. If the worker has to pay contributions to a staff welfare institution, the employer has to match such contributions by payments of at least the same amount. The employer must give the worker the necessary information on his rights *vis-à-vis* the staff welfare institution or the insurance carrier. By a modification of the Code of Obligations and a Federal Act on the Vesting of Occupational Old Age, Survivors' and Invalidity Benefits of 17 December 1993,[166] rules avoiding the loss of Occupational Pensions contributions when the worker changes the employer have been introduced.

165. Frésard-Fellay, G., *Le recours subrogatoire de l'assurance-accidents sociale contre le tiers responsable ou son assureur*, dissertation, Zurich, Basle, Geneva, 2007, p. 239 *seq.*, p. 267 *seq.*
166. *RS* 831.42.

353. Since the coming into force of the Federal Act on Occupational Old Age, Survivors' and Invalidity Pension Provision, the provident funds created in many enterprises continue for that part of a wage which do not come under the compulsory scheme, and for supplementary payments.

Chapter 3. Working Time

§1. Working Time in General

354. The employee has to carry out work during predetermined hours and days. The working hours are in principle fixed by the individual contract of labour – expressly or impliedly – if not by practice. But the working hours may not exceed those which are fixed by public law or, as the case may be, by collective agreement or by a standard labour contract. In one case, however, the employer may demand that the employee performs longer hours than those which are fixed by the individual contract, by practice, or even by collective agreement or standard labour contract; this is when the increase in working time appears necessary (Article 321*c* CO), i.e. essential for safeguarding the legitimate interests of the employer, for example when orders have to be satisfied at relatively short notice, or if there is an unexpected shortage of staff. The employee is bound to perform this additional work if three conditions are fulfilled. In the first place, as has been said, the work has to be necessary for the employer. In the second place, the performance of the work must be possible for the employee; he is not bound to accept the employer's demands if the additional work exceeds his strength or when he cannot accept it for another reason, for instance because he is unable to perform the work for urgent family reasons or, especially when he is doing part-time work, because he is bound by another contract of labour. In the third place, the employee may refuse to perform the additional work when he cannot in good faith be expected to do it, for example when the employer could engage auxiliary workers instead of asking for additional work, or could distribute the work in another way, or when the need for additional work results from a labour dispute. Article 321*c*, para. 1, CO is classified by Article 361 CO as being absolutely imperative, but, notwithstanding the wording of this provision, it ought to be possible to regulate the matter by collective agreement. According to Article 321*c*, paras. 2 and 3, CO, additional work has to be paid by a supplement of 25 per cent of the salary or, with the consent of the worker, to be compensated by a time off of the same duration. The labour contract or a collective agreement can provide for other solutions. Also, according to Article 321c para. 3 CO, if agreed in writing or pursuant to a standard employment contract or collective employment contract, overtime may not be compensated.

355. In every case, the employer has to respect public law provisions on the maximum working time (see below, para. 367).

§2. Recording of Working Hours

356. Article 46 LTr requires the employer to keep registers or every other documents presenting valuable informations regarding the execution of the law and its ordinances at the disposal of the enforcement and supervisory authorities. According to Article 73 OLT1, the first ordinance of the Labour Act, these documents include the daily and weekly hours of work, as well as compensatory work and overtime work, but also half an hour breaks or more.

357. However, two new articles, Articles 73a and 73b OLT1, entered into force on 1January 2016. These two articles bring new exceptions to the automatic recording of working hours. These new provisions provide the possibility, for social partners, a majority of workers in a given enterprise or the employer, to agree on derogations regarding the recording of working hours, but not without the observation of some specific conditions. The idea behind such a modification is to reestablish the legal security and at the same time to relieve the companies of such important and heavy administrative tasks.

§3. Full-time and Part-time Work; Sliding Working Time

I. Full-time and Part-time Work

358. The employee may be engaged to do full-time or part-time work. Part-time work is where the working time is appreciably below the hours normally worked in an enterprise. According to Article 319, para. 2, CO when the employee undertakes to perform regular work in the employer's service on an hourly, half-daily or daily basis, the legal provisions concerning the contract of labour apply. But part-time working may have repercussions on the position of the employee as regards social security. Employees who work fewer than 8 hours a week are not insured through accident insurance against non-professional accidents, except those accidents which occur on the way to work (Ordinance on Accident Insurance, Article 13). Often, part-time workers do not earn SF 21,150 a year, and therefore they do not come under the Occupational Pensions Scheme.

359. Part-time work ought not to be confused with auxiliary work, i.e. with work performed in an irregular manner; in this case, each period of work can be deemed to constitute a new labour relationship. Repeated auxiliary work performed in an irregular manner for the same employer can be considered, after a certain time and in certain circumstances, as a part-time labour relationship for an indefinite period. In this case, the employer has to respect the legal period of notice when he has no more need of the auxiliary worker. It has been seen that travellers who work for an employer only occasionally or temporarily are not deemed to be 'commercial travellers' in the sense of the code (see above, para. 200).

II. Work on Call (Picket Service)

360. A form of irregular part-time work is the work on call (picket service). The worker stays at home (or elsewhere where he can be easily contacted) and the employer determines when he needs him for work. As the Federal Court decided, this form of labour relationship is legally possible,[167] and is more and more used.

167. *ATF* 124/1998 III 249.

But Article 27 of Civil Code (general protection of the workers personality) limits the possible number of picket service hours. The worker is entitled to be paid when he is waiting on call from his employer (see above, paras. 315–317, and below, para. 419).[168]

III. Sliding Working Time

361. For some years, the system of sliding working time has been in operation in many undertakings in Switzerland. Under this system working time is divided into a general schedule and an individual schedule. All employees have to be present during the hours fixed in the general schedule. Within the limits of the individual schedule, however, each worker may fix for himself each day, for the remainder of the working time, the beginning and end of the work, as well as his breaks. If within a fixed period (for instance one month) he does not perform the number of working hours he has normally to perform, he has to make them up in a subsequent period.[169]

362. Sliding working time should be distinguished from variable working time. In the latter, the worker may choose from among different schedules the one which is most convenient for him; he then has to maintain this choice. Variable working time does not create specific legal problems, while such problems do arise in the case of sliding working time, mainly concerning compensation for missing working hours.

§4. Limitation on Working Hours

363. Working hours are submitted to public law limitations. These bear on the number of working hours, the beginning and ending of the working day, the provision of breaks during working time and in some cases on the limitation of the daily hours of work. The statutory provisions nevertheless allow some exceptions, whereby the employer is authorized to exceed the normal limits.

I. According to the Employment Act

364. The principal rules governing this matter are to be found in the Employment Act and apply to enterprises subject to this Act.

168. See the sentence of the Federal Court of 21 May 2015, 8C_318/2014.
169. See the sentence of the Federal Court of 24 October 2016, 4A_227/2016 for the difference between overtime and cumulated positive balance under a flexible work schedule (analysis of the sentence by Fuld S., in Newsletter DroitDuTravail.ch, December 2016).

A. Maximum Working Time

365. The Employment Act determines the maximum weekly hours of work, comprising the hours during which the employee has to remain at the disposal of the employer. These hours are fixed differently for the two categories of employees:

- on one hand, workers employed in industrial enterprises and white-collar workers (office workers, technical staff and other salaried employees) as well as sales staff in large retail undertakings (see above, para. 174);
- on the other hand, other workers, i.e. mainly workers in the construction and craft trades, in commerce and sales staff in small retail undertakings.

366. The maximum hours of work are fixed at 45 hours a week for the first category and 50 hours a week for the second (Article 9), although when the two categories of employees are employed together in an enterprise or part of an enterprise the maximum of 50 hours applies to both.

367. The employer may not, without legal exception, exceed the maximum hours thus fixed. Within these limits the effective hours of work are fixed by collective agreements and individual contracts.

B. Exceptions and Overtime

368. The Employment Act provides for many exceptions, so that the working hours can be extended in many cases:

(1) the SECO may exceptionally allow an extension of four hours a week, mainly in situation where the enterprise is seriously in difficulties (*raisons impérieuses*) (Article 9, para. 4, EA);
(2) the maximum weekly hours of work may also be exceeded in the event of abnormal pressure of work, to allow for stocktaking, the settlement of accounts or liquidations or to prevent or remedy a stoppage if the employer cannot be expected to resort to other measures; such overtime may not exceed two hours a day or 170 hours a year (140 hours for the category of workers for which the maximum hours of work are fixed at 50: see above, para. 366) (Article 12, para. 2, EA).

369. In some cases, the maximum weekly hours may be temporarily extended by four hours, subject to the condition that they are not exceeded as an annual average, namely by four hours in activities subject to seasonal interruptions or fluctuations, if the maximum weekly hours are not exceeded as an average over six months (Article 9, para. 3, EA, Article 22, para. 1, Ordinance I).[170]

170. See also Article 22, para. 2, Ordinance I for other possible extensions.

370. When work has been suspended for a short time because of a stoppage in the undertaking or because the undertaking has been closed down for a holiday period, the time lost may be made up over a reasonable period. For this purpose the maximum hours of work may be exceeded, but the overtime may not exceed two hours a day (Article 11 EA); the same provision applies when missing hours of work have to be compensated for in sliding working time.

371. For several important categories of enterprises (more than 40 categories altogether, Articles 15–52), for which it has been admitted that it would be difficult to comply with the provisions of the Employment Act respecting working time, special provisions have been enacted in Ordinance II.

372. These provisions of Ordinance II thus partly replace those of the Employment Act, in order to meet the needs of the professionals concerned; they apply, for instance, to clinics and hospitals, doctors' practices and chemists' shops, clinics for animals, hotels, restaurants, cafés, undertakings in the entertainment and sport industry, editorial offices of newspapers, bakeries, slaughterhouses, etc. Thus, for example, night work or Sunday work can be ordered by the employer, for some of these special categories, without authorization (Article 4, paras. 1 and 2).

373. The discrepancies between normal working hours and those allowed for some categories of enterprises had been much criticized. If it was understandable at the time of the adoption of the Bill, i.e. in 1964, to allow for a transitional period an increase of the working hours for those establishments which, before the passing of the Act, had not been subjected to the regulation of the working hours, it is not reasonable that, more than 50 years afterwards, the same situation still prevails. The trade unions have asked for the repeal of such provisions, but without success until now.

374. From the legal provisions about maximum working time, one naturally has to distinguish the number of working hours effectively accomplished. This number is influenced by collective agreements, which have provided for a progressive reduction in the number of working hours. According to the agreement in the machine industry,[171] the normal working week, fixed at 44 hours in 1978, was cut down to 43 hours in 1979, to 42 hours in 1983, to 41 hours in 1986 and to 40 hours in 1988 (Article 12.1) until now in 2017; but workers had to support a part of the cost of the reduction. In the watch-making industry, too, the duration of working hours has been cut down to 40 hours (Article 13.1).[172]

375. The normal working week has been as follows in the years 1990 to 2008:

171. Collective agreement of the machine industry of 1 July 2013 to 30 June 2018.
172. Collective agreement of the watch-making industry of 1 January 2017 to 31 December 2021.

Table 12. Normal number of weekly working hours

	1990	2008	2015
Industry and crafts	41.6	41.2	41.3
Building and civil engineering	43.5	41.6	41.4
Services	42.3	41.7	41.9
General average	42.2	41.6	41.7

Source: Statistical Yearbook of Switzerland 2010 and FOS, DTN, Neuchâtel 2016.

The number of worked hours is steadily declining: in the period 1985–2008, the reduction has been 1.8 hours.

C. Daily Working Time: Night Work

376. According to the Employment Act, the daily work and the evening work have to take place within a spread of 14 hours, breaks and overtime work included (Article 10, para. 3, EA). Daily work is defined as work between 6 am and 8 pm, and the so-called evening-work between 8 pm and 11 pm; the latter can be performed only after audition of the workers representation or, if there is none, of the workers concerned by this measure (Article 10, para. 1, EA).

377. With the consent of the workers representation or the majority of the concerned workers, an enterprise may alter the limits fixed for daytime work: it can be extended between 5 am and 12 pm; in such cases the spread shall not be more than 17 hours (Article 10, para. 2, EA).

378. Night work is in principle prohibited (Article 16 EA). But permission can be given to enterprises to regularly or periodically work at night if it is essential for them to do so for technical or economic reasons (Article 17, para. 2, EA). Ordinance I defines the activities for which night work is deemed to be essential and gives a list of activities for which it is presumed that night (and Sunday) work is indispensable: for instance, bakeries; the milk industry for the reception, treatment and processing of milk; printing plants for the printing of daily newspapers; processes in metallurgy, etc. (Article 28 and appendix of Ordinance I). The employer has to give the worker a time compensation of 10 per cent of the night work within one year (Article 17*b*, para. 2, EA, which also provides for some exceptions). Night work may also be permitted, as a temporary measure, in cases of duly proven urgency between 5 and 6 am and 11 and 12 pm (Article 17, paras. 3 and 4, EA). In both cases, no worker can be forced to night work without his agreement (Article 17, para. 6, EA).

379. The Employment Act and its general ordinance contain special provisions on continuous work or work in two or more shifts (Articles 24–25 EA, Articles 34–35 and 36–39 Ordinance I).

380. When it is essential, for technical or economic reasons, for enterprises to operate continuously, they may be given permission to do so. In such cases, maximum weekly working hours are replaced by average weekly working hours, which have to be respected over a period of 16 weeks (Article 24, para. 5, EA). The weekly working hours may not exceed 52, or exceptionally 60 hours (Article 38, para. 2, Ordinance I). When work in two or more shifts does not imply an encroachment on night working time (see above, para. 376), workers may not be employed for more than 11 hours a day, breaks included (Article 34, para. 3, Ordinance I).

D. Breaks and Daily Rest

381. Work has to be interrupted by breaks. They must last for at least one hour if the working day is more than nine hours in length, half an hour if it is more than seven hours in length, and a quarter of an hour if it is more than five and a half hours in length. In the case of continuous work, when exceptionally the daily hours of work exceed nine hours, the break must be of at least two hours. Breaks are considered as time worked if the worker is not allowed to leave his workplace (Articles 15 EA, 18 and 38, para. 3, Ordinance I).

382. The worker has a right to a daily rest of at least 11 hours, exceptionally, once a week, of 8 hours (Articles 15*a* EA, 19 Ordinance I).

II. In Transport Enterprises

383. In transport industries the situation is different. The employees do not benefit from a fixed time-table of working hours, as do employees in industry and commerce. Their work is interrupted by idle periods, during which they are not free to dispose of their own time. They are not able to return home every evening; in the case of seamen, they can seldom return to their home at all. Special provisions have been enacted with a view to taking these peculiar circumstances into account.

384. For public transport enterprises, the Act on Work in Public Transport Enterprises does not provide for maximum weekly hours of work, but in the traffic services, rather for a daily average of a maximum 7 hours of work over a year (Article 4, para. 1); this average can be raised to 7 hours 40 minutes if, within the working time, there are more than 2 hours of mere attendance (Article 4, para. 2). The average duration of the 'service turn' (i.e. working time plus breaks) may not exceed 12 hours over a period of 28 days (Article 6, para. 1). In certain circumstances, the service turn may be extended to 15 hours, but it may not exceed an average of 12 hours over three consecutive days (Article 6, para. 2). When compelling reasons, such as *force majeure* or operational disruption, forces to exceed the maximum duration of the extension of service set out in para. 2 for more than 10 minutes, compensation must be paid within three working days (Article 6, para. 3). Towards the middle of the working time, the employee must have a break of at least one hour; if the break is taken outside the work place, 30 per cent counts as working time (Article 7). Night work – i.e. work done between midnight and 4 a.m. – may not be done (except by workers engaged exclusively for such work) for more than 7 consecutive days or for more than 14 days in every period of 28 days (Article 9). Work done between 10 p.m. and 6 a.m. gives the worker a right to a time bonus between 10 and 40 per cent (Article 4 *bis* of the Act and Article 6 of the Ordinance).

385. The Drivers' Ordinance contains special provisions concerning employees – as well as independent professional drivers – on the roads. In terms of running time of the vehicle, the hours of work may not exceed 9 hours a day, but can reach up to 10 hours a day, maximum twice a week. For employees, the maximum weekly hours of work are fixed at 56 (however, a maximum of 90 hours cannot be exceeded over a period of two consecutive weeks) (Article 5).

386. In maritime shipping, the ordinance of 20 November 1956 provides for normal working hours of 8 hours a day on deck service and 9 hours a day in general services (Articles 23 *et seq.*).

III. Home Work

387. In the case of home work, where the worker does not work under the control of the employer, it was naturally not possible for the law-maker to fix maximum hours of work. The Act on Home Work (Article 7, para. 2) got round the difficulty by prescribing that the delivery time has to be fixed so that the worker is not obliged to work for more than 8 hours a day or on Sundays.

§5. Weekly Rest

388. According to the Code of Obligations, the employer is bound to grant the employee one day off every week. This rest day ought in principle to fall on a Sunday, unless this is impossible in the given circumstances. Exceptionally, and if the employee agrees to it, the rest day may be replaced by two half-days, or several rest days may be granted consecutively (Article 329, paras. 1 and 2, CO).

389. For those employees who come under it, public law extends and regulates the right to a weekly rest. According to the Employment Act, the weekly rest is fixed at one and a half days per week (i.e. one half day more than according to the Code) – in principle on Sunday and a supplementary half day (Articles 18 and 21 EA).

390. Enterprises may, in conditions similar to those for night work, have permission for work to be done on Sundays (see above, para. 378).[173] When an employee is occupied at work on a Sunday for more than five hours, he is entitled to a compensatory rest of at least 24 consecutive hours during the preceding or following week (Article 20, para. 2, EA). In the same cases, except for continuous operations, the weekly rest has to bc on a Sunday at least once a fortnight (Article 20, para. 1 EA). In continuous operations, at least 26 rest days have to be on a Sunday – 17 where the working hours never exceed 8 per day and 13 if the daily working hours never exceed 8 and the weekly hours never exceed 42 (Article 37 Ordinance I). For certain categories of undertakings, as for working time, exceptions are provided by Ordinance II (see above, para. 371).

391. Public holidays, which are assimilated to Sundays, are fixed by the cantons; for employees who come under the Employment Act, the public holidays thus fixed may not exceed eight per year. The National Day, 1 August, is fixed by the Employment Act and also assimilated to a Sunday (Article 20*a*, para. 1 EA).[174]

392. The Employment Act allows the cantons to make other provisions, notably on Sunday rest and the opening hours of retail selling enterprises, restaurants, cafés and entertainment enterprises (Article 71 EA). It may also impose rules on the obligatory closing of shops for one and a half days a week. Naturally, the cantons may also oblige employers to give employees who are not protected by federal public law a longer weekly rest than that which is provided by civil law.

393. According to the Act on Work in Public Transport Enterprises, employees in public transport enterprises are entitled to 62 paid rest days per year, of which 20 have to be on a Sunday (Article 10, para. 1). Exceptions are provided for with regard to tourist traffic. Special provisions are also provided for car drivers by the Drivers' Ordinance and for seamen by the Ordinance on Navigation.

§6. Annual Vacation

394. While the provisions relating to daily and weekly rest have their origin in the 19th century, those which govern the annual vacation are more recent. After the recognition of the right of civil servants to an annual vacation, and the incorporation of such a right in many collective agreements, cantonal legislation has introduced this right within the framework of public law since 1931. In 1964 it was decided to unify, on a national scale, the provisions governing the annual vacation, which were then included in the Code of Obligations and deprived, therefore, of any public law effect.

---

173. On Sunday work under the previous Employment Act, *see* for instance the sentence of the Federal Court of 28 February 2000, *ATF* 126/2000 II 106.

174. On the question of remuneration of public holidays, see Federal Court 4 May 2010, decision 4A_54/2010.

395. The right to an annual vacation means that the employee benefits each year from a certain number of consecutive leave days; in taking his annual vacation he not only enjoys a cessation from work which enables him to rest and to have leisure, but this interruption enables him to leave his ordinary residence so he can enjoy more complete relaxation, travel and benefit from life in a manner previously unknown in workers' circles.

396. The employer is bound to grant annual leave to his employees; the minimum leave has been fixed by the Code at four weeks per year for adult employees and at five weeks for young employees and persons learning up to 20 years of age (Articles 329*a*, para. 1 and 345*a* para. 3, CO).

397. Of course, the collective agreements and standard labour contracts may also provide for a longer vacation. Generally, in collective agreements, the length of the vacation is graduated according to the age of the employee. In the machine industry, the duration of leave is fixed between 25 working days for employees from 20 years of age, to 27 working days for employees over the age of 40 years of age. This duration reaches then 30 working days for employees over the age of 50 years of age. For young workers and apprentices, the duration varies according to the age or the year of apprenticeship from seven to five weeks of vacation (Article 13.1). In the building industry,[175] the employees over 20 years and under 50 years of age have a vacation of five weeks; for those under 20 years or over 50 years, the duration of the leave is fixed at six weeks (Article 34).

398. The problem of the entitlement to leave of an employee who has been prevented from doing his work during a part of the year is solved by Article 329*b* CO. If the absence from work is due to the fault of the employee, the employer may reduce, where the absence has lasted for more than one month, the length of the leave; this reduction being by 1/12 for each month of absence. If, on the other hand, the absence is due, without fault of the employee, to personal reasons such as sickness, accident, compliance with legal obligations or discharge of a public office, the employer is not entitled to reduce the annual leave when the absence has lasted for not more than one month (two months for a woman in the case of pregnancy and confinement). This provision has to be interpreted in the sense that, in this last case, the reduction does not bear on the first month (or the first two months in the case of pregnancy or confinement), but that the employer may then reduce the leave by 1/12 per month from the second (or third) month of absence; when there has been a fault the reduction may also bear on the first month.

399. In the aforesaid cases, the length of the reduction may be modified by a collective agreement or a standard labour contract insofar as the latter lays down a regulation which on the whole is at least equally favourable for the employee (Article 329*b*, para. 4, CO).

---

175. Collective agreement of the building industry of 1 January 2016..

400. The employer has to continue the payment of the wage during the stoppage of work due to the vacation, i.e. he has to pay the wage which the employee would normally have received during the same period if he had worked (Article 329*d*, para. 1, CO). The advantage resulting from the vacation would indeed be illusory if during the period of leave the worker did not receive his wage.

401. The dates when leave is to be taken up are in principle fixed by the employer. As a principle, the employer has to announce the date of the leave early enough to the worker and to respect legitimate needs of the worker in fixing it. The collective agreement in the watch-making industry refers to the recommendation of the employers' organizations, according to which the enterprises should be closed during the last two or three weeks of July and during a third or fourth week immediately before or after this period. However, enterprises may also grant leave individually to each employee (Article 15.4). When fixing the period of leave, the employer has to have due regard for the employee's wishes in so far as they are compatible with the interests of the enterprise or the household (Article 329*c*, para. 2, CO). According to some collective agreements (for instance, in the building industry, Article 36), the date of the vacation is agreed between the employer and the employee. The leave period must include at least two consecutive weeks (Article 329*c*, para. 1, CO).

402. Annual leave has, as a rule, to be granted during the qualifying year of employment (Article 329*c*, para. 1, CO). The Federal Court has ruled, in some cases, that after the following year, the right to annual leave was considered to have lapsed. But the wording of the provision of Article 329*c* which provided that leave, if it had not been taken in the qualifying year, had to be taken in the following year, has been modified by an Act of 16 December 1983, and this requirement no longer appears in the law. Naturally, the employee may require that the leave be given in the qualifying year and if not, in the following year, but if he did not receive the leave in due time, he may exercise his right until the end of the period of limitation, i.e. for five years (Article 128 CO). When holidays have not been granted in due time, entitlement to vacation cumulates itself from one reference period to the next.

403. According to Article 329*d*, para. 2, CO, a mandatory provision, as long as the contract is in force, the vacation cannot be replaced by a sum of money. However, cantonal and Federal Courts have ruled that exceptions are possible. One of which is where there is, at the end of the contract, not enough time to effectively grant the vacation so that the latter may be replaced by a sum of money. The payment of leave in cash has to be given to the worker, when the contract has been terminated at a relatively short notice, for instance two or three months (*ATF* 117/1991 II 270). The other exception is when the contract provides for a part-time work with irregular schedules and has been concluded for short time. Here again the worker is assumed not to have enough time to take his vacation. In that case, in order for it to be valid, the contract and the wage sheets must stipulate clearly that a sum of money is substituted for leave.[176] Sometimes, the vacation wage is included in the wage paid for the work done by the employee. Such a practice is unlawful, except in the case where the part of the wage representing the vacation wage is determined in a percentage or in figures.[177] If the vacation lasts four weeks a year, the vacation wage ought to represent 8.33 per cent of the wage paid for the work done; for a vacation of five weeks, the vacation wage ought to represent 10.64 per cent of the said wage.[178] In both exceptions and in addition to the conditions previously mentioned, the employer must provide the worker with enough time to take effectively his vacation. If he does not, the employer may be required to pay the wage linked to vacation a second time. The same will occur if the employer substitutes a sum of money for leave when the conditions mentioned above are not realized.[179]

404. The employer has to grant, to each worker who has not reached 30 years of age, a so-called youth leave for a maximum of one week a year with a view to allow him to follow a voluntary activity for a cultural or social organization. This leave may be unpaid unless provided for by an agreement, a standard labour contract or a collective agreement (Article 329*e* CO).

405. When, during a vacation, the worker performs paid work for a third party in violation of his employer's legitimate interests, the employer may refuse to pay the vacation wage or demand the refund of any amounts he has already paid (Article 329*d*, para. 3, CO). The worker nevertheless remains quite free to have another activity which does not violate his employer's interests or to undertake other work.

406. While the rules governing the annual vacation generally have the character of civil law provisions, in the transport industry the matter is regulated by special public law provisions, breaches of which are therefore sanctioned penally. In public transport enterprises, the length of the vacation is fixed at five weeks per year for young people until the age of 20, and for adult workers, four weeks per year until the age of 50, five weeks from 50 to 60, and six weeks from 60 years (Article 14 of the Act on Work in Public Transport Enterprises, Article 21 of the Ordinance for the execution of the Act).

§7. Justified Leave

407. As well as the daily and weekly rest and the annual vacation, the employer has to grant the customary breaks or leaves, especially the necessary leave for family events such as marriage, death of a relative, birth of a child, moving house, or

176. *ATF* 129/2003 III 493.
177. *ATF* 115/1990 II 515.
178. *ARV* 1988, p. 1, 41 and 55.
179. *ATF* 116/1990 II 515.

for public or trade-union activities etc. (Article 329, para. 3, CO). As a rule, collective agreements determine the type and duration of the so-called 'justified' leave. As a rule also, if failing a specific agreement or usage, the employer is not bound to pay a wage in case of leave.

Chapter 4. Remuneration and Benefits

§1. Principle and Determination

I. Principle

408. The wage that the employer has to pay periodically to the employee, is the counterpart of the employee's undertaking to perform the work. The payment of the wage constitutes an essential obligation of the employer by virtue of the contract of labour. When there is no obligation to pay a wage, there is no contract of labour (see above, paras. 200 and 245).

409. In an apprenticeship contract, the payment of a salary does not, as in a contract of labour, constitute a necessary element of the contract. However, since the revision of the Code in 1971, it became a legal obligation of the employer: Article 344*a*, para. 2, CO provides that the amount of wages has to be fixed in the contract. The apprenticeship contract which does not contain a clause relative to the salary is void, for it does not respect the written form prescribed by the law.[180]

II. Determination of Wages

410. The determination of the wage is left to the contracting parties. The state does not fix minimum wages.[181] If the parties do not fix the wage in the contract, then it shall be determined by the usual conditions (Article 322, para. 1, CO). Normally, the wage paid for the same or equivalent work in the enterprise or in the locality may be considered as usual. Collective agreements, while they are very important for the fixing of wages, do not fix the wage directly. They fix minimum wages, or sometimes average wages; they too may leave aside the amount of the wage. The wages effectively paid are very often above the minimum fixed by the collective agreement. When standard labour contracts fix a wage – which they seldom do – they fix it as a minimum wage.

411. On 8 October 1999, the Federal Assembly approved the bilateral agreements concluded by the Federal Council and the European Union, in particular the Agreement on Free Movement of Persons (see above, paras. 24, 125–127 and 135).[182] To implement this agreement, several ancillary measures were passed at the same time.[183] Their aim was to provide remedies against social dumping by regulating the working and wages conditions of posted workers. The Federal Act on Workers posted to Switzerland was therefore passed. In addition and in cases of abuse, minimum wages can be introduced by means of standard labour contract,

180. *ATF* 132/2006 III 753.
181. For apprenticeships, see above, para. 368.
182. See FF 1999, p. 7942, for the Act adopted by the Federal Assembly, and FF 1999, p. 5440 (5695 *seq.*, 5737 and 5779 *seq.*) for the Government's draft and explanation report.
183. FF 1999 VI, p. 5498.

which will then be compulsory (Article 360*a*, CO). This last point is a novelty in Swiss labour law. Since then, numerous standard employment contract containing minimum wages have been adopted, in particular by the cantons of Geneva and Ticino. Finally, collective agreements may be extended more easily in order to improve the working and wages conditions.

412. Article 8, para. 3, of the Federal Constitution (before Article 4, para. 2 accepted in June 1981) sets down the principle that men and women have the right to equal pay for work of equal value. This constitutional provision applies directly to private law and public law relations, but its direct effect is limited to the wages paid in the same establishment or enterprise, or fixed by collective agreements or standard labour contracts.

413. The Federal Constitution forbids all forms of discrimination – direct or indirect. It is not necessary that the discrimination be deliberate; the principle of the equality of wages has to be respected independently of the motivations or intentions of the employer. However, differences in wages do not violate the principle if they are caused by objective reasons such as age, seniority, the existence of dependants, experience, qualification, risks, etc.[184] The Federal Act on Gender Equality adopted in 1995 (see above, paras. 168, 170 and 322, 323) implements Article 8, para. 3, of the Federal Constitution and in that sense goes further. According to Article 5 of the Act and in case of inequality, workers can obtain the accurate wage due to them irrespective of their sex. The Federal Court has specified that the correct wage was due retroactively from the worker hiring, unless a shorter prescription time is specified.[185] According to the Federal Court, disparities of salary due to different opportunities of negotiations or resulting from cyclical fluctuations, must be compensated as soon as it is reasonably possible for the employer, within one year if need be.[186] The Federal Act on Gender Equality overturns, on its Article 6, the burden of proof, which lies with the employer should the discrimination appear to be likely (except for sexual harassment and hiring).[187] On the supposition that workers of opposite sexes have a similar position in the undertaking with comparable specifications, the possible difference of salary between them is presumed to be of sexist nature, so that the employer has to offer the proof of the non-discrimination.[188] When the equivalence between the various functions within a company is not evident, or not established, the judge has to order a specialist report.[189] In addition, it must be said that Article 7 provides that organizations can lodge a complaint against an employer, on specific conditions. In the last years, since the Federal Act on Gender Equality came into force in 1995, the Federal Court has rendered several judgments, mainly

184. *ATF* 113/1987 Ia 107.
185. *ATF* 124/1998 II 436.
186. *ATF* 130/2004 III 145.
187. *ATF* 125/1999 III 368.
188. *ATF* 127/2001 III 207.
189. *ATF* 133/2007 III 545.

in public law contexts. These judgments are useful for interpreting and understanding this Act.[190]

414. In one particular case, i.e. in the case of home work, there used to be public law provisions on the determination of wages. According to the Act on Home Work of 12December 1940, the Federal Government could fix by ordinance the wages for home work which were extraordinarily low and which could not be efficiently regulated by collective agreements. But, after some years, the government abandoned this procedure and the Act on Home Work, of 20 March 1981, did not provide for such a faculty. It nevertheless contains provisions which allow the exercise of control on the amount of wages paid for home work. According to this Act, the wage rate paid for home work has to be equal to the amount paid for analogous activities performed in an enterprise; if such a comparison is not possible, one has to take as a basis the usual wage rate paid for analogous work performed in the same branch and the same area. In making the comparison, one has nevertheless to take equitably into account the differences in labour conditions between work performed in an enterprise and work performed at home, as well as the supplementary charges or savings resulting for the employer and for the worker from the fact that the work is done at home (Article 4, para. 1). These provisions are penally sanctioned (Article 12).

In another case, a control of the amount of wage is allowed, that is, in the case of foreigners requesting a permit to work in Switzerland (see above, para. 264). To be admitted to work in Switzerland, a third State foreigner must obtain the usual payment and working conditions of the place and the branch (Article 22 of the Act on Foreign Nationals). In order to determine the latter, the authorities take legal provisions, collective agreements, standard labour contracts, as well as salaries and conditions granted for a similar work in the same company and the same branch into account (Article 22 of the Ordinance on Admittance, Residence and Employment). Statistical data are nevertheless also to be considered. The mentioned check requires that the authority receives sufficient information regarding the salary. Additionally, Article 22, para. 2, of the Ordinance requires from the employer the production of a written, and at least from the employer, signed labour contract, indicating the duration of the gainful activity, the hire and the salary. The following remark: 'is valid only under reserve of the FOM approval' has to be included in the contract.[191] Regarding EU-8 and EU-2 workers, provisions mentioned above also apply, but only during a transitional period of time (see above, para. 126, 127). After this duration, the aforesaid workers will benefit from a complete free movement, as the EU-17 and EFTA workers already do.[192]

190. *ATF* 124/1998 I 223, 124/1998 II 409, 124/1998 II 436, 124/1998 II 529, 125/1999 I 15, 125/ 1999 I 71, 125/1999 II 385, 125/1999 II 530 and 125/1999 II 541, all regarding the public sector. For the first published case regarding private labour law, see *ATF* 125/1999 III 368.
191. Directives of the Federal Office for Migration on the aliens' field of 1 July 2010, chapter I.4, p. 10.
192. Directives of the Federal Office for Migration on the Agreement on free movement of persons of 1 June 2009, chapter II, p. 67.

§2. DIFFERENT TYPES OF WAGES AND BONUSES

I. Wages Paid in Money or in Kind, Time Wages and Task Wages

415. The wage is normally due in money. It may also be due in kind: when the employee lives in with the employer, his board and lodging are part of the remuneration in the absence of any agreement or practice to the contrary (Article 322, para. 2, CO). Other examples of pay in kind are shares and stock options.

416. According to the legal definition of the contract of labour, wages may be fixed on a time basis (time rates) or on the basis of the work performed (piece or task rates) (Article 319, para. 1, CO; see also above, para. 276).

417. When wages are calculated on a time basis, the time for which the employee has worked is the only criterion to be used for calculating the wage. The employer may not make a deduction because the work performed is not sufficient or because the worker has done defective work.[193] He may only ask for damages if he is entitled to them and then set off his claim against the wages due, within the limits authorized by such a setting off (see above, para. 442). When the worker is required by the contract to do piece work or task work, the employer has to inform him of the rate before the commencement of each individual job. Should the employer fail to give this information, he then has to pay the remuneration at the rate set for similar or identical work (Article 326*a* CO).

418. There are many systems of remuneration according to the results achieved. Their aim is generally to act as an incentive to increase productivity. The work is usually remunerated according to results when the worker does not work under the direct supervision of the employer, especially in the case of home work. The most characteristic of these systems are remuneration according to the number of pieces achieved (piece rate) and remuneration according to the quantity of labour done (task rate); these may be combined with the time rate. It may also be provided that, concerning for instance work performed on time rate, a premium will be paid when a certain quantity of work has been achieved.

II. Work on Call

419. A wage must be paid to the employee when he is on duty (see above, paras. 315–317 and 360). The question at stake here is whether such a wage is due when the worker is waiting for a call, that is, when he does not yet know whether his employer is going to offer him work. The Federal Court ruled that picket time (the time during which the worker, waiting for the employer's call, has to be available) has to be remunerated. However, the amount of this specific remuneration depends on the availability expected from the employee and has to be defined in each

193. *ATF* 97/1971 II 142.

case.[194] The worker also has a right to be paid an average salary during the legal period of termination, if the employer does not call him for work.[195]

III. Commission

420. The wage may consist, totally or partially, of commissions on certain transactions made or prepared by the employee. This kind of remuneration is common for commercial travellers; it is also used, as a complement to their salary, for certain employees who are members of the sales staff of retail undertakings. If the contract of a commercial traveller provides that the wage consists totally or mainly of the payment of a commission, such a provision is valid only if the said commission constitutes reasonable remuneration for the employee's services (Article 349*a*, para. 2, CO). The Federal Court estimated that this rule was to be respected not only in the case of a contract of a commercial traveller but with all workers under the benefit of a wage in a form of a commission.[196] Where a commercial traveller is the sole agent for a particular area or group of customers, he is entitled to the agreed or usual commission on all business concluded by himself or by his employer with customers in his area or group (Article 349*b*, para. 1, CO).

IV. Participation in Profits

421. A part of the wage may consist of participation in profits or sales or participation in the returns of the enterprise in another way. In such cases this part is calculated on the basis of the returns of the business year, established in accordance with the legal provisions and accepted principles of good business practice (Article 322*a*, para. 1 CO). The employee has the right to receive the necessary information, but the employer may refuse to give this information directly to the employee; access to the accounts has then to be given, in so far as is necessary, to an expert appointed by common agreement or, if this is not possible, by a judge (Article 322*a*, para. 2, CO). Where the agreement provides for a share in the profits of the enterprise, the employee who has requested it receives a copy of the profit and loss account for the business year (Article 322a, para. 3, CO).

V. Bonuses and Supplements

422. The basic wage may be increased by different kinds of bonuses and supplements.

423. A wage supplement has to be paid for overtime work. According to the Code of Obligations, any overtime not compensated for by time-off must be paid by

194. *ATF* 124/1998 III 249.
195. *ATF* 125/1999 III 65.
196. *ATF* 139/2013 III 214.

the employer at a rate that is at least a time-and-a-quarter times the standard wage, unless there is an agreement made in writing, or other provision made by collective agreement or standard labour contract (Article 321*c*, para. 3); thus an agreement could provide that the wage supplement is included in the standard wage.

424. A wage supplement is due, according to the Employment Act, for night work in cases where a temporary authorization has been given for such work because of proven urgency (see above, para. 378); this supplement also amounts to a minimum of 25 per cent (Article 17*b*, para. 1, EA). The same is true for Sunday work, but the wage supplement then amounts to a minimum of 50 per cent (Article 19, para. 3, EA). These supplements are not due in cases where night work or Sunday work are permanently authorized and are permanently rather than casually performed; in such cases, it is presumed that the wage has been fixed accordingly. In the case of permanently authorized night work, the Employment Act prescribes a compensatory time bonus of 10 per cent within a year. This bonus is not due when the night work does not exceed seven hours a day or four nights a week (Article 17*b*, paras. 2 and 3, EA).

425. According to the collective agreement or the contract, a cost-of-living bonus may be added to the standard wage as compensation for price increases. Either the contracting parties have to decide periodically as to the amount of the bonus, or else it is fixed automatically according to the price index. In the watch-making industry, if the parties to the agreement do not reach an understanding, the matter is submitted to the arbitral court of the industry which decides (Article 18.5, para. 1).

426. Many collective agreements, for instance the agreements in the machine industry and the watch-making industry, provide for the payment of a 13th month's wage. The 13th month's salary is widespread in practice. It constitutes an element of salary of which the principle, the amount and the unconditional term are fixed beforehand. It distinguishes itself from a gratification of which the principle and the amount are optional. A gratification obeys the *principe de l'accessoriété*, according to which it is incidental to wage and can only be of a secondary importance in the worker's remuneration. Contrary to what has been said, in certain circumstances, gratification may become mandatory. First, when the bonus consists of a very high amount in comparison with the annual salary, being equivalent to, or even higher than the regular salary, it must be considered that it is a variable salary even if the employer retained the optional salary. Second, the regular payment made uninterrupted for several years and without any reservation as to its optional nature may give rise to an assumption by the employee of future bonuses. The bonus becomes a compulsory part of the salary when the employer pays it without reserve for three consecutive years. Thirdly, even a reservation on the voluntary nature of the bonus may, in some cases, become ineffective. This is the case when, for 10 years, the employer has paid a bonus each year to an employee. The worker is therefore entitled to believe, in accordance with the rules of good faith, that the bonus is due to him and consequently he is entitled to a payment.

427. Indeed, the Code of Obligations prescribes that when the employer grants a special bonus on certain occasions, such as Christmas or the end of the year, the employee is entitled to such a bonus if there is an agreement to this effect (Article 322*d*, para. 1). It is, however, difficult to know if a gratification is compulsory or optional in actual practice, in the absence of any written agreement. The Federal Court tried to find a solution to this problem in its various court rulings. The agreement may indeed be an implicit one; if the employer has paid such a bonus for many years (more than three years consecutively), without any reservation, it becomes an integral part of the contract of labour; the same is true when the employer regularly pays the bonus to most of the employees.[197] This bonus can then be said to have been integrated into the usual conditions of remuneration in the enterprise (*see* also *above*, para. 168). If the employment relationship is terminated prior to the date on which the special bonus falls due (for instance, at the end of the year), the employee is entitled to a proportional share of the bonus only when an agreement has been reached to that effect (Article 322*d*, para. 2, CO); such an agreement may be an implicit one.

428. For some time, the TF has been imposing specific rules for high wages. As for one, the *principe de l'accessoriété* doesn't apply in case of high wage. In order to determine whether a wage should be considered as a high one, that is to say an income exceeding five times the median wage, it is necessary to rely on all remunerations that have penetrated the worker's patrimony, whatever their designations or legal origins are, therefore including gratifications.

429. Regarding the determination of the gratification attribution date to certain period, it is the date of payment that shall be decisive and not the year to which it relates.

430. The forms of gratification and profit-sharing of workers become diversified. For some years, the validity of profit-sharing plans (stock option plans, share plans) in Swiss law has been admitted. This type of plans offers numerous advantages for the employer. They enable to develop a bond between the undertaking and the middle/senior executives and to motivate the employees. Yet, a distinction has to be made as to the profit-sharing plan constituting a salary or a bonus.[198]

431. Gratuities which are paid by the customer, and not by the employer, are also to be considered as wages in those professions where the giving of tips is usual; this means that when the employee is ill, the employer who pays him his wage (see above, para. 450) also has to pay him compensation for the tips that the employee should have received if he had worked. The same is true concerning vacation wage, for the calculation of which the employer has to take into consideration the tips which the employee would have received if he had not been on leave. Tips which constitute an important part of the worker's income are considered as wages for the payment of social insurance contributions.

197. See Federal Court 25 October 2004, decision 4C.244/2004.
198. *ATF* 130/2004 III 495, 131/2005 III 615.

432. Other bonuses may be paid to employees, especially by virtue of collective agreements, such as family benefits, special bonuses for work performed in special circumstances (dirty work, dangerous work, underground work, etc.).

§3. Refunding Costs

433. Besides the payment of wages, the employer has to refund to the employee all the necessary expenses entailed in the performance of work, including living expenses when work is performed away from the normal place of employment. Nevertheless, a fixed allowance such as a per diem or a lump sum may replace the reimbursement of costs – but only if this has been agreed in a written contract or stipulated by a collective agreement or standard labour contract, provided that such an allowance must be sufficient to cover all the necessary expenses. Any arrangement to the effect that the employee himself is to bear all or part of the necessary expenses is void (Article 327*a* CO). For commercial travellers, the law goes further, in the sense that any arrangement whereby all or part of the compensation for expenses is included in the fixed salary or commission is void (Article 349*d*, para. 2, CO).

434. When the employee, with the employer's consent, uses his own motor vehicle or a motor vehicle provided by the employer for his work, he has to be reimbursed for running expenses for the use and maintenance of the vehicle to the extent that it is used for his work. If he uses his own motor vehicle, he is entitled to recoup the taxes levied on the vehicle and third-party insurance premiums, and further to receive reasonable compensation for the depreciation of the vehicle to the extent that it is used in the performance of the work (Article 327*b* CO). For the cost of the supply of materials and accessories by the worker, see above, paras. 325 and 326.

§4. Payment of Remuneration

435. The remuneration has to be paid, unless otherwise agreed or customary, in legal tender and during working hours (Article 323*b*, para. 1, CO). It may naturally be paid into a bank account if the worker can dispose of the money within the legal or conventional term of payment. A pay slip has to be given by the employer.

436. The wages have to be paid at the end of the month, unless shorter (not longer) intervals or other dates have been agreed upon or are usual; but the collective agreement or standard labour contract may prescribe other intervals (longer intervals too) or dates. The same intervals and dates apply to the payment of the commission unless, in respect of transactions which take longer than half a year to conclude, the date on which the commission falls due has been deferred by written agreement. As for shares in the returns of the undertaking, they have to be paid as soon as the amount of the returns has been determined, and at any rate not later than six months after the end of the business year (Article 323 CO).

437. In the case of home work, when the worker works for the employer on a continuous basis, the wage has to be paid every half-month, but it may be paid at the end of the month if the worker so agrees. If the worker does not work on a continuous basis, the payment has to be made on delivery of the completed work (Article 353*a* CO).

438. In case of need, the employer, if he is in a reasonable position to do so, is bound to grant the worker an advance in proportion to the work already performed (Article 323, para. 4, CO). If the sum paid is higher than the amount which would have corresponded to the work already done, it will then not be considered as an advance but, partially or totally, as a loan; in that case, it cannot be deducted from the wage but only set off against the employee's claim (see below, para. 442).

§5. Deductions From the Wage

439. The employer is entitled, or even obliged, to make some deductions from the wage. The main types of deductions are mentioned below.

440. The employer has to deduct from the wage, if he does not want to bear it himself, the workers' proportion of social insurance premiums. For the federal old-age, survivors' and invalidity insurance, together with the compensation for loss of earnings for persons on military service or maternity leave, the worker's part is calculated at the rate of 5.125 per cent of the wage; the same amount has to be paid by the employer. Further to a decision of the Federal Council and the 4th revision of the Act, for unemployment insurance, the worker's and the employer's proportions are, for each of them, 1.1 per cent of the wage, but only up to an annual wage of SF 148,200 per employment relationship. In order to stabilize the finances of the unemployment insurance, a part of 0.5 per cent of the wage is taken on the wage exceeding SF 148,200 (the same amount is due by the employer). For non-professional accident insurance, the deduction from the wage is calculated as a function of the group of risk to which the employer of the assured person belongs. The employer has to bear the premiums of professional accident (industrial injuries) insurance, which vary according to the trade or enterprise. The premiums for the Occupational Pension Scheme are fixed by the relevant provident institutions. Premiums for sickness insurance are usually paid by the employees, but some collective agreements or private pension funds may prescribe the deductions to be made by the employers.

441. The employer may be obliged to deduct taxes from his employees' wages when there is a system of taxation at source, especially for certain categories of workers (particularly aliens).

442. Advances made on the wage do not give rise to real deductions, because they represent wages already paid. But when the sum paid in advance does not correspond to work already performed and is considered as a loan (see above, para. 438), the employer may set off his debt against his claim, but only to the extent that the wage can be subject to seizure or attachment; that is, only that part of the wage which is not absolutely necessary for the maintenance of the worker and his family. Nevertheless, there is no limit on setting-off claims for damage wilfully caused to the employer (Article 323*b*, para. 2, CO).

443. The employer may deduct a certain sum as a guarantee pledge to cover his claims arising out of the labour contract. In principle, the amount withheld cannot exceed one tenth of the remuneration due on pay day and, in total, one week's pay; but a greater amount may be authorized by collective agreement or standard labour contract (Article 323*a*, paras. 1 and 2, CO).

444. Article 38, para. 1, EA states that the work rules may provide for discipli-naary sanctions 'in a suitable manner'. Thus the employer may, in certain circumstances, deduct fines from the wage (see above, para. 284).

§6. Protection of the Wage

I. Against the Employer

445. As has been said, the employer is subject to limitations in setting-off counter-claims against the claim of remuneration (see above, para. 442).

446. Moreover, arrangements for the remuneration to be used in the interests of the employer are void (Article 323*b*, para. 3, CO). It concerns all agreements which limit the worker's right to freely use his salary. It is, for example, the worker's obligation of consuming all or any of his wage in the purchase of goods belonging to the employer.

II. Against the Worker's Creditors

447. The right to wages may not be transferred to a third person or pledged, except for the guarantee of family support (Article 325 CO). The wage is protected in the procedure of distraint. A seizure may only be made on the part of the wage which is not absolutely necessary for the maintenance of the worker and his family.

III. Against the Employer's Creditors

448. In the event of the employer's bankruptcy, the worker's claims in virtue of the labour contract, existing or due for six months before the opening of bankruptcy proceeding or later, constitute a preferential claim, up to the annual maximal amount of insured earnings in accident insurance. Claims, which the worker can assert in return of sureties, are also preferential claims. The same is true for worker's claims resulting from a social plan and existing or due for six months before the opening of bankruptcy proceeding or later (Article 219 of the Federal Act on Debt Collection and Bankruptcy).[199]

199. *RS* 281.1.

Chapter 5. Incapacity to Work

§1. Payment of the Wage during Incapacity

I. The General Conditions of Payment

449. The legal provisions concerning the consequences of incapacity to work are a token showing the recognition of the social character inherent in the labour contract. According to the general rules of the Code of Obligations, a worker unable to perform the promised work ought to be in default. This is not the case when workers are incapacitated from doing their work for personal reasons. The employer has to bear, totally or partially, the damage arising from this incapacity. This obligation arises from the dependence of the employee on the employer, which results in the duty of the latter to grant the employee suitable treatment. Within given limits, the employer is bound to pay wages during incapacity.

450. Such incapacity arises when the employee is prevented from working for reasons which are personal to him or are somewhat related to him. The Code of Obligations gives as main examples the following cases of incapacity: sickness, accident, pregnancy and confinement, compliance with statutory obligations and discharge of public office (Article 324*a* CO). Statutory obligations and discharge of public office include, on the one hand, military service and civil service for conscientious objectors, and on the other hand, such public duties as fall on members of a public authority, a communal council, a jury, witnesses and so on. However, although not mentioned in the Code, the incapacity to work also includes events which have already been mentioned as cases where the employer is bound to grant 'justified leave' (see above, para. 407); for instance, the marriage of the employee or the sickness or death of a near relative, as well as the accomplishment of compulsory work for conscientious objectors.[200]

451. In order to receive his wage during incapacity, the worker has to fulfil two conditions:

(a) The cause of the incapacity must not be the worker's fault. The term 'fault' has to be interpreted in a restrictive sense. For instance, when the worker is sick because he did not take all the necessary precautions, he is not 'at fault' under this provision. However, he may be considered as being at fault if, for example, he creates an accident due to alcohol abuse.
(b) The employee is entitled to receive his wage during his incapacity to work only if the employment relationship has lasted for more than three months or, if this is not the case, if it has been entered into for more than three months (Article 324*a*, para. 1, CO).[201]

200. See *ATF* 122/1996 III 268.
201. See *ATF* 131/2005 III 623.

II. The Duration of Payment

452. If the foregoing conditions are fulfilled, the employee is entitled to receive his wage (including fair compensation for any loss of remuneration in kind) for three weeks in the first year of employment. After the first year of employment has been completed, the wage is paid for a longer period of time, but this period has not been fixed precisely by the Code. In this case, the remuneration shall be paid for a reasonably longer period, taking into account the duration of the employment relationship and the particular circumstances of the case (Article 324*a*, para. 2, CO). Thus, after the first year of service, the duration of payment is not strictly proportional to the duration of service. However it also has to take account of other circumstances, such as previous payments made by the employer in cases of incapacity to work, the time and amount of these payments and the economic position of the employer and the employee.[202] Consequently, the scales fixing the duration of payment of the wage during incapacity to work according to the number of years of employment, which have been laid down by several labour courts and most collective agreements, although they are generally applied in practice, have a purely indicative value; they are not binding on the courts, although the collective agreements are to be considered as laying down minimal rules.

453. The three scales used by Swiss tribunals are the scale of Bern, the scale of Basle and the scale of Zurich. In the French-speaking part of Switzerland, we usually use the scale of Bern.

Table 13. Duration of payment of the wage during incapacity to work

Years of service	Scale of Bern	Scale of Basle	Scale of Zurich
0–1 year	3 weeks	3 weeks	3 weeks
1–2 year	1 month	2 months	8 weeks
2–3 year	2 months	2 months	9 weeks
3–4 year	2 months	3 months	10 weeks
4–5 year	3 months	3 months	11 weeks
5–6 year	3 months	3 months	12 weeks
6–7 year	3 months	3 months	13 weeks
7–8 year	3 months	3 months	14 weeks
8–9 year	3 months	3 months	15 weeks
9–10 year	4 months	3 months	16 weeks
10–11 year	4 months	4 months	17 weeks
11–12 year	4 months	4 months	18 weeks
12–13 year	4 months	4 months	19 weeks

202. *ATF* 84/1958 II 29.

Years of service	Scale of Bern	Scale of Basle	Scale of Zurich
13–14 year	4 months	4 months	20 weeks
14–15 year	5 months	4 months	21 weeks
15–16 year	5 months	5 months	22 weeks
16–17 year	5 months	5 months	23 weeks
17–18 year	5 months	5 months	24 weeks
18–19 year	5 months	5 months	25 weeks
19–20 year	6 months	5 months	26 weeks
20–21 year	6 months	6 months	27 weeks
21–22 year	6 months	6 months	28 weeks
22–23 year	6 months	6 months	29 weeks
23–24 year	6 months	6 months	30 weeks
24–25 year	6 months	6 months	31 weeks

Source: Favre, C., Munoz, C. and Tobler, R. A., *Le contrat de travail – Code annoté,* Lausanne, 2010.

454. Childbirth entitles the worker to allowances of an amount provided in Articles 16b *et seq*. of the Federal Act on Compensation for Loss of Earnings for Persons on Military Service or Maternity Leave. However, pregnancy does not create any special credit. Article 324*a*, para. 3, CO only indicates that the employee, being prevented from working because of her pregnancy, benefits from the right of payment of her salary according to and within the limits of Articles 324*a* and 324*b* CO. There is also a public law provision, regarding partial payment of wages during incapacity to work in case of pregnancy, which applies if the employer cannot offer, to pregnant women working at night or in dangerous jobs, another occupation (Article 35, para. 3, EA) (see below, para. 541).

III. Derogatory Clauses

455. A departure may be made from the legal provisions respecting the payment of wages during incapacity to work in two different ways.

456. In the first place, it ought to be underlined that the foregoing legal provisions constitute only minimum rules; the protection of the worker may be increased by the individual contract, collective agreement or standard labour contract (Article 362 CO).

457. In the second place, a departure may be made from the legal provisions by written agreement, collective agreement or standard labour contract if the arrangement, taken as a whole, is not less favourable to the worker (Article 324*a*, para. 4, CO). For instance, the worker may receive a sum which is lower than the whole wage, but for a longer period. The arrangement is valid if the total sum received by the worker is not lower than that to which he is entitled under the legal provisions. The same provision may apply when the employer has made contributions to a non-compulsory insurance scheme which covers a part of the loss of earning; the insurance benefit may replace the wage, in so far as it has been paid for by the employer's contributions. Judicial precedents and doctrine admit that the equivalence is respected when the employer finances, by paying at least half of the premiums, the payment of daily allowances corresponding to 80 per cent of the salary, after a waiting period before payment of two days, during 720 days, over a maximal period of 900 days.[203] In order for the derogatory agreement to be valid, it has, at the same time, to be concluded in writing and provide equivalent transactions. If one of these conditions is not met, the ordinary legal protection of Article 324a para. 1-3 CO applies.

458. If the employer is bound (by a collective agreement or under labour contract) to conclude an insurance for loss of earnings, according to case law, when the employer partly or totally omits to conclude such a contractual or collective insurance to the advantage of the worker, he has to repair the damage undergone by the concerned person. The due redress covers the worker's interest to the existence of an insurance for loss of earnings, complying with the terms of the labour contract and corresponding to the payment which he would have received from the insurance for the realization of the considered risk.[204]

IV. The Case of Compulsory Insurance

459. In case of illness, accident, pregnancy, military service etc., the loss of earnings may be covered by benefits from the social security schemes. Therefore, when the worker is covered, under a statutory provision, by compulsory insurance against the economic consequences of being prevented from working, the employer is freed, totally or partially, from his obligation to pay the wage. The employer need not pay the remuneration if the insurance benefits, for the period during which the payment of the wage ought to be continued, amount to no less than four-fifths of the remuneration for that period; the employer has only to make up the possible difference between the benefits and four-fifths of the remuneration. If the insurance benefits are paid only after a waiting period (for instance, only from the third day after an accident in the case of accident insurance), the employer has to pay four-fifths of the wage during this period (Article 324*b* CO).

203. See Federal Court 5 December 2002, decision 4C.275/2002.
204. See Federal Court 1 March 2006, decision 4C.9/2006, *ATF* 127/2001 III 318, 124/1998 III 126.

§2. The Continuation of Employment

460. When the worker is prevented from working because of illness, accident, pregnancy and confinement or military service, the employer is not free to terminate the contract of labour. The Code of Obligations institutes some limitations to his liberty to act as such. This will be examined later (see below, paras. 475 and 476).

Chapter 6. Termination of the Contract

§1. In General

461. The protection given by Swiss law to workers against dismissal is limited. The legal provisions on the termination of the labour relationship apply in principle equally to the employer and the employee, and the employer who wishes to terminate a contract of labour may terminate it without special justification, except when the said termination constitutes a misuse of rights.

462. As to the manner of terminating the relationship, a distinction has to be made between contracts for a definite period and contracts for an indefinite period. A contract concluded for a definite period automatically terminates at the end of the period agreed upon by the contracting parties (see above, para. 232). Before the end of this period there is in principle no possibility for one of the parties to terminate the relationship upon notice, with the exception of termination for just cause (see below, para. 479).

463. On the other hand, a contract concluded for an indefinite period terminates after a period of notice given by one of the parties (see above, para. 235) – that is the so-called 'ordinary termination' (see below, §2) – or at any time, i.e. without prior notice, if one of the parties has a 'just cause' to terminate it – so called 'extraordinary termination' (see below, §4).

Swiss law provides for two kinds of protection against dismissal:

1. the protection against termination during incapacity of work (below, §3);
   2.1 the protection against misuse of the right of terminating the contract (below, §5); and
   2.2 the protection against collective dismissal is a particular form of this second kind (below, §6).

464. Both kinds of protection apply by 'ordinary termination' but have quite different effects. While the first one is an absolute protection, i.e. makes an irregular termination void, the second one only brings a relative protection: an irregular termination is not void, but just gives right to indemnity.

§2. Terms of Notice

465. Between the notice of termination and the termination of the contract itself, there ought to be a given period called the period of notice. This period is fixed by contract or by statute. The periods fixed by contract may not be different for the employer and for the worker; if there has been an agreement to the contrary, then the longer period of notice is valid for both parties (Article 335*a*, para. 1, CO). The equality principle is violated when, the period of notice being apparently the same, only one of the parties has in a given situation the right to give notice.[205] Where the employer has expressed his intention to terminate the contract or has terminated it for economic reasons, the shorter period of notice stipulated for the employee by individual agreement, collective agreement or standard labour contract is valid in this case (Article 335*a*, para. 2, CO).

466. The party (employer or employee) who terminates the contract has to give, in writing, the grounds for the termination if the other party asks for it (Article 335, para. 2, CO). The fact that the said party does not comply with this request or that it delivers a false reason does not affect the validity of the termination, but in the case of litigation, the court may take into account such a refusal either in relation to the evaluation of proofs or in the awarding of costs.[206]

467. During the trial period, i.e. normally during the first month of work, the contract may be terminated at seven days' notice. A written agreement, a collective convention or a standard labour contract may provide for other terms, but the trial period may not exceed three months (Article 355*b*, paras. 1 and 2, CO) (see above, para. 236).

468. After the end of the trial period, the contract may be terminated at one month's notice during the first year of employment, at two months' notice after the first year of employment up to the ninth year, and after the completion of the ninth year at three months' notice. But the period of notice can take effect only at the end of the following month (Article 335*c*, para. 1 CO). Thus, not only a period of notice, but also a specific term is provided for. Both parties have indeed to be protected against the possibility of a termination without notice or at very short notice: the employer has to look for another employee and the employee to look for another job. But it would be more difficult to find another employee or another job, as the case may be, during the month. Most changes in occupation take place at the end of the month, traditionally as well as on account of the said provisions of the Code; it is therefore easier for both parties to find a suitable employee or job at that time.

469. It is possible to depart contractually from this provision, but in this case a minimum period of one month (without the observation of a specific term) has to be observed. Such a departure may be stipulated in a collective agreement or in a standard labour contract; if it is stipulated in an individual contract, it is valid only if it has been put in writing. For the first year of employment, a collective agreement may provide for a term below one month (Article 355*c*, para. 2, CO).

470. If a contract of labour has been concluded for more than ten years – or for life – it may be terminated by the worker or by the employer at any time after the expiry of ten years subject to six months' notice to be given for the end of a month (Article 334, para. 3, CO).[207]

205. *ATF* 116/1990 II 145.
206. *ATF* 121/1995 III 60, Federal Court 1 March 2007, decision 4C.282/2006.
207. See Federal Court 27 February 2006, decision 4C.321/2005, 8.1.

471. Special provisions of the Code of Obligations govern the termination of contracts concluded for an indefinite period by commercial travellers. When the commission to which they are entitled amounts to no less than one fifth of the total remuneration and is subject to considerable seasonal variations, travellers who have been employed until the end of a season may give notice, before the beginning of the next season, for a term expiring not earlier than the end of the second month following the notice. An employer who, in the same circumstances, has had a traveller in his service since the end of the preceding season may only give notice of the termination of the contract for a term expiring not earlier than the end of the second month following (Article 350 CO).

472. When a seaman's contract of labour has been concluded for an indefinite period, it may be terminated by notice given in writing seven days in advance; but the termination of the contract is adjourned until arrival in the next port if the term expires during a journey (Article 77, para. 2, of the Federal Act on Navigation under the Swiss Flag).

473. The contracting parties are allowed to end a labour contract any time by means of a termination agreement, as long as it is not used with the objective of circumventing mandatory provisions prevailing in labour law. No specific form is required. Such an agreement needs nevertheless the real and mutual intention of both parties. However, a litigious termination agreement must be interpreted in a restricted manner.[208] In case of an invalid agreement, the legal protection system applies.[209]

474. Thereby, a worker can give up the protection against termination of the contract during incapacity to work, by using a termination contract. The validity of the latter depends however on the fact that the agreement contains mutual concessions.[210]

§3. During Incapacity to Work

475. When the worker is prevented from working, the right of the employer to terminate the contract is, after the expiration of the trial period, subject to the following limitations.

The employer may not give notice of termination:

(a) while the worker is on compulsory military or civil service or civil protection service under federal legislation and if the worker is doing service for more than 11 days, during the four weeks preceding and the four weeks following such service;

208. See Federal Court 13 February 2009, decision 4A_474/2008.
209. Federal Court 17 June 2005, decision 4C.37/2005.
210. See *ATF* 118/1992 II 58, Federal Court 17 June 2005, decision 4C.37/2005.

(b) during a total or partial incapacity of work resulting from sickness or accident not due to the worker's fault, i.e. during 30 days in the first year of employment, during 90 days from the second to the fifth year of employment and during 180 days from the sixth year of employment;
(c) during pregnancy and the 16 weeks following confinement;
(d) while, with the agreement of the employer, the worker is taking part in a foreign aid project on the orders of the federal authority (Article 366*c*, para. 1, CO).

476. Notice of termination given within a prohibited period is null and void (Article 336*c*, para. 2, CO). The period of protection starts to run with the beginning of the incapacity to work, so that if it encroaches on another year of service, the period of the longest protection applies as far as the incapacity continues at the start of the new year of service.[211] The Federal Court ruled that it is possible for an employee to cumulate the different types of protection provided by Article 336*c* CO.[212] A worker can, for instance, be the victim of an accident and, within the same year of service, do three weeks of military service (*cumul interlittéral*). He can also get sick on several occasions and benefit each time from a new protection, as long as the sicknesses are of a different nature (*cumul intralittéral*).[213]

477. Where notice of termination has been given by the employer before the commencement of a period of prohibition, and the term of notice runs into such a period, the effects of the notice are suspended and recommence after the period has ended (Article 336*c*, para. 2, CO). In such a case, if the termination of the contract is to take effect at the end of a month, a working week or a similar term, and this term does not coincide with the end of a period of notice that has recommenced after suspension, the period of notice is extended into the following final term (Article 336*c*, para. 3, CO). According to the Federal Court, the term of notice in virtue of Article 336*c*, para. 2, CO does not begin to run from the reception of vacation by the worker, but must be retroactively calculated from the term of the contract.[214]

478. The same limitations apply to the worker if one of his superiors who he can stand in for, or the employer himself, is prevented from doing his job for the reasons mentioned under (a) (see above, para. 475 and 476) and must in his absence be replaced by the worker; in such a case, the worker may not therefore terminate the contract during the same periods of prohibition (Article 336*d* CO).

§4. Termination for Just Cause

479. When there is a contract of labour concluded for a definite period or an indefinite period both the employer and the employee may at any time terminate the

211. *ATF* 133/2007 III 517.
212. *ATF* 120/1994 II 124.
213. Federal Court 21 September 2016, decision 8C_826/2015.
214. *ATF* 134/2008 III 354. About the calculation and the suspension of the period, see *ATF* 121/ 1995 III 108, 124/1998 III 347 and 124/1998 III 475.

contract, if there is a just cause for termination, without being obliged to observe the period of notice or the normal end of the contract. The term 'just cause' is deemed to cover any circumstances in which the party who has given notice of his determination to terminate cannot in good faith be expected to continue the employment relationship (Article 337, para. 2, CO). It is up to the judge to decide whether such a just cause exists, but the fact that the worker has been prevented from doing his work through no fault of his own cannot be considered just cause (Article 337, para. 3, CO). The Federal Court has ruled that the existence of a just cause has to be admitted when the essential conditions, of an objective or personal nature, under which the contract was concluded are no longer present;[215] in other words, it may be deemed as a case of application of the *clausula rebus sic stantibus*. The question whether the party who prevails himself of the just cause may also put forward for his justification circumstances of which he was not aware at the time of termination as well as circumstances which have occurred after the termination, is controversial. For the Federal Council, it would not be possible to put forward any circumstances which are known by the party terminating the contract only after the notice of termination.[216] The Federal Court ruled that it is possible to put forward circumstances unknown in the moment of the notice of termination which have occurred before the termination if they would have justified a termination for just cause; but it is not possible to put forward circumstances which have occurred after the termination.[217] Finally, the employer may no longer summon facts that occurred before the termination if he had notice of their existence and chose not to put them forward at that time.[218]

480. In most cases, the just cause lies in the faulty behaviour of either the employer or the employee. But a termination for just cause does not necessarily imply that a fault has been committed by the other party. The cause may lie in the party who terminates the contract – for instance, an illness which prevents him continuing the employment relationship or even in a fact external to both parties.

481. The grounds of the termination must be serious enough. A minor fault in the worker's work or one sole absence from work cannot give rise to the existence of a 'just cause'. But many successive faults, which have been followed by appropriate warnings, can constitute such a cause.[219] The party who terminates the contract and who blames the other party must act without delay, namely only within two or three working days;[220] if he does not act immediately he is deemed to have renounced the termination. However, an additional extension of the time of thinking is granted only when the particular circumstances of the case require to admit

215. *ATF* 101/1975 Ia 545.
216. See the report of the Federal Council, in: FF 1984 II, p. 634.
217. *ATF* 121/1995 III 467, 124/1998 III 25.
218. Federal Court 16 August 2016, decision 4A_109/2016.
219. *ATF* 129/2003 III 380, 130/2004 III 213.
220. Federal Court 24 August 2004, decision 4C.348/2003, 3.2.

an exception to the rule.[221] Exceptions can for instance be justified by the requirements of common economic life or when certain situations must been clarified.[222] He has to make clear that it is a termination of the contract for a just cause and has, if the other party asks for it, to give in writing the grounds of his decision (Article 337, para. 1, CO).

482. In the case of an apprenticeship contract, which is normally made for a definite period, the parties may, in some special circumstances, terminate the contract for a 'just cause' even though the general conditions for the existence of a just cause may not be met. These cases are as follows:

(a) if the trainer or his substitute lacks the necessary occupational skill proficiency or personal qualities for the apprentice's training;
(b) if the person learning lacks the physical or mental aptitude indispensable to his training or if his health or morals are prejudiced;
(c) if the training cannot be completed or can be completed only in essentially different circumstances (Article 346 CO).

483. If the employer becomes insolvent the employee may revoke the contract without notice unless he is given surety for his claims under the contract within a reasonable period (Article 337*a* CO).

§5. Misuse of the Right to Terminate the Contract (Unfair Dismissal)

484. According to Article 2 of the Civil Code, an obvious misuse of rights is not protected by the law. Therefore, it could be said that the employer misused his rights when he dismissed his employee making use of the institution contrarily to its ends, with a view to satisfying interests which it was not the aim of the said institution to protect.[223] However, in the case of such a dismissal, it was very difficult to obtain the judicial recognition of the misuse.

485. Therefore, an Act of 18 March 1988 on the termination of the contract of labour has introduced in the Code of Obligations provisions which specify some cases where the termination of the contract constitutes a misuse of rights. The Federal Court specified that the protection against the misuse of the right in the termination of the contract also applied during the trial period.[224] These cases are listed in Article 336, para. 1, CO. According to the said provisions, the termination of the contract constitutes a misuse of rights when it is pronounced by a party to the contract:

221. See *ATF* 130/2004 III 28.
222. Federal Court 24 August 2004, decision 4C.348/2003, 3.2.
223. *ATF* 107/1981 II 169.
224. *ATF* 134/2008 III 108.

(a) for a reason which is inherent to the personality of the other party, unless this reason is connected to the labour relation or creates in an essential matter a serious prejudice to the work in the enterprise;
(b) because of the exercise by the other party of a constitutional right, unless this exercise violates an obligation resulting from the contract of labour or creates in an essential matter a serious prejudice to the work in the enterprise;
(c) when the termination is pronounced only to prevent the birth of legal claims resulting from the contract;
(d) because the other party vindicates *bona fide* claims resulting from the contract of labour;
(e) because the other party is called for compulsory military or civil service or in the civil protection under federal legislation, or is fulfilling a legal obligation which he or she did not ask to assume.

486. Curiously, in all these cases, the legal provisions affect not only the dismissal of the employee by the employer, but also the termination of the contract by the employee. In this sense, they are, at the least, unrealistic. In what case, for instance, would an employee terminate the employment because the employer is called for compulsory military service?

487. Moreover, in three cases, legal provisions are specially protecting the employee against a dismissal by the employer (Article 336, para. 2, CO). Dismissal of the employee is considered a misuse of rights:

(a) because the latter belongs or does not belong to a workers' union, or has exercised in conformity with the law a union activity;
(b) while the employee, as an elected representative of the workers, sits on a works council or in an institution connected with the enterprise; in that case, the employer is deemed to have misused his rights if he cannot prove that he had a valid reason for termination;
(c) when the employer did not respect the procedure provided for by law for collective dismissals (see below, paras. 492–494).[225]

488. Beyond the cases of misuse of rights which are specifically listed in Article 336 CO, it is also possible, in other cases, to refer to a misuse of rights in the termination of the contract based on this article and on the general provision of Article 2 CC. In any case, the listing in Article 336 CO is not exhaustive.[226] Considering

225. This third case has been added by an Act of 17 December 1993 amending Article 336 of the Code of Obligations.
226. *ATF* 123/1997 III 246. For an example, the termination of the contract connected to the offer of taking it back if the employee accepts an immediate deterioration of his working conditions (an immediate decrease of the wage, for example) is considered as a misuse of the right of terminating the contract. The offer of a new and different contract connected to the notice of termination of the contract in force (the so-called *Änderungskündigung*) is, on the other hand, admitted by the Federal Court.

the non-exhaustive nature of Article 336 CO, the Federal Court interprets the concept of dismissal in consequence of misuse of rights in a broad manner. According to case law, the misuse of termination can result not only from the grounds of the release, but also from the way the party who ends the contract exercises this right. The abuse can also be retained in case of patent disproportion of the interests in presence, which becomes socially shocking. A misuse is also possible when the employer's right to end the contract is exercised contrarily to its purpose. A termination pronounced for pure personal suitability can turn out to be unfair.[227]

489. If the termination of the contract constitutes a discrimination against women according to the Federal Act on Gender Equality (see above, para. 170), it is also a case of misuse of the right to terminate the contract (Article 9 of the Act).

490. It ought to be noted that the Federal Act on Gender Equality has introduced a small breach in the Swiss system on termination of the labour contract. Indeed, this Act provides for the first time (except the termination during incapacity of work, which is null and void, as already seen, see above, para. 475 and 476) that a notice of termination can be quashed by the judge, on complaint, in the specific case of the so called 'retaliation' termination. Article 10 of the Federal Act on Gender Equality specifies that the notice of termination given by the employer during an intern or extern procedure or complain on sex equality (reclamation, conciliation or judicial procedure) is 'annullable', unless it is founded on a justified reason (para. 1). Thus, the Act permits to the court to force the employer to reinstate provisionally the worker in the enterprise for the duration of the judicial procedure, when the conditions of an annulment are probably realized (Article 10, para 3, of the Act). This special protection against 'retaliation' dismissal in sex equality matters has a limited duration: it applies only during the period of the (internal or judicial) litigation and for the six months after issue of the latter (Article 10, para. 2).

491. In two cases only, the burden of proof lies with the employer: in case of dismissal of a worker representative (para. 434, case (b)) and in the case of discriminating dismissal of a woman (para. 435). In all other cases, the worker who has been dismissed has to prove that the employer has violated the provisions of the law. Although, according to the Federal Court, account must be taken of the difficulties involved in proving a subjective element, namely the actual reason that pushed the employer to terminate the contract. Therefore, the employee is only forced to present sufficient evidence proving the reasons summoned by the employer are unfounded in order for the judge to assume the existence of an unfair dismissal. However, this presumption of fact does not result in a reversal of the burden of proof. Il merely constitutes a proof by clues. Regarding the employer, as he

227. *ATF* 131/2005 III 535, 132/2006 III 115.

cannot remain inactive, he is forced to provide evidence in support of his own allegations as to the reasons why he delivered such a dismissal (see Article 160 CCP).[228]

§6. Collective Dismissals

492. Until 1993, federal law did not provide any special rules regarding collective dismissals for economic reasons. On 29 April 1975, the central organizations of the employers and of the trade unions passed on a recommendation to their affiliate organizations, encouraging them to conclude collective agreements covering measures to be taken in such cases.

493. However, an Act of 17December 1993 has introduced such rules in the Code of Obligations, largely in response to the Directive 75/129 of the European Community on collective dismissals. According to this amendment of the CO, the employer is still free to dismiss employees for economic reasons, but has to respect a special procedure provided for in the Code. According to Article 335*d* of the Code, there is a collective dismissal when the employer dismisses – within 30 days – a certain number of workers without specific individual reasons. The measures have to affect a minimum of:

- 10 workers in enterprises employing normally more than 20 and fewer than 100 workers;
- 10 per cent of the workers in enterprises employing normally between 100 and 300 workers;
- 30 workers in enterprises employing normally more than 300 workers.

Small enterprises (employing fewer than 21 workers) are not covered by these rules.

494. When the employer does not respect the procedure provided for in the Code, the dismissal is considered as a misuse of rights, which gives the worker the individual right to make a claim (see below, para. 503).

495. Before pronouncing a collective dismissal, the employer has to consult with the workers' representative or, if there is none, the workers, in order to try to find, in good faith, an agreement. He has to give them written information about his plans and to offer them the possibility to make proposals about how to limit or to avoid collective dismissals or to attenuate their consequences (Article 335*f* CO). The plan for a collective dismissal and the results of the workers' consultation have to be notified to the cantonal labour authority, which tries to find solutions to the problems (Article 335*g* CO).[229]

---

228. Federal Court 15 November 2011, decision 4A.408/2011, 5.2.
229. *ATF* 132/2006 III 406, 134/2008 III 67.

§7. CONSEQUENCES OF TERMINATION

I. General Consequences

496. The notice given by one of the parties to the other party terminates the contract of labour. In the following cases, the contract continues despite the notice:

(a) the party who has given notice has made a mistake: if the term he has applied was too short, then his decision has to be corrected (if he refuses to apply the correction, then the situation is the same as if he had wrongly terminated the contract for a just cause; see below, para. 499);
(b) the notice itself has not been given in the prescribed form (for instance, it has been given verbally although the collective agreement states that it has to be given in writing);
(c) it has been given, contrary to the statutory provisions, within a protected period of incapacity to work.

497. In one case, as already said, the 'retaliation' dismissal, the notice of termination given contrary to Article 10 of the Federal Act on Gender Equality, may be quashed by the court (see above, para. 490).

498. On expiry of the contract, all claims arising from the employment fall due. However, an exception may be made through a written clause of the contract when the employee is entitled to commission on business conducted wholly or partly after the termination of the contract. As for shares in the returns of the undertaking, they are to be paid at the same time as for the other employees (Article 339 CO).

II. Termination without a Just Cause

499. When the employer terminates the contract with immediate effect and without a just cause, he has to compensate the employee for the damage which has thus been caused to him. This compensation includes the amount the employee would have earned if the labour relation had lasted until the end of the period of notice or until the end of the contract concluded for a determined period (Article 337*c*, para. 1, CO). But the employee may have to suffer a deduction, which bears on the amounts which he has not disbursed because of the termination of the contract or which he has earned by doing other work, or the amount of any earnings he deliberately forgoes (Article 337*c*, para. 2 CO). Moreover, the employer may be bound to pay a supplementary compensation to be fixed by the court, which has to take into consideration all the circumstances of the case; but this supplementary compensation may not be in excess of six month's wages (Article 337*c*, para. 3, CO). The Federal Court considers that, contrary to the legal text ('the judge can'), the compensation is due as a rule, apart from exceptional cases, for any dismissal with immediate effect and without a just cause. However, the court cannot accord simultaneously the supplementary compensation in case of unjustified immediate termination of the contract and the compensation in case of misuse of the right to terminate the contract (see below, para. 503).[230] In such a case, the judge will only allocate a compensation based on Article 337*c*, para. 3, CO.

III. Termination for a Just Cause

500. If the just cause for the termination of the contract without notice is a breach of its terms by one of the parties, the party at fault has to make good the full damage caused, taking into account all the claims arising from the employment relationship (Article 337*b*, para. 1, CO). Thus, if the party at fault is the employee, the employer may ask for compensation for the damage entailed by the difficulty of immediately finding another employee; if it is the employer, the employee may ask for compensation for the loss of the wage until the normal expiry of the contract or until the expiry of the next term of notice, as well as for all other prejudice. However, this provision does not allow to allocate to the worker a compensation exceeding the effective loss of earnings. The employer cannot be sentenced to the payment of a punitive and repair compensation as in the case of a dismissal with immediate effect and without a just cause.[231]

501. In other cases, such as when no party is at fault or when they are both at fault, it is up to the judge to assess the financial consequences of the termination of the contract, taking into account all the relevant circumstances (Article 337*b*, para. 2, CO). He may share out the damage between the parties or he may decide that the damage will be borne by the party who has terminated the contract.

IV. Where the Employee does not Report for Work

502. When the termination of the contract is due to the fact that the employee did not report for work or has left his job without notice and without a valid reason, the employer is entitled to compensation to the amount of one quarter of the monthly remuneration, plus damages for any additional loss or prejudice (Article 337*d*, para. 1, CO). The judge, at his discretion, may nevertheless reduce such compensation if no loss or prejudice has been caused to the employer or if the loss or prejudice entailed does not reach an amount corresponding to one quarter of the monthly remuneration (Article 337*d*, para. 2, CO). The claim for such compensation must be asserted by instituting judicial proceedings or an action for recovery within 30 days of the date on which the worker failed to report for work or left his job (Article 337*d*, para. 3, CO).

---

230. *ATF* 121/1995 III 64.
231. *ATF* 133/2007 III 657.

V. Misuse of Rights

503. In the case where one of the parties to the contract has misused his rights in terminating the contract, the other party, if he intends to prevail himself of this misuse, has to raise a written objection with the author of the termination; this objection has to be filed not later than the expiry of the period of notice (Article 336*b*, para. 1, CO). The objection must contest the reasons summoned by the employer as well as the termination itself and the employee has to show his willingness to continue the working relationship.[232] If the parties do not reach an agreement, the party who has received the declaration of termination has to assert his claim by instituting an action for recovery within 180 days of the termination of the contract (Article 336*b*, para. 2, CO). If the court finds that the author of the termination has misused his rights, it will fix a compensation sum to be paid to the other party; this compensation must, however, not be in excess of the amount of six months' remuneration of the worker, the compensation due for another ground being reserved (Article 336*a* CO). In cases of non respect of the procedure provided for by the law for collective dismissals (see above, paras. 492–495), the compensation shall not exceed the amount of two months' remuneration (Article 336*a*, para. 2, CO). It ought to be noted that the party who asks for the compensation does not have to prove that he has suffered damage. Nevertheless, the nature of the compensation amount has a double character: On the one hand, it is a penalty for the employer's unjustified dismissal of the worker, on the other hand its aim is also to compensate for the damage suffered by the employee.[233]

504. Although the employer may be deemed to have misused his rights, the termination of the contract is valid; the court cannot force the employer to reinstate the worker in the enterprise (see nevertheless above, para. 436 for 'retaliation' dismissal in sex equality matters).

VI. Long-service Leaving Grant

505. When the employment relationship of an employee aged 50 years or more is terminated after 20 or more years, the employer has to pay him a long-service leaving grant (Article 339*b*, para. 1, CO).

506. Calculating the length of the employment relationship may present some difficulties: in the case of an interruption in the relationship the question arises whether there has been only one – all inclusive – relationship between the parties, or whether there have been two or several successive relationships. The mere interruption in the course of the 20 years does not necessarily mean that the same

---

232. Federal Court 8 September 2014, decision 4A.320/2014.
233. *ATF* 123/1997 III 391, 123/1997 V 11 (according to the latter, the compensation amount is not subject to social insurance premiums), Federal Court 27 February 2007, decision 4C.370/2006.

employment relationship was not taken up again after the interruption. The question is to be solved according to the circumstances and the will of the parties. There is no interruption when the employment relation has been transferred in the interest of the former employer to a company economically identical to the latter.[234]

507. The amount of the grant may be fixed by written agreement, collective agreement or standard labour contract, with a minimum corresponding to the equivalent of two months' remuneration (Article 339*c*, para. 1, CO); if not, it is up to the judge to assess this amount at his discretion, taking into account all the relevant circumstances, and with the maximum amount in this case being equivalent to eight months' remuneration (Article 339*c*, para. 2, CO). The grant may be reduced or not paid at all if the employee has terminated the contract without a valid cause, if the employer has terminated the contract immediately for a just cause, or if the payment of the grant would cause hardship to the employer (Article 339*c*, para. 3, CO).

508. The grant shall be paid at the end of the labour relation, but the term of payment may be postponed by a written agreement, a collective agreement, a standard labour contract or a judicial decision (Article 339*c*, para. 4 CO).

509. The benefits of a provident fund which have been received by the employee are deducted from the amount of the grant insofar as these benefits have been financed by the employer or by the provident institution through the employer's contributions (Article 339*d*, para. 1, CO). The employer is also exempted from the obligation to pay a long-service leaving grant if he undertakes to pay in the future provident benefits to the employee (Article 339*d*, para. 2, CO).

§8. Transfer of the Employment Relationship

510. When the employer transfers the enterprise or a part of it to a third party, the employment relationship is transferred to the new employer with all rights and duties attached (Article 333, para. 1, CO). If the employment relationship is also ruled by a collective agreement, the latter has to be respected by the new employer for at least one year, if it does not end before by expiration of the period agreed upon or by termination by a party (Article 333, para 1bis, CO). Article 333, para. 1, CO is a mandatory provision. The employer who transfers the company and the new employer cannot conclude any derogatory agreement.[235] The employee may nevertheless refuse such a transfer (Article 333, para. 1, CO). In such a case, the employment relationship is terminated at the expiry of the statutory term of notice. Until such date, the employee and the person who has acquired the undertaking are bound to execute the contract (Article 333, para. 2, CO). The former employer and the new

234. *ATF* 112/1986 II 51.
235. *ATF* 132/2006 III 32.

employer are jointly and severally liable for debts towards the employee which have fallen due prior to the transfer and which subsequently fall due up to the date on which the employment relationship could normally be terminated or is in fact terminated as a result of the employee's refusal (Article 333, para. 3, CO). The Federal Court considered that the joint liability established by Article 333, para. 3, CO did not apply in case of purchase of an undertaking in a situation of bankruptcy proceeding.[236]

511. In other cases, the employer is not entitled to transfer any rights arising from the employment relationship to a third party, unless the contrary has been agreed or ensues from the circumstances of the case (Article 333, para. 4, CO).

§9. Merger, Demerger and Transfer of Assets and Liabilities

512. The Federal Act on Mergers, Demergers, Transformations and Transfers of Assets and Liabilities entered into force on 1 July 2004.[237] This Act provides that the transfer of the employment relationships as part of a merger, a demerger or a transfer of assets and liabilities is ruled by Article 333 CO. In case of failure to respect information duty and consultation procedure, the workers' representative can demand from the court to forbid registration into the trade register.

§10. Death

I. Death of the Employee

513. The contract of labour, due to its personal character, terminates with the death of the employee (Article 338, para. 1, CO). The employer is, however, bound to pay, on the death of the employee, remuneration for one further month reckoned from the day of death or, after five years of service, for two further months if the employee leaves a surviving spouse, a same-sex partner, minor children or other persons towards whom he had maintenance obligations (Article 338, para. 2 CO). When the employee has fulfilled the conditions for receiving a long-service leaving grant, such a grant shall be paid to the said persons (Article 339*b* CO).

II. Death of the Employer

514. On the death of the employer, the contract, in principle, continues. However, if the contract essentially relates to the employer's person, for instance in the case of a personal secretary, a domestic worker or a nurse, the death of the employer terminates the employment relationship. In the first case, the contract is transferred

236. *ATF* 129/2003 III 335.
237. *RS* 221.301.

to the employer's heirs, and the provisions relating to the transfer of the employment relationship (see above, para. 510) apply (Article 338*a*, para. 1, CO). In the second case, the employee may claim equitable damages for loss or prejudice sustained by him as a result of the premature ending of the contract (Article 338*a*, para. 2, CO).

Chapter 7. Protection of Special Categories of Worker

§1. Young Workers

I. General Remarks

515. The special protection given to young workers has been an essential part of public labour law since the enactment of the first Factories Act in 1877 (see above, para. 101).

516. According to the Employment Act, 'young workers' are workers of either sex who are under 18 years of age (Article 29, para. 1, EA). The provisions of the Employment Act also apply to young workers in public transport enterprises (Act on Work in Public Transport Enterprises, Article 16). For seamen, the relevant age is 18 years (Ordinance on Navigation, of 20 November 1956,[238] Article 16).

517. In principle, the Employment Act does not apply to the children and grand-children of the head of the enterprise or to his spouse's children (Article 4 EA). It however applies when children and grand-children work collectively with other employees (Article 3, para. 2, Ordinance V).

518. Young workers who are employed in enterprises or occupations which are not submitted to the provisions of federal protective legislation – such as agricultural workers or domestic workers – may be protected by cantonal law.

519. The employer must have due regard for a young worker's health and he has to make arrangements to safeguard his morals. When he engages a young person, he has to require evidence of his age (Article 29, paras. 2 and 4, EA).

II. Minimum Age

520. Enterprises submitted to the provisions of the Employment Act are forbidden to employ young persons under 15 years of age (Article 30, para. 1 EA).

Nevertheless, exceptions are made, in particular:

(a) young persons over 13 years of age may be entrusted with errands and light work. During the school year, they may be employed for nine hours per week and three hours a day, while during half of the school holidays or two weeks of work experience, they may be employed for 40 hours per week and eight hours a day (Articles 30, para 2, EA and 11 Ordinance V);
(b) young persons under 15 years of age may work on the occasion of cultural, artistic or sport events, as well as in advertising. This type of activities must

238. *RS* 747.301.

however be announced 14 days before the said work to the competent cantonal authority (Articles 30, para. 2, EA and 7 Ordinance V);

(c) young persons over 14 years of age who are not required to attend school may, in cantons where the maximum age for compulsory schooling is under 15 years, be authorized to take a regular job (Articles 30, para. 3, EA and 9 Ordinance V).

521. These exceptions are allowed provided that the jobs in question are not harmful to the health of the young workers and do not prejudice their school work.

522. 15 years of age is also the minimum age for admission to work in public transport enterprises, in maritime shipping and in the home (but the home-worker may be helped by his children who are under 15 years of age).

523. Nevertheless, in the federal legislation, there are no provisions which would provide for a minimum age in occupations that are not regulated either under the Employment Act or under the Act on Work in Public Transport Entreprises, the Act on Home Work and the Act on Navigation under the Swiss Flag. In those cases, the competence of establishing a minimum age lies exclusively with the cantonal law-maker. In practice the problem is partly resolved, in each canton, by the law on obligatory scholarship.

III. Forbidden Operations

524. Young workers may not be employed in some kinds of operations, such as work with machines, tools or apparatus which involve a great risk of accidents or require too strenuous an effort, or work which involves a great risk of fire, accident, sickness or poisoning, or underground work in galleries and mines, etc. Even more operations are forbidden to young workers who are not 16 years of age. They may not work in enterprises such as circuses, cinemas, etc., and in customers' services in hotels, restaurants and cafés. Young workers who are not 18 years of age may not be employed in the customer services department of entertainment businesses (Articles 29, para. 3, EA, 4–6 Ordinance V, Ordinance of the Federal Department of Economy on Dangerous Work for Young People).[239]

IV. Hours of Work

525. Special rules govern the hours of work of young workers. In undertakings regulated by the Employment Act, their daily hours of work may not exceed nine, including time spent in working overtime or attending compulsory courses during working hours; neither may their hours exceed those of other workers in the same undertaking or, where there are no other workers, the hours recognized by local custom (Article 34, para. 1, EA). The spread of a young person's daytime work may

239. *RS* 822.115.2.

not be more than 12 hours including breaks. Young persons under 16 years of age may not be occupied after 8 p.m.; after 16 years of age they may not be occupied after 10 p.m. (Article 31, para. 2, EA).

526. Young persons under 16 years of age may not be assigned to do overtime or incidental jobs beyond the normal hours of work (Article 31, para. 3, EA).

527. Nevertheless, exceptions to the above-mentioned provisions can be made for some categories of enterprises, such as clinics and hospitals, medical practices, hotels, restaurants and cafés, etc. (see above, para. 371).[240]

528. The hours of work for young workers under 13 years of age who are authorized to accept certain jobs in an enterprise are subject to special limitations (Article 10, Ordinance V) (for young workers over 13 years of age, see above, paras. 520 and 521).

V. Medical Certificate

529. Federal law does not oblige the employer who engages a young worker to request a medical certificate, except if the young worker, who is over 14 years of age and is not required to attend school, is authorized to take regular work (Article 9, para. 2, Ordinance V) (see above, paras. 520 and 521).

§2. Women

I. General Remarks

530. As well as protecting young workers, Swiss federal legislation has, from the beginning, ensured the protection of women workers. This protection presents two aspects: the protection of all women workers and special protection during pregnancy and confinement.

531. For the first form of protection – which extends to all women workers – one ought to distinguish between the measures designed to prevent discrimination and those measures which limit the employer's right to employ women in certain kinds or forms of work. The prevention of discrimination is provided for in Article 8, para. 3, of the Federal Constitution, which proclaims the equality of rights between men and women (see above, para. 412). The other so-called 'protective measures' have been subject of controversy: the question arose whether they are consistent with the principle of equality. This second form of protection has now been abolished by the revision of the Employment Act of 20 March 1998 (for an exception, see below, para. 533). Some of the aspects of the general protection of

240. See the Ordinance of the Federal Department of Economy on Dispensations for Night and Sunday Work Prohibition During the Initial Vocational Training, *RS* 822.115.4.

women have been extended by this revision on all workers having family responsibilities (see below, para. 543).

II. The Protection of Women in General

532. Previously, the Employment Act stated that the employer must have due regard for a woman's health and that he has to make arrangements to safeguard her morals (old Article 33 EA) – which is indeed a patriarchal conception of protection!

A. Forbidden Operations

533. The Ordinance I still forbids the employment of women in underground construction (with the exception of scientific activities, some forms of short occupations, etc.: Article 66 Ordinance I). This prohibition has been maintained because of Convention No. 45 of the ILO, ratified by Switzerland.

B. Hours of Work

534. Before the revision of 20 March 1998, the Employment Act also provided for some special arrangements on hours of work for women in general, in particular a prohibition, in principle, of night and Sunday work (old Article 34 EA). This special protection has now disappeared: women are generally treated like men in this respect.

III. Protection against Discrimination

535. Article 8, paras. 2 and 3, of the Federal Constitution intends to oppose sex discrimination, proclaiming the principle of equality between women and men. As has been said, this provision provides specifically for the right of men and women to receive equal pay for work of equal value (see above, para. 412). The Federal Act on Gender Equality gives since 1995 concrete expression to this principle (see also above, para. 170).

536. This Act contains a prohibition of every kind of direct or indirect discrimination based on the sex of the worker, also in the fields of hiring, distribution of tasks and working conditions as in the fields of remuneration and vocational training. It also contains special provisions against sexual harassment in the enterprise.

537. In all these fields – with the exception of discrimination in hiring and in the case of sexual harassment – the burden of the proof has been inverted: women only have to prove the plausibility of a discrimination (Article 6 of the Act). The

Act provides, as sanctions, that the employer may be condemned to stop the discrimination and to pay the worker an indemnity up to three months' wages, potentially of six months (Article 5 of the Act).

IV. Protection in the Case of Pregnancy and Nursing

538. According to Article 35, para. 1, EA, the employer has to employ pregnant women and nursing mothers in such a manner that their health and the health of the child are not compromised. The Ordinance I prohibits occupation of pregnant women in some risky jobs, such as work in very cold or hot environment, carrying heavy loads, exposure to harmful radiation, etc. However, the employer has the possibility of proving by a risk evaluation, provided for in the ordinance, that the activity does not contain any risk to the woman's or the baby's health (Article 35, paras. 1 and 2, EA and 60 to 66 of the Ordinance I).

539. Pregnant women and nursing mothers may not be employed without their consent (Article 35*a*, para. 1, EA). Women who have been confined may not be employed during the eight weeks following their confinement, after, and until the sixteenth week after the confinement, they may only be employed with their consent (Article 35*a*, para. 4, EA). During eight weeks before the confinement, pregnant women may not be employed between 8 p.m. and 6 a.m. (Article 35*a*, para. 4, EA). The employer has to offer to pregnant women and women between the eighth and sixteenth week after the confinement who worked between 8 pm and 6 am similar work between 6 am and 8 pm (Article 35*b*, para. 1, EA).

540. Pregnant women may be excused work or may leave their work without any formality other than that of notifying their employer. The employer has to grant nursing mothers the necessary time for nursing (Article 35*a*, para. 2, EA).

541. Since the 1998 revision of the Employment Act, the employer who cannot offer other employment to a woman working in a risky environment prohibited by the ordinance (see above, para. 533) or working between 8 pm and 6 am, has to pay her 80 per cent of her wage (Articles 35, para. 3, and 35*b*, para. 2, EA). The payment of wages during incapacity for work in general and the protection of women against termination of the contract in case of pregnancy and confinement are provided for under civil law for all women workers (and not just for those who come under the federal protective law) by the provisions of the Code of Obligations (see above, paras. 450, 475 and 476). The women having given birth also benefit from allowances of the federal maternity insurance.

542. The Act on work in Public Transport Enterprises provides for the application of the Employment Act regarding health protection, employment, replacement work and wage payment in case of pregnancy (Article 17).

§3. PERSONS WITH FAMILY RESPONSIBILITIES

543. Special protection is granted to persons of either sex who have special family responsibilities. Family responsibilities are defined by the Employment Act as the education of children until a maximum age of 15 years and taking charge of relatives and close relations needing care. According to the Employment Act, the employer must have due regard for such employees when fixing the hours of work and rest (Article 36, para. 1, EA). He must, if they so request, grant them a midday break of at least an hour and a half (Article 36, para. 2, EA). If their children are sick, the employer has to accord them the necessary time to take care of them (up to three days) (Article 36, para. 3, EA). They cannot be assigned, without their consent, to overtime work (Article 36, para. 2, EA).

Chapter 8. Covenants of Non-competition

§1. The Problem

544. While in principle the employee may not, during the existence of the contract, compete against the employer (see above, para. 288), he is naturally freed from this obligation when the contract has expired. A general prohibition against the employee competing with his former employer would constitute an inadmissible infringement of personal rights (Article 27 CC) and morality (Article 20 CO). There are, nevertheless, circumstances in which the employer has a legitimate interest in ensuring that an employee who has just left his enterprise is prevented from immediately competing against him by making use of the knowledge he has gained during his employment. With a view to taking reasonably into account the interests of both the employer and the employee and making a just balance between them, the law-maker has authorized the conclusion of a covenant of non-competition. The conclusion of such covenants is strictly regulated both as to their validity and as to their effects.

545. By the covenant of non-competition the employee undertakes to refrain from competing against his employer in any manner after the termination of the contract, and in particular to refrain:

(1) from operating a competing business on his own account;
(2) from working for such a business;
(3) from having an interest (i.e. a relevant interest) in such a business (Article 340, para. 1, CO).

A competing business is considered to be a business which operates in the same field and which appeals to the same customers.

§2. Conditions of Validity

546. To be valid, the covenant has to meet the following conditions:

(1) The employee has to have, as a result of the employment relationship, access to the employer's customers or manufacturing or business secrets (Article 340, para. 2, CO). A secret is something that the employer wishes to keep from the knowledge of his competitors.
(2) In making use of the above-mentioned secrets, the employee may cause significant prejudice to the employer (Article 340, para. 2, CO). In other words, there ought to be a causal relationship between the use of the secrets and the possibility of prejudice, and this possible prejudice ought to be significant.
(3) The covenant may only bind a worker who has full legal capacity. Thus, a worker who is not of age may not sign, personally or through his guardian, a covenant of non-competition.

(4) The undertaking has to be made in writing, i.e. it has to be incorporated in a written clause, counter-signed by the employee (Article 13 CO).

547. An undertaking which does not meet these conditions is null and void. For instance, it has been ruled that when the relationship between the employer and his customers is an essentially personal one, based on the ability of the employer, the acquaintance of the customers by the employee is not likely to cause any real prejudice to the employer; this is mainly the case for professional people like lawyers, dentists or doctors and in these activities a covenant of non-competition will not usually be considered valid.[241]

§3. Restrictions

548. The prohibition against competition ought not to impair the employee's earning prospects in an unreasonable manner. To this end, it has to be restricted from three points of view: the place, the time and the type of operation. The extent of the restriction will vary from case to case: according, for instance, to the activity and to the size and nature of the enterprise. If the place in which the covenant is to take effect is very small, the time may be longer, and vice versa. As to time, a limit of three years has been fixed; this limit may nevertheless be exceeded in special circumstances (Article 340*a*, para. 1, CO); among these circumstances may be mentioned the case where the employer has undertaken to pay the employee his wage or a part of it during the period of prohibition, which is usual in some industries.

549. The fact that these restrictions have not been mentioned in the covenant does not render it invalid.[242] It will then fall to the judge to fix the extent of the restrictions as he has to do when the employee argues that the restrictions laid down in the covenant are not adequate. If the judge holds that the prohibition is excessive he can reduce it at his discretion taking into account all the relevant circumstances and giving due weight to any benefits granted by the employer in return for such a pledge.[243]

§4. Violation of the Covenant

550. An employer whose former employee has broken the covenant may ask for compensation; the damages he receives are to compensate him for the loss he suffered because of the violation (Article 340*b*, para. 1, CO). In such a case, assuming

241. See ATF 138/2012 III 67, 2.3.2 = JdT 2012 II 287 = SJ 2012 I 297, Federal Court 13 July 2007, decision 4C.100/2006, 2.3 and 2.6.
242. *ATF* 96/1970 II 141.
243. *ATF* 130/2004 III 353.

the validity of the covenant, no distinction is drawn between damage due to the use of knowledge of customers or of secrets and damage due to the personal ability of the former employee. The employer has to be compensated for the loss of orders or sales during the validity of the covenant.

551. The covenant often stipulates a penalty for non-performance. In such a case, in the absence of any agreement to the contrary, the employee may free himself from the prohibition by paying the stipulated amount. The judge may nevertheless reduce the penalty if it is deemed excessive, i.e. when it is obviously unreasonably high.[244] In actual practice, annual salary represents a maximum, which is only rarely allocated.[245] Conversely, the fact that a penalty has been stipulated does not prevent the employer from asking for compensation for any damage in excess of the amount of the said penalty (Article 340*b*, para. 2, CO); he has then to prove the extent of the prejudice and the fault of the employee.[246]

552. Normally the employer may not ask the court to order that the employee should abstain from violating the covenant. But, if there is an express agreement in writing to that effect, he may demand, in addition to the penalty and further compensation, that the other party cease and desist from such violation, on the following conditions:

(1) the demand is warranted by the extent of the prejudice suffered or threat to the employer's interests;
(2) it is also warranted by the employee's conduct – it may be by violating the covenant or by the manner in which he has terminated the contract of labour (Article 340*b*, para. 3, CO).[247]

553. In actual practice, the real fulfilment is an *ultima ratio* and the judge has to follow it up only in a very restrictive way. A real fulfilment must be limited to very serious violations of the prohibition which coincide with an act of unfair competition.[248]

554. According to the Code of Obligations, no departure either to the employer's or the employee's detriment may be made from provisions concerning the consequences of an infringement of a prohibition against competition (Article 361 CO). But this provision is inconsistent and cannot be applied; as the conclusion of a covenant of non-competition is optional it is not possible to declare 'null and void' a clause which would withhold from the employer the whole of the damages he could demand according to the Code.

---

244. *ATF* 91/1965 II 372, 109/1983 II 120.
245. *ATF* 130/2004 III 353.
246. *ATF* 92/1966 II 31.
247. *ATF* 131 III 473, c. 3.2, 103/1977 II 120.
248. *ATF* 131/2005 III 473.

§5. TERMINATION OF THE PROHIBITION AGAINST COMPETITION

555. Naturally, the prohibition against competition terminates at the end of the prescribed time. But, in some cases, a covenant of non-competition, although perfectly valid, may lapse before the expiry of this time.

556. This is the case if it has been established that the employer no longer has a significant interest against the maintenance of the employee's undertaking (Article 340*c*, para. 1, CO); for instance, when the employer gives up the activity which is the object of the covenant or when the manufacturing secret becomes widely known.

557. Furthermore, the prohibition may lapse according to the manner in which the contract of labour has terminated. When the contract has been terminated by the employer he may no longer exercise his rights according to the covenant unless the employee has given him a good cause (*motif justifié*) to do so; this good cause is not necessarily a 'just cause' (*juste motif*) in the sense of Article 337 CO (see above, para. 479) – it is enough that it is a reason which reasonably leads him to terminate the contract. When the contract has been terminated by the employee the prohibition is maintained, unless he has terminated it for a good cause which can be imputed to the employer (Article 340*c*, para. 2, CO).[249] A regular work overload despite warnings delivered to the employer or a wage clearly set under the usual commercial terms should be considered a good cause. The Federal Court has ruled that when each of the parties is responsible for the termination the covenant of non-competition is in principle maintained, but the judge has to take the consequences of the termination into account in assessing the damage due to the employer.[250]

249. *ATF* 130/2004 III 353.
250. Federal Court 26 April 2007, decision 4C.13/2007, 4.2.

Chapter 9. Intellectual Property: Inventions by the Employee

§1. Property of the Invention

558. When the employee makes an invention or creates a design while working in the employer's service the invention or the design may, according to the circumstances, belong to him or the employer. A distinction has to be drawn as to whether this invention or this design has been made as part of the employee's duties under the contract or not. If it has been, it is the property of the employer, irrespective of whether or not a patent can be taken out on it. This rule also applies when the employee has had a part in the invention or the design under the same conditions (Article 332, para. 1, CO).

559. To this end it is not necessary that the employee has been specially engaged to make inventions or designs. The Federal Court has held that it may be deduced from the circumstances and from the position of the employee that his employer expected inventive activity from him; for instance, this applies to a senior technical director.[251]

560. If, conversely, the invention or design, while still being made by the employee in his employer's service, had not been made as part of the duties of the said employee under the contract, the invention belongs to the employee. This is so when the employer does not expect inventive activity from the employee. Nevertheless, the employer may, by written agreement, have reserved an option to acquire the right to such inventions and designs (Article 332, para. 2, CO). If this option has been reserved, the employee who has made the invention has to inform the employer in writing. The employer has then to notify the employee in writing within a period of six months as to whether he intends to acquire the rights to the invention or design or to waive these rights in favour of the employee (Article 332, para. 3, CO). In the absence of such notification, it is taken to mean that the employer has waived his rights.

561. In both cases, the name of the inventor has to be given to the Federal Institute of Intellectual Property and written down in the letters patent unless the inventor renounces it (Articles 5–6 of the Federal Act on Patents for Inventions).[252]

562. It ought to be added that the provisions of the Code of Obligations relating to inventions also apply to public servants (Articles 6, para. 2, of the Federal Act on the Personnel of the Swiss Confederation). However, Article 322 CO is not to be applied in case of an invention occurring in a public working relationship.[253]

251. *ATF* 72/1946 II 270.
252. *RS* 232.14.
253. See Tissot, N., 'Logiciels et brevets d'inventions réalisés par les professeurs des universités et des écoles polytechniques suisses' in Medialex 2014, p. 59.

Besides, according to the Ordinance on the Personnel of the Swiss Confederation,[254] inventions of public servants are encouraged (Article 74). Thus, another provision is to be mentioned in this context, that is, Article 17 of the Federal Act on Copyright and Neighbouring Rights (LDA).[255] The latter specifies for the 'software programs' that their exclusive rights are automatically transferred to the employer. It should also be mentioned that Article 17 LDA does not apply in public working relationship. In case of software created in such conditions, the applicable public laws shall be observed.[256]

§2. Remuneration of the Employee

563. When the employer is the owner of the invention or the design from the beginning because it has been made by the employee as part of his duties under the contract, he is not bound to pay remuneration to the employee; the parties are expected to have taken possible inventions and designs into account when fixing the wage. But if the employer has acquired the invention or the design, which has not been made by the employee as part of his duties under the contract, he has then to remunerate the employee: he has to pay him special compensation at an equitable rate taking into account all the circumstances of the case, such as the financial value of the invention, the degree of collaboration of the employer and his staff and the use made of his operational facilities, as well as the expenses incurred by the employee and his position in the enterprise (Article 332, para. 4, CO).

254. *RS* 172.220.111.3.
255. *RS* 231.1.
256. See De Werra, J., in: Commentaire Romand de propriété intellectuelle (2013), p. 154, n° 8.

Chapter 10. Jurisdiction in Labour Disputes

§1. General Remarks

564. The settlement of individual disputes has, as in most countries, to be distinguished from the settlement of collective disputes. Individual disputes, which are dealt with in the present chapter, are in principle submitted to the courts, while most collective disputes – and especially conflicts of interest – are settled by arbitration panels or other special organs (see below, para. 739).

565. Before 1 January 2011, each canton had its own civil procedure and its own judiciary organization. The procedures were thus different in each canton for the first two instances. However, the Code of Obligations (Article 343 aCO) and the Recruitment Act (Articles 10 and 23 LSE)[257] provided for a number of procedural rules which applied throughout Switzerland. These provisions essentially required that a conciliation hearing be held before a court composed of a joint tribunal. The Swiss Code of Civil Procedure came into force on 1 January 2011, abolishing the cantonal rules in this area. The principles laid down in the Code of Obligations concerning the procedure to be followed for labour disputes are sustained, as in cases regarding judiciary organization, although this matter remains in the responsibility of the cantons.

§2. Geographical Jurisdiction

566. Generally, in civil litigation, the competent jurisdiction is that of the canton where the defendant is domiciled (Article 30, para. 2, Cst). The Code of Civil Procedure also provides for a general forum of domicile or seat of the defendant, unless it establishes a special forum (Article 10 CCP). This is the case in the employment contract since Article 34 para. 1 CCP provides that the action may be brought, in addition to the general forum, in the place where the worker usually undertakes his professional activity. Article 34 para. 2 CCP similarly provides that the court of the place of commercial establishment of the lessor of service or the intermediary with whom the contract was concluded is also competent to rule on the actions of job seekers or workers governed by the Recruitment Act.

567. The forum for labour law is a semi-imperative forum. According to Article 35 CCP, workers or job seekers cannot waive, either in advance or by tacit acceptance, the forum provided for in Article 34 CCP. This protection only applies to the weak party to the contract, and therefore to the worker or job seeker. In practice, this means that the employer can only act in respect of Article 34 CCP, unless expressly accepted by the worker, after the action has been filed. On the other hand, the worker may bring his action to a forum different from the one provided for in Article 34 CCP and the action will only be declared inadmissible only if the

257. *RS* 823.11.

employer challenges the forum, otherwise it will be deemed to have been tacitly accepted by the latter.

§3. Procedure before the Cantonal Courts

568. In labour law, trials generally start with a conciliation attempt (Article 197 CCP) on simple request of the Plaintiff, in written or oral form (Article 202 CCP). The parties can nevertheless renounce the conciliation proceeding by mutual agreement, when the amount at issue totals at least SF 100,000 (Article 199, para. 1). Such a renouncement is also possible unilaterally, for disputes regarding the Federal Act on Gender Equality (Article 199, para. 2) or when the domicile or the seat of the defendant is based abroad or is unknown (Article 199, para. 2, lit. a and b CCP). This phase is aiming at reaching an agreement on the dispute, to avoid a complete procedure, which is why the content of the discussions is confidential and not recorded (Article 205 CCP) and the parties are in principle required to attend the conciliation hearing personally (Article 204 CCP). If the plaintiff is absent, his action is withdrawn and deemed not to have been pending, which may have a consequence in the presence of an expiry or limitation period (for example, the initiation of an action to challenge unfair dismissal within 180 days after the end of the employment relationship under penalty of expiry, Article 336b para. 2 CO). If the conciliation results in an agreement, the latter shall have the effect of a binding decision (Article 208 CCP). On the other hand, if the parties cannot reach an agreement, the plaintiff is granted an authorization to proceed and must submit a claim within three months following the issuance (Article 209 CCP), with the consequence otherwise of seeing his claim withdrawn and the action deemed not to have been pending

569. Articles 210 and 212 provide that the conciliation authority can, in certain situations, put forward a ruling and even pronounce a judgment. The parties can also agree to turn to mediation in place of conciliation (Article 213, para. 1). Mediation (like conciliation, *comp.* Article 124 para. 3 CCP) is however also possible at all times of the proceeding, by means of a common request (Article 214, para. 2 CCP).

570. The conciliation procedure can also be avoided if the plaintiff makes a claim by following the procedure of the clear case (Article 257 CCP *cum* Article 199 letter A CCP). Such a procedure is admissible where the state of affairs is not contentious or is provable immediately and when the legal situation is clear. If these conditions are not fulfilled, the action is inadmissible and the plaintiff must applicate for conciliation. Such an action can thus only be admitted or declared inadmissible, but cannot be dismissed on its merits.[258] It only applies in relatively clear situations, for example, in labour law, so that the worker obtains the turnover allowing to determine his wage or so that the employer obtains the return of all the documents entrusted to the worker within the framework of the contract.[259]

258. *ATF* 140/2014 III 315.
259. *ATF* 141/2015 III 23, regarding the clarity of description of required documents.

571. After the conciliation fails, the procedure continues with the filing of a claim. There are two principal forms of procedure, namely the ordinary procedure and the simplified procedure. The type of procedure applicable is determined mainly by the value in dispute of the action. If it is less than or equal to CHF 30,000.- the simplified procedure applies (Article 243 para. 1 CCP). It should be noted that in proceedings under the Federal Equality Act or the Federal Act on Information and Consultation of Workers in Enterprises, it is always the simplified procedure that applies (Article 243, para. 2 letter a and e CCP). Still regarding this matter, it should be pointed out that when the case is not of a financial nature, the trial will be conducted in accordance with the ordinary procedure.[260]

572. The value in dispute is determined by the prayers for relief. Interest, costs of the ongoing proceedings or a possible publication of the decision and the value of possible subsidiary claims are not taken into account (Article 91 para. 1 CCP). If the prayers for relief do not specify a sum of money, the court shall determine the value in dispute if the parties are unable to reach an agreement or if the information they provide is manifestly incorrect (Article 91 para. 2 CCP). According to Article 92 para. 1 CCP C, recurring usage or services have the value of the capital they represent. Article 92 para. 2 CCP specifies that if the duration of the recurring usage or services is unknown or indefinite, the annual usage or services multiplied by twenty is deemed to be the value of the capital; in case of a life annuity, the amount of the capital corresponds to the actual cash value. In the case of an action and counterclaim, the value in dispute is determined by the action with the higher value (Article 94 para. 1 CCP). For the purpose of determining the costs, the values of the action and the counterclaim are added together insofar as they are not mutually exclusive (Article 94 para. 2 CCP). It must be pointed out that the action for the issue of a work certificate does have a value in dispute, which is determined in the light of the circumstances of the case in question, depending on the importance the certificate has for the worker and for the subject-matter of the dispute, namely delivery or rectification.[261]

573. The simplified proceedings (Article 243 CCP) is, as the name suggests, less formal than the ordinary proceedings. It may be initiated in writing or by oral procedure (Article 244 paragraph 1 CCP) and may contain a legal and factual development. In particular, the plaintiff does not have to allege the relevant facts and evidence in his claim, but may do so at the hearing (article 244, paragraph 2 CCP) with the assistance of the judge (Article 247 para. 1 CCP).[262] In the area of labour law, where the simplified proceedings apply, the judge has to establish the facts of the claim *ex officio* (Article 247, para. 2 CCP).[263] It is not limited by the means of evidence offered by the parties and has a duty to seek relevant evidence if it is aware

260. *ATF* 142/2016 III 145: in the field of labour law, actions of former employees of banks seeking to prohibit the handing over to foreign judicial authorities of data concerning them are deemed to be considered, in general, as non-pecuniary.
261. See Bohnet, F., CPC annoté, Neuchâtel 2016, Article 91 no 19.
262. *ATF* 141/2015 III 569, c. 2.3.1.
263. Dietschy, P., 'Le déroulement de la procédure simplifiée', in *Procédure civile suisse – Les grands thèmes pour le praticien*, Neuchâtel, 2010, pp. 188–189.

of it on the basis of the record and may invite a party to supplement the evidence it has offered.[264] This *ex officio* investigation does not, however, release the parties from their burden of alleging the facts and their duty to propose adequate means of proof. The absence of such allegations or evidence will result in the loss of the trial.[265] In any event, the judge remains entirely free in his assessment of the evidence (Article 157 CCP). Finally, it should be pointed out that, regarding the legal argument, the judge is not bound by the juridical assertions of the parties (Article 57 CCP).

574. The ordinary proceedings (Article 219 CCC) are more cumbersome and time consuming and the parties have more responsibilities. Thus, the principles of production of evidence apply without limit and the judge has no power of enquiry (Article 55 CCP). The procedure is written (article 220 CCP) and generally includes two written rounds (Article 225 CCP). In this procedure, the judge freely assesses the evidence (Article 157 CCP) and applies the law *ex officio*. (Article 57 CCP).

575. It should also be noted that the claimant can directly bring action before the superior cantonal court, if the amount at issue is at least SF 100,000 and if the defendant gives his consent (Article 8, para. 1 CCP). Ordinary proceedings apply in this case.

576. Regarding court costs, none of them are charged in disputes relating to the Federal Act on Gender Equality, those relating to an employment contract or the Recruitment Act up to an amount in dispute of SF 30,000 and for those relating to the Participation Act, whether it is for the conciliation step (Article 113, para. 2, lit. a, d and e CCP respectively) or the litigation proceeding in case of conciliation fail (Article 114, para. 2, lit. a, c and d CCP respectively). The cantons may provide for further exemptions from procedural costs (Article 116, para. 1 CCP).

577. As regards party costs, the Code provides that it is not allocated for the conciliation phase (Article 113 para. 1 CCP). Each party therefore assumes costs related to this phase (mainly lawyer fees). If, however, the conciliation fails, the unsuccessful party must compensate the successful party at the end of the litigation (again mainly lawyers' fees, Article 95 para 3. CCP cum Article 106 para. 1 CCP).

578. Court and party costs may nevertheless be charged in cost-free proceedings to a party who proceeds in a vexatious manner or in bad faith (Article 115 CCP).

579. The Code of Civil Procedure no longer provides, as it was the case before, situations in which the professional representation of a party to a court may be prohibited. Article 68 para. 1 CCP provides that representation may be performed on a non-professional basis without restriction by a person of trust, whereas Article 68

264. Federal Court 12 November 2007, decision 4A_214/2007, c. 7.
265. *ATF* 130/2004 III 102, c. 2.2.

para. 2 CCP provides that professional representation may be carried out before all authorities by lawyers who are members of the bar (letter a) and, before special courts in the field of labour law, by professionally qualified representatives (letter d, ex: employees of a trade union).

§4. Organization of Cantonal Courts

580. The courts, before which individual disputes arising from contracts of labour may be brought, vary according to the cantonal constitution or legislation (the cantons are competent in judiciary organization, cf. Article 122 para. 2 Cst. and Article 4 para. 1 CCP). There are three main systems, but the situation is complicated by the fact that in some cantons, there are differences according to the communes or the category of workers concerned. The main systems are as follows:

- litigation is brought before the ordinary civil courts;
- litigation is brought before a special court (labour court, industrial court, *tribunal de prud'hommes*) when the amount at issue does not exceed a given sum (in most cases SF 30,000). Over this amount the ordinary courts are competent;[266]
- litigation is brought, whatever the amount at issue, before a special labour court. This is the case in some cantons, for example: Geneva and Jura.

581. In most of the cantons where there are special labour courts these courts consist of a lawyer (generally, but not everywhere, a professional judge who is a member of a civil court) and, in equal numbers, representatives of the employers and employees. In some cantons the president is competent to decide small cases on his own. In Geneva, for exemple, there is no professional judge; the *tribunal de prud'hommes* consists of representatives of the employers and employees elected from five professional groups and presided over by an employer's representative and an employee's representative alternately. The president is assisted by an employers' representative and an employees' representative.

582. These three categories are found both at the conciliation stage and at the first instance. In disputes under the Gender Equality Act of 24 March 1995[1], the conciliation authority shall comprise a chairperson and an equal number of representatives of the employer and employee and of the public and private sectors; the genders must be equally represented (Article 200 para. 2 CCP).

583. At cantonal level, the appeal is brought before an ordinary civil court of appeal.

---

266. The Neuchâtel Cantonal Court ruled that the composition of the court should not necessarily be parity for it to be considered 'special' Neuchâtel Cantonal Court 31 August 2015 (ARMC.2015.28).

§5. Federal Jurisdiction

584. Generally, sentences pronounced in the last cantonal instance may be referred to the Federal Court. An ordinary (civil law) appeal, for a violation of federal law (including constitutional rights), international law, cantonal constitutional rights and intercantonal law, may in principle be lodged only if the amount at issue is at least SF 15,000, if the value is indeterminate or if the litigation raises a basic legal question.[267] If this is not the case, or for a violation of cantonal law, a ancillary constitutional appeal is possible: the cantonal sentence may in such cases be rendered null and void if a constitutional right has been violated. This is so, in case where for instance, the sentence is deemed to be arbitrary and thus violates equality before the law (i.e. it violates a clear and undisputed principle of law), or is deemed to violate the right to be heard, or when the dispute has not been brought before the correct judge, or when the constitutional principle of equal pay for men and women has been violated. In working relations of public law, an appeal in public matter to the Federal Court can be made, if the value of dispute is higher than SF 15,000 or raises a basic legal question.

585. The Federal Court has no special chamber for cases arising out of contracts of labour. These disputes are submitted either to civil law chambers or public law chambers, according to the case.

§6. Arbitration

586. According to Article 354 CCP, any claim can be the subject of arbitration, insofar as it comes within the parties' free disposal. In the field of labour law, the latter provision must be put in connection with Article 341, para. 1, CO, according to which the worker cannot give up, during the duration of the contract and during the month which follows the end of this one, on the claims resulting from mandatory provisions of the law (Article 361 et 362 CO) or from a collective agreement.

587. Few collective agreements provide that individual disputes between employers and employees shall be brought before arbitration panels.

588. A stipulation in a collective agreement providing for an arbitration clause may not be extended by public authority to employers and employees who are not personally bound by the agreement (Article 1, para. 3, of the Federal Act on the Declaration of General Application of Collective Employment Agreements).

---

267. For example, the Federal Court considers that when it has never come to a clear decision on a topic, the party can refer to the basic legal question. See *ATF* 134/2008 III 354.

Part II. Collective Labour Relations

Chapter 1. Trade Union Freedom

§1. Trade Union Freedom and Freedom of Association

I. The Principle

589. For a long time Switzerland has not had specific constitutional or legal provisions regarding trade union freedom. The latter was considered as an aspect of the general principle of freedom of association, which was guaranteed by Article 56 of the previous Federal Constitution. Today, with the new Federal Constitution of April 1999, trade union freedom has his specific guarantee in Article 28 of the Constitution. According to this disposition, workers and employers and their organizations have the right to unionize for the defence of their interests, to form unions and to join them or to keep out of them. Moreover, Article 28, paras. 2–4, contain provisions regarding strike and lock-out (see below, para. 722).

590. Switzerland has also ratified Convention 87 of the International Labour Organization, concerning Freedom of Association and Protection of the Right to Organize. According to this convention workers and employers, without any distinction whatsoever, have the right to establish and, subject only to the rules of the organization concerned, to join organizations of their own choosing without prior authorization (Article 2); workers' and employers' organizations have the right to draw up their constitutions and rules, to elect their representatives in complete freedom, to organize their administration and activities and to formulate their programmes (Article 3). The provisions of the first part of the Convention, concerning freedom of association, are self-executing and have to be applied by the courts in the same manner as Swiss law (see above, para. 192).

591. Moreover, Switzerland is a party to the European Convention on Human Rights. Article 11 of this Convention declares that everyone has the right to freedom of association with others, including the right to form and to join trade unions for the protection of his interests. In Switzerland this principle has the same force as a constitutional provision and has to be directly applied by the courts.[268] In cases of violation of this right, a petition may be brought before the European Court of Human Rights. Similar guarantees are given by the International Covenant on Civil

268. *ATF* 101/1975 Ia 67, 102/1976 Ia 379.

and Political Rights (Article 22) and the International Covenant on Economic, Social and Cultural Rights (Article 8).

II. The Legal Framework

592. According to Article 60 CC, political, religious, scientific, artistic, charitable, recreational or other associations which do not have an economic purpose acquire legal personality as soon as they express in their rules the will to be organized corporately. The Federal Court has held that groups of individuals whose purpose is of a general economic nature, but which do not themselves exert an industrial or commercial activity, may constitute associations; this is notably the case for associations of employers and workers.[269] Thus, it is enough for a trade union to express in its articles of association the will to be organized corporately and to draw up the necessary provisions about the purpose, the pecuniary means and the organization of the association. There is no need to declare or to register the association or to ask for any official authorization.

593. Infrequently, a trade union chooses to be a co-operative society instead of an association. Such a society, whose main purpose is to encourage or ensure, through a common activity, the realization of the specific common interests of its members (Article 828 CO), acquires legal personality after being registered on the Trade Register. It may naturally carry out industrial or commercial activity.

594. Trade unions and employers' organizations, whatever kind of organization they have chosen, are absolutely free to constitute themselves and no official control is exerted on their constitutions or on their activities. They are subject to the general rules governing associations or, as the case may be, co-operative societies. Except for some matters which are the object of mandatory provisions, an association may organize itself freely. For co-operative societies the mandatory provisions are more numerous. But the activities of a trade union are governed primarily by its articles of constitution. Within the provisions of its constitution it may pass decisions which are binding on its members. The competent body of the union may impose restrictions on the personal liberty of its members which are deemed to be necessary with a view to achieving the purposes of the association.[270]

§2. The Right to Organize

595. Anyone is free to join a trade union. He merely has to be admitted, in accordance with the union's constitution, by the competent body of the union. The state does not exert any control or impose any restrictions.

---

269. *ATF* 90/1964 II 333.
270. *ATF* 85/1959 II 525.

596. But the main problem is that which occurs in the relationship between worker and employer. The employer may not forbid the employee to belong to a union: such a prohibition would be contrary to the right of personality (Article 27 CC) and to the specific obligation of the employer to protect and respect the employee's person and individuality (Article 328, para. 1, CO).[271] Nevertheless, Swiss law gives little specific protection to the worker against discrimination in employment; the employer is absolutely free to hire or not to hire a worker, whatever the reasons for his decision. But there are special legal provisions under which the dismissal of an employee on the grounds that he belongs or does not belong to a union or because of a union activity is considered a misuse of rights; indeed, the employer who misuses his rights can only be condemned to the payment of damage, and the amount of the latter may not exceed six months' remuneration (see above, para. 499).

597. Moreover, there is difficulty in proving the real cause of the dismissal, and therefore, it is in practice not easy for the worker to win his case.

598. The most important collective agreements provide for the protection of the right to organize. For instance, in the watch-making industry, the agreement provides that freedom of association is guaranteed to the worker in Switzerland as well as in affiliated firms abroad, in the sense of conventions Nos. 87 and 98 of the ILO and of the Guidelines for Multinational Enterprises of the OECD, and that no measures whatsoever may be taken against a worker because he is a member of a union (Article 1.4). Trade unions consider that Switzerland does not protect enough union activists and that it does not respect its international commitments.

§3. The Problem of Union Security

599. Although a person is free to join a trade union, he is also free not to join one.

600. At the end of the 19th century, a certain number of collective agreements included clauses whereby employers and workers tried to compel everybody in their trade to belong to their respective organizations. Such clauses were in the mutual interests of both parties. The employers undertook not to hire workers who were not members of the contracting union; reciprocally the trade unions undertook that their members would not work for unorganized employers. Thus, in agreement with the employers' organizations, the trade unions struggled against those employers who, by not being members of employers' organizations, could sell their products or offer their services at a lower price, since they were not bound to pay their workers the wage agreed upon by the parties to the agreement. In some cases, however, the agreement merely stipulated that when a worker was taken on, he had to be a member of a trade union – whichever one it might be – or that he had to join the

271. Sentence of the Federal Court of 9 March 1979, *Semaine Judiciaire* 1981, p. 317.

contracting union within a given period of time. In other cases, the employers undertook to give preference to organized workers.

601. The Federal Court ruled at first that a closed-shop clause in a collective agreement was lawful, the union in a given occupation being the natural and obvious representative of the workers in many matters, including conditions of employment.[272] At that time there was a single trade union movement. But later on minority unions, notably Christian, were formed. In this new situation the Federal Court declared unlawful the demand of a trade union for the dismissal of a worker who was a member of a minority trade union;[273] it later upheld the same opinion in more general terms.[274] Finally, in 1956, when the legal provisions regarding collective agreements were amended, a provision prohibiting closed-shop clauses was inserted in the Code of Obligations. This provision is now Article 356*a*, para. 1, according to which any clause in a collective agreement or arrangement between the parties to compel employers or workers to join a contracting organization is null and void. In 1998, the Federal Court ruled that cantonal subsidies for companies could not be subject for the latter to join a trade union because such a requirement was out of proportion and infringed the freedom of association.[275]

602. The aforesaid provision of the Code of Obligations entails no consequences in public law, only in civil law. An individual or a union may claim before the court that a closed-shop clause included in a collective agreement or an arrangement between the contracting parties causes him an injury and is null and void; he may also claim damages.

603. In the same way, the Federal Act on the Declaration of General Application of Collective Employment Agreements provides that a collective agreement may not be extended if it infringes the freedom of association and in particular the right to join or not to join an association (Article 2, No. 5; see above, para. 601).

604. While a closed-shop agreement is at present not recognized as valid, the parties to a collective agreement may resort to a kind of agency shop system, the so-called system of 'loyalty to the agreement'. Under this system, employers are not required to abstain from engaging workers who are not members of the contracting workers' organization, but they are required to engage only those workers who pledge themselves to comply with the provisions of the collective agreement. The Federal Court ruled in 1949 that the obligation to adhere to a particular workers' organization and the obligation to adhere to a collective labour agreement are two fundamentally different things; it is difficult to see how a workers' rights as an individual would be harmed by compelling him to adhere to an agreement which had in fact been concluded in his interests.[276]

272. *ATF* 30/1904 II 271.
273. *ATF* 51/1925 II 525.
274. *ATF* 75/1949 II 305, 82/1956 II 308.
275. *ATF* 124/1998 I 107.
276. *ATF* 75/1949 II 305.

605. Under this system, a worker who is an outsider cannot be obliged to pay a contribution to the union, but the collective agreement to which he may be compelled to adhere generally contains a clause under which he has to pay a 'solidarity contribution' which will be deducted from his wage. It would not be fair, ruled the Federal Court in the case mentioned above, to allow an outsider to benefit from the many advantages afforded by a collective agreement without making any financial sacrifice, especially since in negotiating and implementing collective agreements the contracting organizations have incurred considerable expenditure which has to be met out of their members' contributions. But the amount of such contributions has been limited by judicial practice so that it cannot be as high as union members' contributions to their union.

606. The principles laid down by the Federal Court have been sanctioned in the Code of Obligations, with the institution of the adhesion of outsiders having been expressly provided for by Article 356*b* CO. Such individual adhesion to an agreement may, with the agreement of the parties, be given by an employer who is not a member of the contracting employers' organization, as well as by a worker who, being employed by an employer bound by the agreement, is not a member of the contracting workers' organization (Article 356*b*, para. 1, CO). If the conditions set down are inequitable, as in the case of excessive contributions, the judge may cancel them or reduce them to a fair amount. Any clause or arrangement to fix contributions to the advantage of a single party is to be declared null and void (Article 356*b*, para. 2, CO). Some agreements provide that their normative provisions must be applied by the bound employer to all his employees, whether the latter are member of a trade union or not. In 1997, the Federal Court ruled that a worker not bound by the agreement could not require its application on the basis of such a provision, which is compulsory only for the employer.[277]

607. In order to preserve the freedom of action of the minority trade unions, it has been provided that arrangements between the parties to a collective agreement to compel members of employers' or workers' associations to accept the terms of the agreement are null and void where such associations are not free to become parties to the agreement or to conclude similar agreements (Article 356*b*, para. 3, CO). Thus 'loyalty to the agreement' cannot be required from members of workers' organizations which have asked to be allowed to accede to the agreement or to conclude 'parallel' agreements but have not been allowed to do so. On the other hand, when a workers' organization deliberately decides to remain outside the agreement, its members may be denied the opportunity of finding work in an undertaking whose owner is a member of the contracting employers' organization if they refuse to sign a personal declaration of adhesion and to pay the solidarity contribution. But the Federal Court has ruled that the parties to a collective agreement cannot, without legitimate interest, oppose the accession to the agreement of a sufficiently representative minority trade union.[278]

---

277. *ATF* 123/1997 III 131.
278. *ATF* 113/1987 II 37.

Chapter 2. The Trade Unions and Employers' Associations

§1. The Role of the Social partners

608. The social partners – trade unions and employers' associations – play a prominent part in the social, economic and even the political life of the country. According to the Federal Constitution (Article 147), the interested economic groups have to be consulted by the federal authorities as regards the drawing up of Acts relating to the implementation of constitutional provisions about economic and social matters.

609. The consultation of the social partners is twofold. Before the drawing up of an important Act the government sets up a special committee to study the matter. The social partners always have, in social and economic matters, representatives on these committees. Secondly, before the Bill is presented to Parliament, the government arranges a 'consultation procedure' in which the trade unions and the employers' associations, as well as other groups and the cantons, are officially consulted about the matter.

610. Furthermore, many leaders of trade unions and employers' associations are members of Parliament, where they have great influence. In the exercise of direct democracy, too, the trade unions and employers' associations play an important role: they may launch popular initiatives with a view to amending the Federal Constitution or ask for a referendum against an Act which has been passed in Parliament. They often support, in elections at the federal, cantonal or even communal level, the political parties which are closest to them.

611. The trade unions and employers' associations have representatives on many federal consultative committees in economic and social matters; they are represented on the governing boards of some official institutions, especially in social insurance, such as on the Swiss Accident Insurance Fund.

612. Finally, one ought to recall the importance attached in Switzerland to collective agreements in industrial relations. These agreements, which play a decisive role in the establishment of labour conditions, are bargained and concluded by the trade unions and, for a great part, by the employers' associations.

§2. The Capacity to Take Action at Law

613. The capacity of the industrial associations (employers' associations and trade unions) to take action at law has to be examined from two different points of view: at public law level and at private law level.

614. Associations of employers and interested workers can appeal against sentences of cantonal and federal authorities (Article 58 EA). According to case law, a provision authorizing these types of associations to defend the interests of their members has nevertheless to appear in their statutes.[279]

615. At private law level, industrial associations may take action at law when they intend to defend a collective interest: not only the collective interests of their members, but also the interests of those people who, not being members, follow the same trade. They may act on the condition that they are empowered by their statutes to safeguard the economic interests of their members and that the latter are themselves qualified to take action at law for the same purpose. But they are not empowered to ask for compensation for damage suffered personally by their members. According to Article 89 CCP, associations and other organizations of national or regional importance that are authorized by their articles of associations to protect the interests of a certain group of individuals may bring an action in their own name for a violation of the personality of the members of such group. For instance, the trade unions are qualified to act in case of an infringement of the personal rights of the workers as well as of an infringement of the Federal Act on Information and Consultation of Workers in Enterprises.[280] Moreover the Federal Act on Unfair Competition[281] (Article 10, para. 2) empowers the industrial associations and economic organizations whose statutes allow them to defend the economic interest of their members to take action at law when these economic interests are threatened or infringed by an act of unfair competition. Finally Article 7 of the Federal Act on Gender Equality[282] provides that organizations can take action at law if they have been set up for two years, they aim to ensure equality between women and men or to defend worker interest and if a great number of persons will be concerned by the results of the process. Before acting the organizations are required to attempt a conciliation with the employer. Apart from that, they act in their own name and have the same rights as any individual complainant.

§3. The Trade Unions

616. Only a minority (estimated at 20.2 per cent in 2013)[283] of workers are organized in trade unions, but their influence is still very great. It is generally recognized that they represent workers as a whole. The trade union movement is not unified and several trade unions are in competition, but one organization undoubtedly plays a leading role: it is the Swiss Federation of Trade Unions.

617. The trade unions have created, alone or by means of collective agreements, many institutions for the benefit of workers. In the field of social security, they created institutions of unemployment insurance (as well as some institutions of health insurance) which are now integrated into the Swiss social security system.

279. See Federal Court 5 May 2000, decision 2A.578/1999.
280. *ATF* 114/1988 II 345, 123/1996 III 176.
281. *RS* 241.
282. See above, paras. 142, 144, 371–372 and 435–436.
283. See www.bfs.admin.ch/bfs/portal/fr/index/themen/03/22/publ.Docuement.197367.pdf.

I. The Swiss Federation of Trade Unions

618. As has been said, the Swiss Federation of Trade Unions[284] (in German: *Schweizerischer Gewerkschaftsbund* – SGB; in French: *Union syndicale suisse* – USS) is the most important federation of trade unions. It groups together the majority of organized workers. It was created in 1880 and thus celebrated its 100th anniversary in 1980. It is affiliated to the ICFTU and the ETUC. It is neutral on religious matters and politically independent. This political independence means that it is quite autonomous. It is not affiliated to any political movement, decides its own political attitudes and takes positions on all the great questions which have an influence on public opinion. It is close to the Social-Democratic Party and several of its leaders play an important role in the socialist group in Parliament of which they are members. In the case of a popular vote it makes recommendations to the electorate and conducts campaigns. In some cantons, the trade union section members of the Federation put candidates on the same panel as social-democratic candidates. The Federation has launched some popular initiatives for the introduction of new constitutional provisions in the Constitution: in 1971, in common with other federations of trade unions, for workers' participation, and in 1979 for holidays with pay, for example.

619. According to its statutes of 1998, the Swiss Federation of Trade Unions fights for social justice and its purpose is to safeguard the interests of workers and unemployed persons at international, Swiss, cantonal and regional level, and especially:

(a) to restore and ensure full employment;
(b) to ensure that everyone can have a professional activity in the same way;
(c) to promote social economy and safeguard the natural bases of life;
(d) to improve life quality and ensure higher living standards to workers and unemployed persons;
(e) to carry out equality of treatment between men and women in all domains;
(f) to promote training of workers and unemployed persons, etc.

620. The platform for the 1980s, adopted by the Trade Union Congress in October 1980, puts as a priority economic democracy and the humanization of labour. Among the present main priorities of the Swiss Federation of Trade Unions, we may quote the achievement of sex equality, the struggle against unemployment and for the development of employment, the upholding of the *acquis sociaux* and in particular the introduction of minimum wages (since the Congress of November 2010).

621. The Swiss Federation of Trade Unions is a confederation of federations of trade unions. While it is involved in the economic and social policy of the country, it does not become involved in industrial relations at the level of the various branches of economic life. Collective bargaining does not fall within its province,

284. See the website: http://www.sgb.ch/f-index.php.

but within that of its affiliated federations. Only exceptionally has it signed agreements with employers' associations or with the other federations of trade unions, an example being the recommendation concerning redundancy in 1975.

622. In 2015, the Swiss Federation of Trade Unions had 361,208 members. It groups together 16 affiliated federations of trade unions, organizing the workers in one or some trades or in one or some occupations. The most important of them are Unia (201,164 members), the Swiss union of transportation personnel (42,167 members), public service workers (35,141 members), syndicom (35,665 members), the Confederation staff association (9,333 members) and the Swiss Union of Bank Clerks (7,997 members).

623. Furthermore, in every canton there is a trade union federation in which are grouped the trade union sections which are active in the canton. These federations have to monitor the development of social policy within the canton. They cannot themselves launch a claim dispute, for this lies within the province of the federations of the different trades.

624. The supreme body of the Federation is the Congress, which meets every four years. It is composed of representatives of the federations of trade unions and of cantonal federations. A smaller body, the Assembly of Delegates, meets at least twice a year. The executive organ is the Steering Committee, which takes day-today decisions.

625. The affiliated federations are usually constituted in the same manner as the Federation: they have a congress, where the individual sections are represented, and smaller bodies which do the day-to-day work. In most cases the individual members may be called upon to vote, for instance about whether a collective agreement is to be accepted or whether a strike is to be launched.

II. Travail.Suisse

626. With 152,108 members in 2015, Travail.Suisse is the second most important federation of trade unions in Switzerland. It currently brings together eleven federations of trade unions of which the largest are Syna, an interprofessional trade union (59,956 members) and the Socio-Christian Organization of Ticino (41,688 members). This federation was constituted in 2002, by the Swiss Confederation of Christian Trade Unions and the Federation of Swiss White-collar Unions. As the Swiss Federation of Trade Unions, Travail.Suisse is religiously and politically neutral. Already very active, it launched, in December 2007, a popular initiative for the introduction of six weeks holidays for everyone.[285]

285. See the website: http://www.travailsuisse.ch/.

III. Unia

627. Unia is the largest trade union of Switzerland. In 2015, it had 201,1664 members, all coming from various professions (80 different branches). Unia was created in October 2004, further to the union of the Industry and Building Trade Union, the Industry, Construction and Services Trade Union and the Commerce, Transport and Food Trade Union. The supreme body of Unia is the statutory Congress, which meets every four years. In the meantime, the statutory Congress is represented by the delegate meeting. The executive body is the Board of Directors. Unia also has an enlarged executive body in the form of the central managing board. Finally, Unia is the possessor of the largest unemployment office of Switzerland.[286]

IV. Trade Union Statistics

628. As well as the main federations which have already been mentioned, there are some smaller organizations of salaried employees. Table 14 gives a list of all these organizations and their membership in 2015.

Table 14. Organizations and their membership in 2015

Organizations	Membership
Swiss Federation of Trade Unions	368,108
Unia	201,164
Travail.Suisse	152,108
Syna	59,956
Swiss Union of Business Employees	48,000
Swiss Union of Teachers	53,029
Swiss Union of the Transportation Personnel	42,167
Socio-Christian Organization of Ticino	41,688
Public Service Workers	35,141
Syndicom	35,665
Total Membership	737,850

Source: http://www.bfs.admin.ch/bfs/portal/en/index.html.

§4. The Employers' Associations

629. The employers are strongly organized in three central associations whose members are trade or regional associations. These associations are economiesuisse, the Swiss Employers' Union and the Swiss Crafts Union.

286. See the website: http://www.unia.ch/English-Window.593.0.html?&L=1.

630. It ought to be mentioned that the law has given the employers' associations a leading role in the organization of the 'equalization funds' which administer a great part of the social security scheme (old age, survivors' and invalidity insurance, family benefits, etc.).

I. Economiesuisse

631. Economiesuisse, the Federation of Swiss Undertakings, was created in September 2000, following the merger of the Swiss Union of Commerce and Industry (*Vorort*) and the Society for the Development of the Swiss Economy. It is now the largest federation of employers' in Switzerland. It plays an important role in the economic and political life of the country and its advice carries great weight with the federal government. According to its statutes, its aim is to defend and to promote its members' interests as regards economic policy. It works for optimum economic conditions and for competitiveness of the Swiss economy and Swiss undertakings. Economiesuisse also stands up for the free-market economy, but accepts its social and ecological responsibilities (Article 1 of the statutes).

632. In 2010, economiesuisse had different kinds of members:

(a) about 100 trade associations, which are divided into two sectors: services and industry;
(b) 20 Chambers of Commerce, which group associations of industrialists and businessmen at cantonal level and defend their common interests;
(c) about 50 individual members, mostly important groups and undertakings.

633. Economiesuisse is organized as follows: the General Assembly is formed by representatives of all members, each member having one vote; the Board of Directors and the Committee, whose members are elected for three years; the Committee of Associations Directors, which is only an advisory council.[287]

II. The Swiss Employers' Union

634. The Swiss Employers' Union is the employers' body which is especially entrusted with the problems of conditions of work and training. It was created in 1908 with a view to confronting the trade unions. It collaborates closely with economiesuisse and is a member of the International Organization of Employers.

635. In 2010, 35 associations of employers of branches and 40 regional associations of employers were members of the Swiss Employers' Union. Many of these were members of economiesuisse at the same time. The organization is similar to

287. See the website: http://www.economiesuisse.ch/web/en/pages/default.aspx.

that of economiesuisse: an Assembly of Delegates, a Central Committee and a Board of Directors.

III. The Swiss Crafts Union

636. The Swiss Crafts Union, created in 1879, aims to safeguard the interests of crafts and of small and medium-sized undertakings. It works especially in the defence of individual enterprises. Like the other employers' associations, it plays an active part in the economic and political life of the country. It is affiliated to the International Association of Crafts and Small and Medium-Sized Enterprises.

637. The members of the union are divided into different categories:

(a) the cantonal craft unions – in 2010 there were 26 cantonal unions;
(b) the trade associations – 271 associations, the most important trade groups being hotels, restaurants and transport, commerce and the building industry;
(c) 14 other organizations aiming to promote small and medium-sized undertakings.

638. The organs of the union are: the General Conference in which all individual members may take part; the Congress or Assembly of delegates, which meets every three years; the Swiss Crafts Chamber, whose members are elected for the greater part by the Assembly; and the Board of Directors, elected for three years by the Chamber.[288]

288. See the website: http://www.sgv-usam.ch/nc/fr.html.

Chapter 3. Collective Relations in the Enterprise

§1. Constitutional Provisions

639. Article 110, para. 1(b), of the Federal Constitution empowers the federal state to pass legislation on relations between employers and employees, especially about the regulation in common of questions concerning enterprises and trade. This provision was originally adopted in 1947 to meet the demands of the trade unions who wanted to introduce legislation on the 'trade community', although at that time they were not eager to introduce an 'enterprise community'.

640. But, some years later, the trade unions changed their minds, and having seen the German legislation on *Mitbestimmung*, asked for a similar law in Switzerland. The Swiss Federation of Trade Unions united, for the first time in history, in a common action with the two Christian trade unions,[289] and the three federations started a constitutional initiative with a view to introducing into the Constitution a provision empowering the federal state to pass legislation on the participation of workers and their organizations in the decisions of enterprises and administrations. The trade unions held that the constitutional provisions then in force were not sufficient to bring in a law about participation in the decisions of the enterprise. But while they asked in their propaganda for the introduction of such participation, they restricted themselves in the constitutional initiative to asking for a mere extension of the competence of the federal state. The Federal Parliament opposed the initiative with a much more restricted counterproposal, but proposal and counterproposal were rejected by the people in 1976.

§2. Legal Provisions

I. Participation Act

641. For a long time no Act was passed in execution of Article *34ter* para. 1 (b), of the former Constitution (now Article 110). In 1993, with a view to approximating Swiss social legislation with that of the Directives of the European Community and despite the Swiss rejection of the accession of Switzerland to Europe, the Federal Assembly passed the Federal Act on Information and Consultation of Workers in the Entreprises, commonly named the Participation Act. According to this Act, in enterprises with at least 50 workers, the latter may elect representatives (Article 3). For smaller enterprises, workers themselves act as representatives (Article 4). The representatives have to be informed on all matters on which they need information in order to fulfil their tasks, and they have to be consulted on the following matters (Article 10):

289. At that time, the Evangelic a (Protestant) trade union had not yet merged with the Christian Confederation.

(a) security at work and health protection;
(b) transfer of undertakings;
(c) collective dismissals;
(d) affiliation to an occupational institution and termination of an affliation contract.

It must be said that this Act applies to private enterprises which permanently offer work in Switzerland (Article 1).

642. The Participation Act is a framework agreement. It guarantees the minimum rights to information and of participation, in particular its procedural aspects. Thus, Article 15, para. 1 provides that the Labour Courts are competent in case of disputes resulting from the application of the Act. In such a case, employers as well as workers and their associations can be parties (Article 15, para. 2). It is not clear whether the representatives have the ability to take the case to court. Apart from its procedural rules, the Participation Act refers to other more specific rules. Article 10 stipulates that representatives have, regarding the fields mentioned above (see above, para. 641), particular rights of participation set out notably in the Code of Obligations (Articles 333 and 333*a* for the transfer of undertaking and Articles 335*d* to 335*g* for the collective dismissals) as well as those set out in the Federal Act on Accident Insurance (Article 82 for the security and the protection of health), the Employment Act (Article 48 for the protection of health). In addition the Participation Act remains subsidiary to the collective agreements (Article 2).

II. Employment Act

643. The Employment Act contains a provision about the possibility of constituting a representative body of employees in the enterprise. The employer in an industrial enterprise who is bound to set out work rules may either prepare these rules himself after consultation with his employees, or reach written agreement on the text of such rules with a freely elected workers' delegation (see above, para. 167). This delegation is deemed to have been freely elected when its election has been carried out in accordance with a collective agreement or analogous arrangement (Article 37 EA and Article 67 Ordinance I). The written agreement between the employer and the workers' delegation is not a collective agreement which has to be concluded with a trade union. But the possibility provided by Article 37 EA has not been used in practice.

644. In other provisions of the Employment Act reference is made to the representation of the workers in an enterprise. The competent authority, when granting an hours-of-work permit, may, as an exceptional measure, make minor departures from the legal provisions if the application of such provisions would involve unusual difficulties and if the majority of the workers concerned or their representatives in the enterprise so agree (Article 28 EA). Furthermore, according to Article 48 EA workers or their representatives must be informed and consulted by their employer about the issues relating to:

(a) health protection;
(b) the organization of working time and its schedule;
(c) specific measures linked to the night work (Article 17*e*).

Workers or their representatives must be consulted by their employer before the latter takes a decision on the issues mentioned above. In cases of disagreement, workers have a right to know why their opinion has not been taken into consideration.

III. Other Acts

645. In the Federal Act on Work in Public Transport Enterprises and in the Ordinance for the execution of this Act, there are a number of provisions which refer to the obligation of the employer to consult the workers or their representatives, or which even provide that some exceptions to the normal hours of work may only be made with the consent of workers or their representatives.

646. Other legal provisions concern the representation of workers in the administration of provident funds. Provident funds in favour of employees have to be transferred by the employer to a foundation, co-operative society or public establishment (Article 331, para. 1 CO). In the case of a co-operative society, the administration is elected by the beneficiaries. But, in general, the fund is transferred by the employer to a foundation, either constituted by himself or which he has joined. In this case, the workers take part in the administration of the fund in proportion to their contributions; as far as possible they elect representatives chosen from among the employees of the enterprise (Article 89*a*, para. 3, CC). According to the Federal Act on Occupational Old Age, Survivors' and Invalidity Pension Provision of 25 June 1982, an employer whose workers are compulsorily insured under the terms of the Act must, if he is not affiliated to a provident institution, choose such an institution in agreement with his employees or their representatives; if agreement cannot be reached the choice is made by an arbitrator (Article 11). The institution is then administered by a body consisting of equal numbers of representatives of employers and of employees. This governing body has to establish the rules of the fund, to take decisions about the financing of the latter and about the investment of the assets (Articles 50 and 51 of the Federal Act on Occupational Old Age, Survivors' and Invalidity Pension Provision). When employers' associations create equalization funds which take part in the administration of old age, survivors' and invalidity insurance, at least one-third of the members of the steering committee of the funds have to be nominated by the workers' unions (Article 54 of the Act on the Old Age and Survivors' Insurance). As regards accident insurance, workers who are not insured with the Swiss Insurance Accident Fund have the right to participate in the choice of the insurance company with which they will be insured (Articles 68 and 69 of the Federal Act on Accident Insurance).

§3. COLLECTIVE AGREEMENTS

647. The first works councils were created at the end of the last century by some employers. But, since the national collective agreement for the brewery trade in 1906, the constitution of works councils in enterprises has been provided for by collective agreements. Now, the main nationwide collective agreements provide for the constitution of such councils, which are elected by the workers and represent them to management. But these councils have no power to participate in the management of the enterprise, which is administered by the employer himself (for individual enterprises) or by a governing body. Their main functions are to discuss the internal problems of the enterprise, in so far as they relate to labour or to relations between management and labour. When reviewing these competences a distinction is generally drawn between: (a) the right to be informed; (b) the right to be consulted; (c) the right to take part in decisions (co-determination). There are no recent statistics about the number of enterprises which have workers' representation, but it has been estimated that more than half of workers are employed in an enterprise which has such representation.

648. We may give as an example the 2013 collective agreement for the machine industry. This collective agreement provides that, when in an enterprise there is no workers' representation, one-tenth of the workers may ask for a ballot. If the result of the ballot shows that the majority of the workers want workers' representation established, then this representation has to be created (Article 38.1, para. 2). All workers coming within the scope of the agreement may vote and be elected, but as to eligibility, particular conditions about the number of years of service may be fixed by mutual agreement between the management and the workers' representation. A proportional representation of the different sectors of the enterprise has to be secured. If there is no member of a contracting union among the elected members, the candidate who is a member of a union and who has obtained the greatest number of votes may be considered as elected, if his union represents at least 20 per cent of all electors who come into the scope of the concerned unit of representation. If members of only one of the contracting unions have been elected, the enterprise may designate as a supplementary member the candidate of another representative trade union who has obtained the greatest number of votes (Article 38.3). Facilities are given to the members of the workers' representation to deal with urgent matters (Article 38.6, para. 3). Members of workers' representations may not be dismissed or disadvantaged because of their normal activities as workers' representatives; in cases of dismissal, a special procedure is provided for by the collective agreement (Article 38.5); those members also have the right to special educational vacations (Article 38.7). The management has to periodically inform the workers' representation about the state of business and about all questions which may be important to the workers (Article 38.10, para. 2). The mode of co-operation between management and workers' representation is fixed in each enterprise by mutual agreement. The collective agreement mentions the principal points which ought to be included in this co-operation, such as working time, a plan for annual leave, protection of health, prevention of accidents, and so on (Article 38.12).

649. While legislation does not provide for the formation of health and safety committees in the enterprise, such committees have been created in collective agreements.

650. Apart from the Participation Act (see above, para. 641) the law does not recognize any special rights for trade unions within the enterprise, but such rights are recognized by some collective agreements. In the watch-making industry, it is provided that the contracting trade union may nominate a union delegate in each enterprise; this delegate is chosen by the union, in agreement with the management; he has the same status as the members of the works committee (Article 4.6). In the printing trade[290] the 'confidence men' of the union and the works council are regarded as trade union bodies, and they have the right to represent the interests of the personnel in the enterprise on questions of union or legal relevance and to ensure the observation of pertaining provisions (Articles 111 and 303). In the agreement for the chemical industry in Basle[291] it is provided that the unions may affix bills in the enterprise and that twice a year they may call together their confidence men for meetings during working hours for which the enterprise has to give unpaid holidays (Articles 35 and 36). But such provisions are exceptional.

§4. Social Plan

651. The notion of social plan is developed by the recent Articles 335h to 335k CO. A social plan is an agreement in which an employer and employees set out measures to avoid redundancies or to reduce their numbers and mitigate their effects (Article 335h para. 1 CO) The notion of social plan proposed by Article 335h al. 1 CO is not new, as Article 335f al. 2 CO still and previously showed the same objective in its consultation procedure in case of mass redundancies. On a more complete version of the definition, the social plan is intended, specifically in case of collective redundancy, to deliver to such concerned employees, in order to reduce the consequences of the latter, some additional benefits, as a result of negotiations with workers' representation, trade unions or workers themselves (Article 335i para. 3 CO).[292] As an example of benefits, we could summon offers made to the dismissed employees to obtain a priority in the hiring made by other firms of the same group or the protection of one of the two members of a couple if the same two are named in the collective redundancy. It should nonetheless be emphasized that establishing a social plan is not an obligation.

652. However, Article 335i CO imposes an obligation to negotiate for a social plan in case of an employer employing at least 250 employees in the same establishment and willing to dismiss at least 30 employees of this same establishment within 30 days (Article 335i para. 1 CO). Redundancies over a longer period of time

290. Collective agreement for the graphic industry, 2009-2012.
291. Collective agreement of the chemical industry in Basle, valid from 1 May 2008.
292. Wyler, R., Heinzer, B., p. 556.

that are based on the same operational decision are counted together (Article 335i para. 2 CO).

653. If the employer violates its obligation of undertaking negotiations or delays them without any good reasons, the notice of termination is deemed to be considered unlawful (Article 336 para. 2, lit. c, CO). In such case or if the parties are unable to agree on a social plan, an arbitral tribunal is appointed (Article 335j para. 1). The arbitral issues the social plan in a binding arbitral award (Article 335j para. 2). However, in any case, the social plan must never jeopardise the continued existence of the company (Article 335h para. 2 CO).

654. Finally, the provisions on the social plan do not apply to mass redundancies that occur during bankruptcy or composition proceedings that are concluded with a composition agreement (Article 335k CO).

Chapter 4. Collective Bargaining

§1. The Role of Collective Bargaining

655. The regulation of labour conditions is based for the most part on collective bargaining. Collective agreements ensure the protection of workers rather than depending on public protective law. The politics of government, as well as, in many cases, that of the trade unions, is that in matters of labour law the passing of an Act is necessary only if the matter cannot be settled by collective bargaining. It is currently accepted that legal provisions ought only to have a 'subsidiary' function: the action of the law-maker appears useful inasmuch as the problem involved cannot be solved without the intervention of the state, notably by means of collective bargaining.

656. Characteristic of this situation is Article 51, para. 3, of the Employment Act. According to this provision, when a contravention of the Act also constitutes a breach of a collective agreement, the cantonal authority may make appropriate allowance for the measures that the contracting parties have taken to ensure that the agreement is respected.

657. But legislation, whatever the extent of collective bargaining, cannot be totally replaced by collective agreements. There are trades where the trade unions are not powerful and efficient enough to achieve advantages by means of collective bargaining. The law of the state gives a minimum of protection; this protection can be gradually increased by the conclusion of collective agreements. The state may then follow up this development, setting a new minimum for all workers, whether members of a trade union or not.

§2. The Parties to a Collective Agreement

658. Collective agreements may be entered into:

(a) on the employers' side, by one or several employers, or by one or several employers' organizations;
(b) on the workers' side, by one or several workers' organizations.

659. Before the 1956 Act employers could conclude collective agreements with non-organized workers. This faculty has been suppressed; the so-called 'house agreements' were merely drawn up by employers and were not the result of collective bargaining. Such 'agreements' now have no more effect than individual contracts and in this sense bind the employer and the employees who have signed them.

660. Collective agreements may be concluded at different levels. In 66 per cent of the cases, they are concluded with one sole employer and cover the employees in his undertaking. In 34 per cent of the cases, they are concluded with one or more employers' organizations; they then cover a plurality of undertakings, either at trade level, industry level or even, but rarely, on particular matters, at an interprofessional level. However, the employees covered by the agreements concluded with one or more employers' organizations represent 82 per cent of the total number of the employees covered by collective agreements, approximately 53 per cent of all the workers being covered by collective agreements.[293]

661. Generally, collective agreements concluded with an employers' organization cover a trade, and especially the blue-collar workers in that trade. The workers' organizations have tried to obtain the inclusion in the agreement of part of the salaried staff and the supervisors. In the machine industry, the organizations of white-collar workers became parties to the agreement which now extends to all the workers employed by the undertakings, with the exception of senior employees (Article 1, para. 2).

662. The agreements vary too as to their geographical scope. The most important are naturally the national agreements which are concluded between the central associations of employers and of employees and which tend to regulate a trade over the whole country. The national agreements cover, on 1 May 2007, 35 per cent of the total number of employees covered by collective agreements (i.e. 588,200 out of 1,682,900). Some of these agreements are only outline agreements, which may be completed by regional, cantonal or local agreements (this is the case, for instance, in the watch-making and the building industries); naturally, the latter have to respect, as a minimum, the provisions of the national agreement.

663. The Code of Obligations does not restrict the right of employers' and workers' organizations to bargain and to conclude collective agreements. The contracting parties are not bound to prove the importance of their membership or their representativeness. The Code does not expressly prohibit the employers' organizations from negotiating and concluding agreements with a minority trade union, instead of the majority trade union. Nor are these organizations bound to negotiate the conclusion of an agreement. But the Federal Court has stated that an employer or employers' organization which refuses, without any reasonable grounds, to discuss the conclusion of a collective agreement with a trade union with a view to weakening the position of the workers and thus bringing about a gain for themselves, would be acting unlawfully, such an attitude being contrary to the fundamental ideas of the law of collective bargaining.[294] The same can be said of an employer or employers' organization which negotiates with a minority trade union, with a view to weakening the position of the workers in the same way. According to another judgment of the Federal Court, the parties to a collective agreement cannot, without legitimate interest, oppose the accession to the agreement of a sufficiently representative minority trade union.[295]

---

293. The percentages above date from 1 May 2007.
294. *ATF* 74/1948 II 158.
295. *ATF* 121/1995 III 168.

664. For the conclusion of a collective agreement, a sole condition has to be realized on the workers' side: the workers' organization must have acquired legal personality, that is, it has to be an association or a co-operative society. Such a condition is not asked for on the employers' side, as the agreement may be concluded not only by employers' organizations, but also by one or several individual employers.

665. Table 15 contains information about the number of collective agreements concluded at the different levels.

Table 15. Statistics of collective agreements (CA) in 2014

	Number of CA	Number of employees covered
CA between organizations	211	1,647,200
CA with undertakings	391	327,800
Total of which	602	1,975,100
obligatory declared CA	73	992,000
production sector	5	900
manufacturing sector	224	643,700
service sector	368	1,143,600
unclassifiable	5	186,900

Source: Federal Office of Statistics, *Convention collectives de travail selon le type, la taille et le secteur économique*, March 2014.

§3. THE OBJECT OF A COLLECTIVE AGREEMENT

666. Before the 1956 Act the object of the collective agreement was, according to the Code of Obligations, to regulate the conditions of employment; that is, to deal with the individual contracts between employers and workers bound by the agreement. The revised provisions of the Code (Article 356 CO) apparently maintain the same legal definition – by the collective agreement, the parties establish in common provisions on the conclusion, the contents and the termination of the individual contracts of labour – but add that the collective agreement may also embody other provisions on condition that they concern relations between employers and workers, and that they may even be restricted to such provisions; in addition, they may stipulate the reciprocal rights and obligations of the contracting parties and provide for the supervision and enforcement of the aforesaid provisions. In other words, the collective agreement may embody any provision concerning relations between the parties to a contract of labour and between employers' and workers' associations in the field of labour relations.

§4. Form of the Collective Agreement

667. The collective agreement is valid only if it is made in writing (Article 356*c*, para. 1, CO), that is, the clauses of the agreement must be embodied in a written document, signed by the competent organs of the parties or by the party itself (in the case of the employer). The same rule applies to amendments to the agreement, to its termination by agreement of the parties, to its denunciation and to the accession of a new party. The individual adhesion of an outsider must also be in writing, as must be the consent of the contracting parties to such an adhesion.

§5. Legal Effects

668. As they may embody different kinds of provisions, collective agreements produce different kinds of legal effects. We can distinguish the effects on parties to individual labour contracts, the effects on the contracting parties themselves, and the effects on the relations between the contracting parties on the one hand and the parties to the individual labour contracts on the other hand.

I. Effects on the Parties to the Labour Contract

669. Traditionally, the first aim of collective agreements has been to fix the conditions of labour of workers who are bound to an employer by a labour contract. As has been said, collective agreements establish provisions about the conclusion, the contents and the termination of individual labour contracts. These provisions have a direct and mandatory effect on employers and workers bound by the agreement during its term of validity (Article 357 CO). The direct effect of the collective agreement means that it becomes part of the individual contract of employment; the mandatory effect means that any agreement to the contrary between the parties to an individual labour contract is null and void. The terms of the collective agreement apply in the same way as if they had been embodied in an Act with mandatory effect. The provisions of the individual contract which are void are replaced by those of the collective agreement. To put it more briefly, the collective agreement thus has a 'normative' effect. These provisions of the codllective agreement create objective law and have to be interpreted in the same way as the provisions of civil law. The violation of a stipulation of the agreement with normative effects is a violation of the federal civil law.[296]

670. But the collective agreement is in principle an instrument of protection for workers. It follows that if the individual contract provides more favourable terms for the worker, such better terms remain valid notwithstanding the provisions of the agreement.

296. *ATF* 98/1972 II 205.

671. As a consequence of the normative effect of the collective agreement, the worker cannot validly, during the contract and in the month following its termination, waive any claim arising from the agreement, just as he cannot waive a claim arising from a mandatory provision of the law (Article 341 CO) (see above, para. 157).

672. But the normative effects of the agreement can be cancelled out by a provision in the agreement; the latter may indeed provide that there will be no such effect. In that case the collective agreement will have effect only on the contracting parties.

673. The normative effects of the collective agreement apply to employers and workers who are bound by it; that is, employers who have personally signed it or are members of an employers' organization which has signed it, and workers who are members of a workers' organization which has signed it. They do not, in principle, apply to outsiders, except to those who have acceded to it (see above, para. 604). But, in practice, the provisions of the agreement relating to the conditions of labour are applied by employers to all workers, whether or not they are members of a contracting union. Furthermore, clauses of a collective agreement which have a normative effect apply to all members of the trade when they have been extended by the public authority (see below, para. 695).

674. The collective agreement may include clauses which apply to all workers, even if they are not members of a contracting union. Such clauses have no normative effect, so that, for example a non-organized worker may not sue the employer for not paying him the wage under the collective agreement; but the payment of this wage constitutes an obligation for the employer arising from his duties as a member of the contracting employers' organization. The fulfilment of this obligation by the employers' organization may be required by the workers union (see below, para. 679).

675. Collective agreements also have indirect effects. Their terms are generally considered as being the norm (see above, para. 175). Other indirect effects may arise from cantonal regulations about the employment of foreign workers; in such cases, where an employment permit is required, the permit may be granted only if the employer undertakes to respect the collective agreement governing his trade. For the European workers, the bilateral agreements and in particular their implementation measures, recently concluded between Switzerland and the European Union provide that the Federal Act on Workers posted to Switzerland applies. According to the latter, the Swiss working conditions, regarding minimum wages for instance, apply to European workers posted to Switzerland (Article 2, para. 1) (see above, paras. 135 and 410, below 710).

II. Effects on the Contracting Parties

676. All important agreements concluded between employers' and workers' organizations include terms dealing with the rights and duties of the parties to the agreement themselves; that is, the 'contractual' effects of the agreement. Some of these effects derive directly from the law; others from the terms of the agreement.

A. *Effects Deriving from the Law*

677. The first effect, deriving implicitly from the law, is the duty of the contracting parties to observe the agreement. The agreement is a contract and, as such, binds the contracting parties as would any other contract.

678. Other obligations which are specifically provided by the law (Article 357*a* CO) are the obligation to ensure the implementation of the agreement (*Einwirkungspflicht*) and the obligation to preserve industrial peace (*Friedenspflicht*).

679. In order to ensure the implementation of the agreement, the associations have to exert their influence on their members; they have to make use, where necessary, of the means of action available to them under their statutes and under the law. This means that they are responsible to the other contracting party if they do not take action against one of their members who has violated the agreement, expelling him from the association if necessary. The obligation to ensure the implementation of the agreement adds to its effectiveness; it gives the agreement an impact which, going beyond its normative effect, comes from the action of the contracting parties.

680. The duty to preserve industrial peace, which, as we have seen, is also prescribed by the Code, means that the contracting parties have to refrain from any coercive action, such as strikes, lock-outs, boycotts and so on. Unless there is a special provision in the agreement, this duty extends only to matters which are dealt with in the collective agreement (see below, para. 733).

681. Must this duty be respected when the other party does not respect the clauses of the agreement? The matter is controversial. But it appears that in the presence of a crass violation of the rights of the workers, the workers' organization may retaliate, applying analogously the *exceptio non adimpleti contractus* (Article 82 CO). It is not possible in such a case to demand from the workers that they continue their work while waiting for a judicial decision, which can come belatedly. But their action has to respect the principle of proportionality.

682. The parties may also include an 'unlimited' peace obligation in the collective agreement; that is, they pledge themselves to respect the peace obligation even in matters which are not regulated by the agreement. Thus, the Code distinguishes between the relative or limited peace obligation and the absolute or unlimited obligation, this latter obligation arising from a special provision of the agreement.

B. Effects Deriving from the Agreement

683. Since the beginning of the century, some collective agreements have included provisions for an unlimited peace obligation. Already in 1929, half of the employees covered by a collective agreement were subjected to such an obligation. In 1937 two of the main collective agreements in Switzerland provided for this obligation: indeed, provisions with this object were included in the collective agreement for the watch-making industry in 1937 and in the same year in the agreement for the machine industry, which was, according to the number of workers covered, the most important collective agreement in Switzerland. In 2000, 71 per cent of the workers covered by a collective agreement concluded with an association were subject to an unlimited peace obligation, which is often considered as one of the bases of industrial relations in Switzerland. Such provisions provide for a prohibition of all forms of opposed action – such as blacking, strikes, lock-outs, etc., for any purpose whatever. The counterpart of the obligation is the setting up of a procedure for settling conflicts by negotiation, conciliation and arbitration (see below, para. 741). Although the principle of the peace obligation has been controversial within the trade unions (especially in French Switzerland), it has been constantly maintained and, in recent times, the number of strikes has been very small (see below, para. 763).

684. The main collective agreements do not limit themselves – besides regulating relations between employers and workers – to regulating the general obligations between the contracting parties deriving from the law or the unlimited peace obligation. They create specific obligations for the parties, such as, for example, the payment of contributions for special aims in the interests of the workers. They also create collective institutions, such as joint committees comprising an equal number of representatives on each side, arbitration tribunals, equalization funds, employment offices, and so on. The joint committees are very important institutions which are usually entrusted with the implementation of the agreement; they have to decide on the interpretation of the agreement, administer common institutions and sanction contravening employers or workers. The powers and structure of these institutions are fixed by the collective agreement. In such cases the collective agreement has not only a contractual, but also an institutional effect. When an arbitration tribunal has rendered a sentence it has to be respected not only by the contracting parties, but also by individual employers and workers. Thus, the clauses of collective agreements which create such tribunals have an indirect normative effect.

III. Effects on the Relations between the Parties to the Collective Agreement and the Parties to the Labour Contract

685. It has been seen that collective agreements may institute rules about collective relations within the enterprise (see above, para. 647). Such provisions are not directly related to the conditions of labour which are integrated in the individual labour contract, but they do have to be observed by the contracting parties and their members. Where, for instance, an employer does not respect his duty to create a works council in his enterprise as provided for by the collective agreement, the trade union which is a party to the agreement may invite the employers' organization which is a co-signatory of the agreement to oblige its members to observe the provision (see above, para. 679).

686. But the law offers another possibility to the contracting parties in such cases. The Code of Obligations gives them the right to sue jointly in court a member who does not observe an obligation resulting from the agreement. They may do so not only in the aforesaid case, but in all the following cases:

(a) the conclusion, contents and termination of individual labour contracts;
(b) the payment of contributions to equalization funds or other institutions concerned with the employment relationship; the representation of workers in the undertaking; the preservation of industrial peace;
(c) the supervision, deposit of guarantees and contractual fines with respect to provisions covered by (a) and (b) above (Article 357*b*, para. 1, CO).

687. In all these cases the agreement may provide, if it has been concluded on the employers' side by one or more employers' associations (as has been said, this is necessarily the case on the workers' side), that the associations are jointly entitled to enforce the observance of its provisions by the employers and workers who are bound by it. To this end, the contracting parties must have been expressly authorized to include such a faculty in their agreement by their statutes or by a decision of their supreme body (Article 357*b*, para. 2, CO).

688. Thus, the employers' and workers' associations, provided that they act jointly, may bring an action against an employer or, as the case may be, a worker who has failed to observe the collective agreement. However, they may not sue in the courts on behalf of the employee to recover amounts due to him under the agreement; the employee has to sue personally – unless he has transferred his rights to his union, or to both the employers' and employees' associations. They have the right to bring an action for a declaration that the employer is in breach of the agreement, and if the agreement provides for penalties, to sue him for the penalties stipulated which will then be due to the associations acting jointly; while the worker will receive, if he has brought the action himself, the amounts deriving from the individual contract (generally the wage) in relation to the agreement. In most cases, a penalty has already been fixed by the joint committee and the associations will ask the court to confirm this penalty. The court may reduce the penalty if it deems it to be excessive (Article 163 CO).[297] The associations may naturally sue for any other claims which they may have against the employer (or against the worker), such as for the payment of contributions, and so on.

297. *ATF* 116/1990 II 302.

§6. Clauses about Access to an Occupation

689. Two kinds of restrictions apply to the contents of collective agreements. The first of these lies in the prohibition of closed-shop clauses (see above, para. 601). The second kind of restriction relates to clauses in a collective agreement or arrangements between the parties to debar workers from a given occupation or activity, or from acquiring the necessary training, or restricting them in the exercise of such an occupation or activity. Such clauses or arrangements are in principle null and void (Article 356*a*, para. 2, CO). Nevertheless, they are valid if warranted by overriding interests that are worthy of protection, such as the safety or health of persons or the quality of work, but the aim of keeping newcomers from entering the occupation may not be considered as an interest worthy of protection (Article 356*a*, para. 3, CO).

§7. Termination of the Collective Agreement

I. Duration of the Agreement

690. The duration of the agreement is usually fixed in its text: agreements are concluded for a given number of years (generally from two to five years). In most cases, if it is not repudiated, the agreement is tacitly continued according to its terms. If the collective agreement has not been concluded for a definite period (which very seldom happens), it may be denounced after one year with six months' notice (Article 356*c*, para. 2, CO). The same applies to the individual declaration of acceptance of an outsider (see above, para. 604).

691. If an agreement, to which more than one employer or employers' or workers' association is a party, has been repudiated by one party, this affects all the parties.

692. The question whether the collective agreement continues to bind the employer after he has resigned as a member of the employers' organization, was controversial. In 2000, the Federal Court decided that a collective agreement of determined duration applies until its expiry to all employers and employees bound at the time of the conclusion, even though they resign from their organization in the meantime.[298]

II. Effects after the Termination

693. According to the Code of Obligations, the normative effects of a collective agreement continue only during the term of validity of the agreement (Article 357, para. 1, CO); the same is naturally true for the contractual effects.

298. See Federal Court 13 June 2000, decision 4C.7/1999.

694. But this provision does not necessarily mean that after the termination of the agreement its clauses have no effect at all. According to Article 357 CO, the clauses of the agreement may partly replace the stipulations of individual contracts. Thus, the clauses of the collective agreement are integrated, as a minimum, into the individual contract. Stipulations which have been declared null and void do not revive at the termination of the collective agreement. The provisions of the agreement are to be considered as being part of the individual contract and remain in force as such until the latter has been repudiated.[299]

§8. Extension of the scope of Application of the Agreement

695. The public authority may, under certain conditions, extend the scope of application of a collective agreement to employers and workers who are not bound by the agreement. The procedure of extension and its effects are provided for in the Federal Act on the Declaration of General Application of Collective Employment Agreements of 28 September 1956, while some principles have already been laid down in the Federal Constitution (Article 110).

696. The extension may be ordered only if it has been requested by all the associations which are parties to the collective agreement, (Article 1, para. 1) (see nevertheless below, para. 626); naturally no extension is possible if the agreement has been concluded, on the employers' side, by one or several employers and not by one or several associations. The request is officially published (Article 9), and any interested persons or groups may lodge their opposition (Article 10, para. 1). The decision is eventually taken by the Federal Council if more than one canton is involved, and by the cantonal government if the agreement covers only one canton (Article 7). In the latter case, however, the extension still has to be approved by the Confederation (Article 13, para. 2).

697. The conditions to be fulfilled are the following (Article 2):

(a) the contents of the agreement must not interfere with equality before the law, or with freedom of association, or contain anything contrary to the mandatory provisions of the law;
(b) the extension must be necessary, in the sense that the employers and workers bound by the collective agreement may suffer serious hardship if it is not ordered; it must not be contrary to the public interest and must not encroach upon the legitimate interests of other trades or other population groups; it must duly consider the interests of minorities in the trades covered by it when these interests arise out of the diversity of regional conditions and undertakings;
(c) the agreement must have a definite importance: the employers and workers who are bound by it – that is, who are members of the contracting parties or who have personally acceded to the agreement – have to form a majority of employers and workers who would be covered by the extension; moreover, the

299. See *ATF* 130/2004 III 19.

employers bound by the agreement have to employ a majority of all the workers covered. A departure may exceptionally be made from the provision concerning the majority of workers being bound by the agreement;

(d) associations which are not contracting parties must be free to adhere to the agreement if they have a legitimate interest in so doing and if they offer sufficient guarantees for the implementation of the agreement; employers and workers who are not bound by the agreement must have the possibility of entering into a contracting association or adhering personally to the agreement.

698. According to the implementation measures of the bilateral agreements concluded with the European Union (see above, paras. 24, 135, 411 and 675), an easier extension of the scope of the collective agreement is possible in case of dumping of wages, resulting from the free movement of persons. In such a case, provisions of the agreement linked to wage, duration of work and equal control can be extended. According to Article 2, it is only required that the employers bound by the agreement have to employ at least 50 per cent of all workers. Another point is important: the 'tripartite' commission is competent to require the extension (Article 360*b*, CO)

699. The extension may affect only those clauses which bind the employers and workers and which have a normative effect or those which bind the employers and workers to the contracting associations as a whole (that is, the 'conventional community'). It does not necessarily affect all these clauses; the parties, as well as the public authority, may exclude certain clauses from the extension.

700. The legal effect of the extended clauses is the same as that of the agreement itself, with the sole exception that their scope of application is not limited to the members of associations and those employers or workers who have personally adhered to the agreement. It applies to all the employers and workers in the trade covered, save any exceptions that may be provided for by the agreement or by the extension order. While the extension order itself is part of public law, it has in principle no public law effects on individual labour contracts. The state does not supervise the implementation of the extension, which remains within the framework of civil law.[300] The only exception to this principle is where the extension effects adhesion to an equalization fund or to other institutions concerned with the employment relationship; in this case, the said institution is submitted to the control of the authority (Article 5, para. 2). Besides, outsiders may ask the public authority to appoint a special control agency at their own expenses if they don't want to submit themselves to the supervision of the control agency imposed by the collective agreement (Article 6). The implementation measures to the bilateral agreements (*see above*, para. 698) provide for the possibility of all the parties to request the institution of an independent control body.

701. The extension order is given for a limited period; this period having expired, a new request has to be submitted by the contracting parties if they wish to obtain the prolongation of the extension for a new period. At the request of all the

300. *ATF* 98/1972 II 205.

contracting parties, the extension will be revoked before the term provided for. It must also be revoked when the collective agreement is no longer in force or when it has been established that the conditions for the extension do not exist or no longer exist; the same is true in the case of a violation of the principle of equality of treatment or when an equalization fund or other institution covered by the agreement is not correctly administered.

702. Thus, it appears that the basis for the extension must always be sought in the will of the contracting parties. While the state cannot itself order the extension of clauses of a collective agreement if the parties do not request such an extension, neither can it maintain the extension against the will of the parties (see also above, para. 626).

703. In July 2015, there were 77 collective agreements whose scope of application had been extended by the Federal Council or with its approval: 40 at federal level and 37 at cantonal level. The decision taken at the federal level covered 70,450 employers and 658,120 employees; those taken at cantonal level covered 8,795 employers and 64,658 employees.[301]

301. Natale, E., 'Les conventions collectives de travail dont le champ d'application est étendu', *Vie économique*, 11 (2015), p. 67.

Chapter 5. Standard Labour Contracts

§1. Concept

704. The standard labour contract (*Normalarbeitsvertrag, contrat-type de travail*) is a peculiarity of Swiss law. Despite its name it is not a contract, but embodies rules governing individual labour contracts in certain occupations which are established by the public authority. Unlike collective agreements, these rules are not established by the employers and workers or their associations, but this matter is described at this point in the monograph because standard contracts are somewhat linked with collective agreements. Indeed, they are substitutes for collective agreements in occupations where there are no such agreements, mainly where the employers, or the workers, or both, do not belong to an organization which would be in a position to conclude a collective agreement. In the same occupations, the parties to the individual labour contracts generally do not conclude detailed agreements about the contents of these contracts. The standard labour contract has the primary aim of filling in the gaps in such contracts and at the same time bringing to bear some common regulation of their contents.

705. Like collective labour agreements in their 'normative' clauses, standard labour agreements contain rules governing the conclusion, contents and termination of individual contracts; these rules generally affect the duration and termination of the individual contract, the rights of the employee (for instance as regards freedom of association), hours of work, holidays, the payment of wages, sickness insurance and so on. A specific authority is able to enact federal standard contracts determining the amount of wage, for the coming into force of the implementation measures to the bilateral agreements concluded with the EU. This was however already possible with cantonal standard contracts in the past.

§2. Competence

706. Standard labour contracts whose scope comprises more than one canton are enacted by the Federal Council; single canton standard contracts are enacted by the cantonal authority (Article 359*a*, para. 1, CO).

707. The cantonal authorities are bound to enact standard labour contracts for two kinds of occupation: for agricultural workers and for domestic workers. In these standard contracts they have to provide especially for the hours of work and for rest periods, as well as for the working conditions of women and young workers (Article 359, para. 2, CO). For these occupations there are indeed no collective agreements nor any provisions of federal public law, and the standard labour contracts are in some measure substitutes not only for collective agreements, but also for public law provisions (at least where there are no such provisions in cantonal law), although the effect of standard labour agreements remains a private law effect.

§3. Procedure

708. Prior to the decision, the draft standard contract is officially published, setting a time limit for written comments by interested persons or groups. The employers' and workers' associations, as well as other interested associations, have to be consulted (Article 359*a*, para. 2, CO); in fact, standard contracts are often proposed by workers' associations.

709. The standard contract becomes operative after publication in the manner prescribed in the relevant regulations for official publications (Article 359*g*, para. 3, CO). The procedure described also applies to the abrogation or amendment of a standard labour contract (Article 359*a*, para. 4, CO).

710. Further to the adoption of implementation measures to the bilateral agreements, in particular to the free movement of persons, a 'tripartite' commission was formed in every canton and for the Confederation. Each commission must be equally composed of representatives of employers and workers, as well as representatives of the State (Article 360*b*, para. 1, CO). The main task of these commissions is the observation of the Swiss labour market.[302] In the event of an abuse in the domain of wages,[303] the 'tripartite' commission generally tries to find an agreement with the concerned employers. If the commission fails, it suggests to the proper authority the enacting of a standard labour contract providing for minimum wages (Article 360*b*, para. 3, CO). The Act on Workers posted to Switzerland provides that provisions concerning minimum salaries contained in standard labour contracts also apply to European workers posted to Switzerland (Article 2, para. 1). As soon as the situation changes, the Commission can require the abandonment of standard labour contracts.

§4. Legal Effects

711. The rules established by a standard labour contract apply to individual labour relations on all the points where the employer and the worker concerned have not themselves agreed in a specific provision (verbal or written) of their contract. In other words, the individual labour contract has, in principle, precedence over the standard labour contract. Unlike the collective agreement, its effect is purely optional rather than mandatory. Nevertheless, where it does apply, it has a direct effect like a collective agreement (Article 360 CO).

302. *RS* 173.71, also Article 11 of the Ordinance on Workers posted to Switzerland *RS* 823.201.

303. There is an abuse if within an economic branch or profession, usual salaries in the locality, the branch or the profession are the object of an excessive and repeated drop and that there is no collective agreement containing rules relative to minimal salaries which can be extended (Article 360*a*, para. 1, CO).

712. In one specific case, the standard labour contract may have a mandatory effect. As already said, the implementation measures to the bilateral agreements provide that mandatory minimum wages can be fixed by standard labour contract in case of a situation of repeated social dumping (see above, paras. 705 and 710). However, it must be said that mandatory salaries are specific remedies which should be used only in the situation described above. In addition, such a mandatory standard labour contract can be introduced only if the 'tripartite' commission requires it and not if the state does so (see above, para. 710).

713. In certain cases the effect of the standard labour contract is wider: it may provide for arrangements departing from some of its provisions to be valid only if they are made in writing. In such a case, the standard labour contract has a 'qualified' optional effect; it has precedence over verbal arrangements between the parties to the labour contract.[304]

§5. The Standard Labour Contracts Enacted by the Federal State and by the Cantons

714. The federal standard labour contracts now in force deal with working conditions in the following occupations:

(a) educators in foster and boarding schools;
(b) assistant doctors;
(c) nursing personnel;
(d) employees professionally exposed to ionazing radiation (insurance allowances);
(e) dairy personnel;
(f) private gardeners;
(g) domestic workers (standard labour contract with mandatory effect).

Most of these standard labour contracts apply to the whole country.

715. All cantons have enacted standard labour contracts for agricultural and domestic workers, as prescribed by the Code of Obligations; they have also enacted various standard labour contracts in other occupations.

304. The federal standard labour contract applying to private gardeners provides that departures made in individual labour contracts to the workers' detriment are valid only if made in writing. This provision applies to all the clauses of the standard labour contract, and not only to some of them, as prescribed by Article 360 of the Code of Obligations. This does not affect the validity of the provision.

Chapter 6. Minimum Wage

716. Where the wages that are customary for a geographical area, occupation or industry are repeatedly and unfairly undercut within a particular occupation or economic sector and there is no collective employment contract laying down a minimum wage that may be declared universally binding, on application by the tripartite commission as defined in Article 360b CO, the competent authority may issue a fixed-term standard employment contract providing for a minimum wage varied by region and, where applicable, by locality in order to combat or prevent abusive practices (Article 360a para. 1 CO). Such minimum wage must not conflict with the public interest or damage the legitimate interests of other economic sectors or sections of the population. It must have due regard to the minority interests of the affected economic sectors or occupations that stem from regional and business diversity (Article 360a para. 2 CO)

717. The Confederation and each canton establishe a tripartite commission consisting of an equal number of employers' and employees' representatives in addition to representatives of the state (Article 360b para. 1 CO). Employers' and employees' associations have the right to put forward candidates for selection as their representatives within the meaning of paragraph 1 (Article 360b para. 2 CO). The commissions monitor the labour market. If they observe abusive practices within the meaning of Article 360*a* paragraph 1, they normally seek to reach agreement directly with the employers concerned. Where this cannot be achieved within two months, they petition the competent authority to issue a standard employment contract fixing a minimum wage for the affected sectors or occupations (Article 360b para. 3 CO) If labour market conditions in the affected sectors change, the tripartite commission petitions the competent authority to amend or rescind the standard employment contract (Article 360b para. 4 CO). To enable them to discharge their responsibilities, the tripartite commissions have the right to obtain information and inspect any business document necessary to the conduct of their investigation. In the event of a dispute, a ruling is given by a body specially appointed for this purpose by the Confederation or the canton, as applicable (Article 360b para. 5 CO). Where necessary for the conduct of their investigations, on application the tripartite commissions may obtain personal data contained in corporate collective employment contracts from the Federal Statistical Office (Article 360b para. 6 CO).

718. The members of tripartite commissions are subject to official secrecy; in particular they are obliged to keep secret from third parties any information of a commercial or private nature gained in the exercise of their office (Article 360c para. 1 CO). Such duty of secrecy remains in force even after membership of the tripartite commission has ceased (Article 360c para. 2 CO).

719. The standard employment contract as defined in Article 360*a* also applies to employees who work only temporarily within its geographical scope and to employees whose services have been loaned out (Article 360d para. 1 CO). It is not permissible to derogate from a standard employment contract as defined in Article 360a to the detriment of the employee (Article 360d para. 2 CO).

720. Employers' and employees' associations have the right to apply for a declaratory judgment as to whether an employer is in compliance with the standard employment contract as defined in Article 360a (Article 360e CO).

721. A canton issuing a standard employment contract pursuant to Article 360a must forward a copy to the competent federal office (Article 360f CO).

Chapter 7. Strike, Lock-out, Boycott

§1. Principle

722. Among the means of collective pressure which workers and employers may exert reciprocally in the case of a labour conflict the principal means are strikes and lock-outs.

723. A strike is a concerted stoppage of work by a plurality of workers with a view to defending their interests in a conflict with the employer. This definition relates to the strike as such. Other forms of action, connected with strike, such as working to rule, sit-downs or sit-ins, are not usual in Switzerland. Solidarity strikes are not usual either.

724. A lock-out is the collective dismissal of workers by an employer or group of employers in order to protect their own interests – generally in response to a strike.

725. Other means of exerting pressure are boycotts, blacklisting and so on which may accompany a strike or a lock-out or which may be independent of them.

726. For a long time, there was no specific regulation on strikes, lock-outs or boycotts in industrial relations.

727. This situation has changed with the adoption of the new Federal Constitution, which embodies now a specific regulation on the right to strike and to lock-out. In the following paragraphs we will deal only with strikes. There are few strikes in Switzerland and lock-outs are quite exceptional. On the other hand, what is said about strikes may in principle be said about lock-outs.

§2. The Right to Strike

728. The Federal Constitution of 1874 did not contain any regulation on the right to strike. But the doctrine was nearly unanimous that the right of coalition – contained in the freedom of association (Article 56 of the previous Constitution) – enjoyed such a guarantee: one of the essential means of action for the trade unions – as an *ultima ratio* – is the strike. So, this constitutional provision implicitly admits the recourse to struggle in labour matters. Meanwhile, the Federal Court, while mentioning the doctrinal views on the matter, did not come to a definite conclusion, declaring that the question of the constitutional recognition of the right to strike could remain open, the question, arising in the particular case on which it had to find, being that of knowing whether the *ultima ratio* principle had been respected.[305] At last, in 1999, the Federal Court admitted that Swiss labour law contained, also under the former Constitution, a right to strike.[306]

729. The new Federal Constitution now embodies a specific regulation on the right to strike in its Article 28. This article includes the freedom to unionize and admits the recourse to the strike and lock-out as 'permitted when they relate to labour relations, and when they are not contrary to obligations to keep labour peace or to resort to conciliation' (Article 28, para. 3). Strikes and lock-outs have to be an *ultima ratio* in the collective struggle in labour matters: paragraph 2 of Article 28 prescribes that 'conflicts shall be resolved to the extent possible through negotiation and mediation'. So, strikes are permitted under three conditions:

(a) they have to respect the *ultima ratio* principle (para. 2);
(b) they have to refer to labour relations (para. 3);
(c) they have to respect obligations to keep labour peace or to resort to conciliation (para. 3).

When these conditions are respected, strikes as such cannot be repressed by the state, except where they have an unlawful purpose or illegal means are used.

730. It was a matter of controversy whether the right to start a strike was limited to the trade unions. The text of the Constitution itself does not include such a condition and the Federal Assembly refused a proposal to introduce such a limitation of the right to strike in the Constitution in the aim to let this question open. However, the Federal Court decided that this limitation still applied.[307] But, inside the trade unions, there may be statutory provisions limiting the power of the leading bodies of the union and providing in such cases for a general ballot – sometimes with the extra requirement of a specific majority in favour of the strike.

731. However, the use of this right can be controlled or suppressed by the state in particular cases: Article 28, para. 4, of the new Federal Constitution prescribes that 'legislation may prohibit certain categories of persons from striking'. Thus, federal or cantonal legislation can forbid strikes for members of the federal or cantonal civil service, when the public interest – as the guarantee of some public services – requires it.

732. Another problem is constituted by the question of whether the right to strike has also to be recognized for relations between employers and workers; that is, under civil law. It was formerly considered that the strike could be regarded as causing a breach of the contract of labour by the workers who were members of the

305. *ATF* 111/1985 II 253.
306. *ATF* 125/1999 III 277.
307. *ATF* 132/2006 III 122.

group which had decided to strike. But the doctrine has evolved, and since the sentence of the Federal Court in 1995[308] it is certain that the strike only suspends the contract, which except in special circumstances is not violated by the strike.

§3. Industrial Peace Obligation and Collective Agreement

733. As has been said, with the conclusion of a collective agreement the contracting parties are bound to preserve the industrial peace; that is, to abstain from any coercive action in respect of matters which are dealt with in the collective agreement. The contracting parties may also agree on an unlimited peace obligation, which extends to matters which are not regulated by the agreement (see above, para. 680). In this latter case, the collective agreement generally prohibits not only strikes, lock-outs and blacklisting, but also other means of pressure, such as written attacks in the press.

734. In concluding a collective agreement with an unlimited peace obligation the trade union renounces the use of the strike for a limited period. At the end of the validity of the collective agreement the right to strike revives. The situation is naturally quite different from what it would be if the right to strike was forbidden by the state. It was indeed to avoid this threat that in 1937 the trade unions were eager to conclude collective agreements with unlimited peace agreement in the watchmaking and machine industries. The state wanted to arbitrate industrial disputes; the employers and workers were against such a possibility. The renunciation of the right to strike was given in exchange for the creation by the contracting parties of a voluntary mechanism for settling disputes by conciliation and arbitration. The trial succeeded, and the collective agreements have been renewed several times. But at the expiry of the collective agreement each party may naturally regain its liberty.

735. The preservation of the 'peace obligation' which is laid down by the Constitution and by the Code of Obligations for the parties to a collective agreement is required only from these parties and not from those individuals who are parties to a contract of labour and who happen to come within the scope of the agreement. The strike is a collective action; a worker who individually – apart from a collective movement – ceases work is not on strike. But the strike, precisely as collective action, can materialize only by the cessation of work by individual workers. The question then arises as to whether the contracting parties may, in the agreement, provide that the peace obligation applies not only to themselves, but also to all the individuals covered by the collective agreement. Many collective agreements do indeed contain such a provision. For instance, in the collective agreement for the machine industry, it is laid down that the obligation to preserve the industrial peace applies

308. Sentence of the Federal Court of 23 March 1995, see *Plädoyer* 5/95, p. 61, see also now *ATF* 125/1999 III 277.

individually to all employees and employers (Article 2, para. 2). Such provisions are also found in the extended clauses of some collective agreements.[309]

736. Such a clause, if it is valid, carries with it two consequences. On the one hand, the obligation for each individual to preserve the industrial peace creates for the contracting organization the obligation to act against any of its members who may have broken the peace. On the other hand, besides the peace obligation with contractual effect, a normative obligation is created, with each individual covered by the collective agreement being bound to observe the industrial peace within the framework of the individual labour contract. The matter is controversial, but where the contracting parties have created a 'conventional community', that is, where they have regulated relations between the parties to the collective agreement as a whole and the parties to individual labour contracts and provided that the associations are jointly entitled to enforce observance of the agreement (see above, paras. 686 and 687), they may act together against an employer or employee who has broken the industrial peace – for instance, by proceeding against him for the payment of a conventional fine.

737. In practice, the problem of whether a normative obligation of industrial peace may be provided for by a collective agreement has no great impact. A strike which breaches a peace obligation, that is, which is prohibited by the collective agreement, does not suspend the individual contract of labour; a worker who has stopped work may be considered as having broken his contract of labour independently of the question of whether or not the obligation has a normative effect. Moreover, after a strike, all problems are generally settled by the agreement which puts an end to the strike, so the matter is seldom referred to the courts.

§4. Industrial Dispute Statistics

738. Table 16 indicates the number of industrial disputes which have brought about stoppages of work between 1982 and 2015.

Table 16. Industrial disputes with stoppage of work

Year	Number of disputes	Enterprises involved	Workers involved	Days lost
1983	5	5	985	4,438
1984	2	2	50	662
1985	3	10	366	72

309. According to the collective agreement for the wholesale furniture industry, extended by the Federal government on 26 January 1993, 'the employers and employees submit themselves to the obligation of preserving industrial peace for all matters which relate to the conditions of work regulated in the present agreement' (Article 37).

Year	Number of disputes	Enterprises involved	Workers involved	Days lost
1986	1	1	36	72
1987	0	0	0	0
1988	4	4	131	870
1989	2	2	22	265
1990	2	2	578	4,090
1991	1	1	51	51
1992	3	18	220	673
1993	0	0	0	0
1994	8	238	6,901	14,380
1995	2	2	83	381
1996	3	5	5,888	7,266
1997	2	3	327	435
1998	7	12	16,125	24,719
1999	5	129	2,255	2675
2000	8	19	3,894	4,757
2001	3	702	20,098	20,098
2002	4	535	21,947	21,447
2003	9	189	8,111	6,141
2004	8	1,117	24,399	38,915
2005	5	11	338	1,392
2006	3	4	635	7,870
2007	2	571	5,083	7,083
2008	8	59	10,160	13,644
2009	3	3	159	395
2010	3	3	172	2,455
2011	7	10	1,007	2,837
2012	7	50	2,869	2,554
2013	11	65	1,688	5,764
2014	8	35	1,915	4,185
2015	13	164	13,437	13'274

Source: Federal Office of Statistics, Grèves et Lock-out, Neuchâtel 2016.

Chapter 8. Settlement of Industrial Disputes

§1. Conciliation and Mediation

739. The procedure of conciliation lies in the search for an amiable solution to an industrial dispute, either by the organs of the contracting parties themselves or with the help of an external body.

The conciliation of industrial disputes may be organized through different channels:

(a) through bodies created by collective agreements;
(b) through cantonal boards of conciliation;
(c) through the federal Board of Conciliation.

740. Mediation is now provided by the Code of Civil Procedure (see above paras. 568 and 569). But it may also be organized by collective agreements. The mediator has more power than the conciliator; a mediator may not only recommend specific measures – as may the conciliator – but also has some powers of arbitration.

I. Bodies Created by Collective Agreements

741. Collective agreements which have been concluded between associations of employers and trade unions generally provide for the formation of bodies or mechanisms entrusted with the conciliation of disputes. Such mechanisms may be provided either for disputes which have arisen within a particular enterprise and which cannot be settled in the enterprise, or for disputes between the contracting parties. The conciliation body is very often the joint committee created for the implementation of the agreement.

742. In the watch-making industry, the contracting parties have nominated several regional mediators whose task is to open negotiations, hear the parties, make recommendations and as the case may be, propose provisional measures; moreover, they may, in certain circumstances and with the agreement of the parties, act as arbitrators (Article 1.11 *et seq.*).

II. Cantonal Conciliation Boards

743. According to the Federal Act on Work in Factories of 18 June 1914,[310] each canton has to maintain a permanent conciliation board whose job is to try to

310. *RS* 821.41. This Act has been repealed and replaced by the Employment Act, with the exception of its provisions about Conciliation Boards (Articles 30–35) which are still in force.

conciliate labour disputes in industrial enterprises (Article 30, para. 1): in most cantons cantonal law gives these boards the competence to deal with other enterprises too.

744. All the boards comprise a neutral president and an equal number of employers' and workers' representatives. Their task is to conciliate collective disputes between employers and workers about labour conditions, as well as about the interpretation and implementation of collective agreements or standard labour contracts (Article 30, para. 1). Thus, disputes of rights as well as disputes of interest may be brought before the cantonal conciliation boards, although certain cantonal provisions, despite the terms of the federal law, exclude disputes of rights from their competence.

745. The board may act *ex officio*, as soon as it hears that a dispute has arisen; it is not bound to wait for a request from the interested parties. Attendance before the board is obligatory and the procedure is free of charge (Article 31).

746. According to some cantonal provisions, the parties to the dispute may not take any coercive action while the matter is before the board, but it must be said that these provisions have fallen somewhat into abeyance.

747. The board may act only if the employers and workers involved in the dispute are not bound by an agreement which institutes private conciliation or arbitration machinery, in which case this private board alone is competent to act.

748. Where the procedure of conciliation before the cantonal board has failed the parties may, in some cantons, ask for the intervention of another authority, such as the cantonal government.

III. The Federal Board of Conciliation

749. While at cantonal level the boards will meet at the request of any party to a dispute – and even *ex officio* – at the federal level, very curiously, the situation is quite different. According to the Federal Act on the Federal Conciliation Board in Collective Industrial Disputes of the 12th of February 1949,[311] a Federal Board may be constituted, in a given case, only by the decision of the Federal Department of Economy. It shall be constituted, at the request of interested persons, if attempts to bring about conciliation between the parties by direct negotiations have failed, if no joint conciliation or arbitration board exists, and if the dispute goes beyond the limits of any one canton (Article 1). According to the instructions of the Federal Department of Economy, the Federal Board may act only in cases of disputes of interest; that is, essentially, disputes arising out of the making of new agreements or the renewal of agreements which have already expired or are about to expire. Disputes of rights, namely those bearing on the execution or interpretation of existing

311. *RS* 821.42.

agreements, are excluded from the competence of the Federal Board, it being understood that they have to be brought before the courts. Thus, the federal authorities put many obstacles in the way of the conflicting parties when a dispute ought to be conciliated. Luckily, because of the small number of strikes, the consequences of this situation are not far-reaching.

750. The Federal Board of Conciliation, when constituted, is composed of a neutral president and two assessors, representing respectively the employers and the workers, who are chosen by the Department from a list of members established by the Federal Council (Article 2).

751. The procedure is rapid and free of charge. Every person summoned by the Board must appear, assist in the oral proceedings, supply information and produce the documents required. The Board endeavours to obtain agreement between the parties by direct means. If it fails to do so, it proposes a compromise to the parties. When an attempt at conciliation fails and the parties are not prepared to accept arbitration, the board informs the public generally of the state of affairs in any manner which it deems fit (Article 4).

§2. Arbitration

752. Through the arbitration procedure, the dispute is brought before a body which settles it definitively and whose award has the force of a judicial decision. The parties are not compelled by law to submit their dispute to arbitration, but they can undertake in a collective agreement to do so. When the dispute is a dispute of rights, concerning the interpretation or implementation of existing rules, the parties have the choice between arbitration and judicial procedure. In the case of a dispute of interest, which bears not on existing rules but on the establishment of new rules, the ordinary courts are not competent, and arbitration may only settle the dispute if the parties themselves cannot solve it through direct understanding, possibly after an attempt at conciliation.

753. Like conciliation, the arbitration of a dispute may be entrusted:

(a) to arbitration tribunals created by collective agreements;
(b) to the cantonal conciliation boards;
(c) to the Federal Board of Conciliation.

I. Arbitration Tribunals Created by Collective Agreements

754. The main collective agreements provide for the establishment of trade arbitration tribunals. The tasks and competence of these tribunals vary according to the different agreements. The arbitration tribunals can be instituted at two levels: at one level for disputes within an enterprise; at a higher level for disputes between the contracting parties themselves. In the case of disputes of interest, some agreements restrict the competence of the arbitration tribunal to certain specific points on which there are provisions in the agreement; other agreements admit a more general jurisdiction for the arbitration tribunal. In the machine industry arbitration may be brought to bear, if conciliation has failed, on the following matters (Article 10.4): general wage modifications, modification of the normal hours of work, the introduction and application of systems of labour qualification and efficiency wages, the interpretation and application of agreements, the consequences of the closure of enterprises and numerous dismissals; other matters may be submitted to the tribunal only with the agreement of both parties. In the watch-making industry, the mediator, as already said, may, in the case of failure of conciliation, issue an award with the agreement of the parties; in this industry, wages may – and often are – fixed by arbitration; the arbitration procedure may also be used to deal with matters which are not regulated by the collective agreement (Article 1.11 *et seq.*). In the building industry, arbitration may be brought to bear on all disputes arising from the interpretation or application of the collective agreement, except wages.

755. Moreover, the arbitration tribunal is generally competent to deal with breaches of the collective agreement and to inflict penalties on the party at fault.

756. The president of the Arbitration Tribunal is always a jurist (usually a judge), who is assisted by two or more members who, in equal number, are nominated by the employers and by the workers. Often what happens is that the Arbitration Tribunal is entrusted with an attempt at conciliation and takes up arbitration if it does not succeed in conciliating the parties. An appeal before a cantonal court can be lodged against the arbitration award for violation of the law, for instance if the award is deemed to be arbitrary. The award of the Arbitration Tribunal can generally be brought directly before the Federal Court, if the parties do not provide an appeal before the cantonal court (Articles 389–390 Code of Civil Procedure).

757. In some collective agreements it is provided that, despite the termination of the normative provisions of the agreement, the provisions about conciliation and arbitration remain in force until the end of the procedure, or even that the whole collective agreement, despite a notice of termination, remains in force until that time. Thus, the dispute can be arbitrated despite the notice of termination given by either of the parties.

758. Where the scope of application of a collective agreement has been extended by the public authority, the extension may not apply to the provisions of the agreement which submit the settlement of disputes to an arbitration tribunal (Article 1, para. 3, of the Federal Act on the Declaration of General Application of Collective Employment Agreements). In such a case, an award issued by the trade arbitration tribunal has no direct influence over employers and workers who are not bound by the collective agreement itself.

II. Cantonal Conciliation Boards

759. When conciliation before the cantonal board of conciliation does not succeed, the parties may entrust the board with the arbitration of the dispute. For industrial enterprises this option is available, according to the Act on Work in Factories of 18 June 1914, only in given cases and not beforehand in a collective agreement. But the settlement of disputes by the cantonal conciliation board is, in practice, provided for by many collective agreements.

760. The cantonal conciliation board being a public authority, its awards may be brought directly before the Federal Court by means of a public law appeal, if the conciliation board is considered as a judicial authority, what it should be.

III. The Federal Board of Conciliation

761. Where an attempt at conciliation before the Federal Board of Conciliation has failed, it will, if the parties agree, make a compulsory arbitration award. But the social partners do not, in practice, make use of this option.

762. At the request of the parties the Department may form a special arbitration board after the termination of the conciliation procedure.

§3. Statistics about the Settlement of Labour Disputes

763. No statistics are available about the settlement of disputes submitted to the trade arbitration tribunals. The only data published relate to the activities of the public Conciliation Boards.

Table 17. Disputes submitted to the Cantonal Conciliation Boards

Year	Number of disputes	
	Submitted to conciliation	Submitted to arbitration
1988	12	3
1989	37	9
1990	23	4
1991	37	12
1998	15	8
2008	8	2
2014	19	13

Table 18. Disputes settled by the Cantonal Conciliation Boards

Year	By conciliation	By arbitration	Not solved
1988	7	3	5
1989	26	6	14
1990	20	3	4
1991	29	9	10
1998	13	6	4
2008	5	1	3
2014	22	1	9

Source of Tables 17 and 18: Sestito, L., 'Les offices publics de conciliation ont été davantage sollicités en 2014', *La vie économique* (2015).

764. From 1988 to 1998, only once, in 1989, a dispute has been submitted to the Federal Conciliation Board, which declared it inadmissible.

Selected Bibliography

IN GENERAL

Legislation

Federal legislation is published in: *Systematische Sammlung des Bundesrechts – Recueil systématique du droit fédéral – Raccolta sistematica del diritto federale* (three different publications, in each of the three official languages). Legislation on labour law can be found in the following volumes of these collections: Vol. 2,2 (Private Law, Code of Obligations) and Vol. 8,3 (Labour).

The official website of the Swiss Confederation is: http://www.admin.ch/ index.html ?lang=en. However, the Federal legislation is also accessible on the following website address: http://www.admin.ch/ch/e/rs/rs.html.

The main laws and ordinances are published in : Dunand, Wyler, Dupont, Kahil-Wolff, *Droit social, Volume 1, Droit du travail*, 4th edn, Basle, 2014.

Cases

A selection of sentences of the Federal Court is published in:

Entscheidungen des Schweizerischen Bundesgerichts, Amtliche Sammlung – Arrêts du Tribunal Fédéral Suisse, Recueil officiel – Decisioni del Tribunale federale svizzero, Raccolta ufficiale (trilingual publication).

Published sentences of the Federal Court from year 1954 and unpublished sentences from year 2000 are available on: http://www.bger.ch/fr/index/juridiction/jurisdiction-inherit-template/jurisdiction-recht.htm.

www.droitdutravail.ch: Created under the aegis of the Faculty of Law of the University of Neuchâtel, this website contains analysis of some chosen sentences of the Federal court in labour law.

Jahrbuch des schweizerischen Arbeitsrechts (JAR), Bern: Published every year, this book contains multiple recent sentences from Cantonal and Federal courts.

Current Statistics

Such statistics are published by the following monthly journals, issued by the Federal Department of Economy: *Die Volkswirtschaft – La Vie économique*.

Selected Bibliography

Different statistics are also available on Internet, on the Federal Statistical Office's website: http://www.bfs.admin.ch/bfs/portal/en/index.html, and some others in a yearly publication of the Federal Statistical Office: *Statistical Yearbook of Switzerland.*

Constitutional Law

Aubert, J.-F., Mahon, P., *Petit commentaire de la Constitution fédérale de la Confédération suisse du 18 avril 1999*, Zurich, Basle, Geneva, 2003.

Auer, A., Malinverni, G., Hottelier, M., *Droit constitutionnel suisse*, 3rd edn, Vols. 1 and 2, Bern, 2013.

Biaggini, G., *Bundesverfassung der Schweizerischen Eidgenossenschaft – Kommentar*, Zurich, 2007.

Ehrenzeller, B., Schindler, B., Schweizer, R. J., Vallender, K. A. (eds.), *Die schweizerische Bundesverfassung – Kommentar*, 3rd edn, Zurich, Basle, Geneva / Zurich, St. Gallen, 2014.

Fleiner, T., Misic, A., Toepperwien, N., *Swiss Constitutional Law*, The Hague, Bern, 2005.

Häfelin, U., Haller, W., Keller, H., Thurnherr, D., *Schweizerisches Bundesstaatsrecht*, 9th edn, Zurich, 2016.

Haller, W., *The Swiss Constitution in a Comparative Concept*, 2nd edn, Zurich, St Gallen, 2016.

Rhinow, R., Schefer, M., Uebersax, P., *Schweizerisches Verfassungsrecht*, 3rd edn, Basle, 2016.

Tschannen, P., *Staatsrecht der Schweizerischen Eidgenossenschaft*, 4th edn, Bern, 2016.

Labour Law

Cases

Jahrbuch des Schweizerischen Arbeitsrechts (JAR), Bern: Published every year, this book contains multiple recent sentences from Cantonal and Federal courts.

Websites

The website of a service of news consecrated to labour law and social insurance law called ARV/DTA online is: https://www.swisslex.ch/cms_swisslex/slx/index.aspx?skin=arv.

www.droitdutravail.ch: Created under the aegis of the Faculty of Law of the University of Neuchâtel, this website contains analysis of some chosen sentences of the Federal court in labour law.

The Center for Labour Relations Study (Centre d'étude des relations de travail, CERT), attached to the Faculty of Law of the University of Neuchâtel, is at the disposal of companies, public administrations or anyone concerned with matters linked to labour law: www2.unine.ch/cms/site/cert.

Books

Andermatt, A., Bianchi, D., Bruchez, C., Gabathuler, T. *et al.*, *Handbuch zum kollektiven Arbeitsrecht*, Basle, 2009 (also in French).
Aubert, G., *Etudes de droit du travail*, Zurich, 1995.
Aubert, G., 'Commentaire des art. 319-362 CO', in: Thévenoz, L., Werro, F. (eds.), *Commentaire romand, Code des obligations* I, Basle, 2003.
Aubert, G., Lempen, K. (eds), *Commentaire de la loi sur l'égalité entre femmes et hommes*, Bern, Geneva (BFEG, University of Geneva, Slatkine), 2011.
Bigler, F.W., *Kommentar zum Arbeitsgesetz*, 3rd edn, Bern, 1986 (also in French).
Bohnet, F., *CPC annoté*, Neuchâtel, 2016.
Brühwiler, J., *Kommentar zum Einzelarbeitsvertrag*, OR 319–343, 2nd edn, Bern, 1999.
Brunner, C., Bühler, J.M., Waeber, J.B., Bruchez, C., *Commentaire du contrat de travail*, 3rd edn., Lausanne, 2004 (also in German).
Carruzzo, P., *Le contrat individuel de travail – Commentaire des articles 319 à 341 du Code des obligations*, Zurich, 2009.
Dunand, J-P., Mahon, P. (eds), *Commentaire du contrat de travail*, Bern, 2013.
Dunand, J-P., Mahon, P. (eds), *Internet au travail,* Genève, Zurich, Basle 2014.
Dunand, J-P., Mahon, P., Lempen, K. (eds), *L'égalité entre femmes et hommes dans les relations de travail*, Zurich 2016.
Dunand, J-P., Mahon, P., Perrenoud, S. (eds), *Le droit de la relation de travail à la croisée des chemins : convergences et divergences entre le droit privé du travail et le droit de la fonction publique*, Zurich 2016.
Geiser, T., Von Kaenel, A., Wyler, R. (eds.), *Loi sur le travail – Loi fédérale du 13 mars 1964 sur le travail dans l'industrie, l'artisanat et le commerce,* Bern, 2005 (also in German).
Mahon, P., *Réglementation du travail*, Lausanne, 1984.
Portmann, W., 'Der Arbeitsvertrag', in: Honsell, H., Vogt, N.P., Wiegand, W. (eds.), *Kommentar zum schweizerischen Privatrecht (Basler Kommentar)*, Vol. *Obligationenrecht I' OR 319-362*, 4th edn., Basle, Frankfort, 2007.
Portmann, W., Stöckli, J.-F., *Schweizerisches Arbeitsrecht*, Zurich, 2007.
Rehbinder, M., *Schweizerisches Arbeitsrecht*, 15th edn., Bern, 2002.
Rehbinder, M., Stöckli, J.-F., *Berner Kommentar*, Vol. VI/2/2/1, Bern, 2010.
Rehbinder, M., *Berner Kommentar*, Vol. VI/2/2/2, Bern, 1992.
Staehelin, A., *Zürcher Kommentar*, Vol. V 2 C, Zurich 2006.
Stöckli, J.-F., *Gesamtarbeitsvertrag und Normalarbeitsvertrag*, Arts. 356–360 OR, Bern, 1999.
Streiff, U., Von Kaenel, A., Rudolph, R., *Arbeitsvertrag*, 7th edn, Zurich, 2012.
Subilia, O., Duc, J.-L., *Droit du travail, éléments de droit suisse*, reviewed and increased edn. of the *Commentaire du contrat individuel de travail*, Lausanne, 2010.
Tschudi, H.P., *Schweizerisches Arbeitsschutzrecht*, Bern, 1985 (also in French).

Selected Bibliography

Tschudi, H.P., *Geschichte des schweizerischen Arbeitsrechts*, Basle, 1987.
Tschudi, H.P., *Sozialstaat, Arbeits- und Sozialversicherungsrecht, Schriften aus den Jahren 1983 bis 1995*, Zurich, 1996.
Vischer, F., *Der Arbeitsvertrag*, 3rd edn, Basle, Geneva, 2005.
Wyler, R., Heinzer, B., *Droit du travail*, 3nd edn, Bern, 2014.

Journals

Arbeitsrecht/Droit du travail, Zeitschrift für Arbeitsrecht und Arbeitslosenversicherung/Revue de droit du travail et d'assurance chômage (ARV/DTA).
Mitteilungen des Instituts für schweizerisches Arbeitsrecht (ArbR).

SOCIAL INSURANCE LAW

Websites

The website of a service of news consecrated to labour law and social insurance law called ARV/DTA online is: https://www.swisslex.ch/cms_swisslex/slx/index.aspx?skin=arv.

Books

Greber, P.-Y., Kahil-Wolff, B., Frésard-Fellay, G., Molo, R., *Droit suisse de la sécurité sociale*, Bern, 2010.
Kieser, U., *Schweizerisches Sozialversicherungsrecht*, Zurich 2008.
Locher, T., *Grundriss des Sozialversicherungsrechts*, 3rd edn, Bern, 2003.
Riemer-Kafka, G., *Schweizerisches Sozialversicherungsrecht*, Bern, 2008.
Wiedmer, D., *Die Sozialversicherung in der Schweiz*, 6th edn, Zurich, 2008.

Journals

Schweizerische Zeitschrift für Sozialversicherung und berufliche Vorsorge (SZS), Bern.

Index

www.ingramcontent.com/pod-product-compliance
Ingram Content Group UK Ltd.
Pitfield, Milton Keynes, MK11 3LW, UK
UKHW020140290926
15471UKWH00003B/600

9 789041 199607